(Continued)

Harlem on Our Minds

Place, Race, and the Literacies of Urban Youth

Valerie Kinloch

Foreword by Jabari Mahiri
Afterword by Edmund W. Gordon

TEACHERS
COLLEGE
PRESS

Teachers College
Columbia University
New York and London

Published by Teachers College Press, 1234 Amsterdam Avenue, New York, NY 10027

The author wishes to express gratitude for use from the following:

"Take A Stand," written in 1996 by Geoffrey Canada and originally published on the Harlem Children's Zone Web site (http://www.hcz.org/what-is-hcz/about-geoffrey-canada). Copyright © 1996. Used by permission of Geoffrey Canada and the HCZ.

Some of Chapter 4 appeared in different form in "'The White-ification of the Hood': Power, Politics, and Youth Performing Narratives of Community" by Valerie Kinloch, *Language Arts, 85*(1), September 2007. Copyright © 2007. Used by permission of the National Council of Teachers of English.

Some of Chapter 5 appeared in different form in "Youth Representations of Community, Art, and Struggle in Harlem" by Valerie Kinloch, *New Directions for Adult and Continuing Education Journal, 116*, 2007. Copyright © 2007. Used by permission of the author and John Wiley & Sons, Inc.

Library of Congress Cataloging-in-Publication Data

Kinloch, Valerie, 1974–
   Harlem on our minds : place, race, and the literacies of urban youth / Valerie Kinloch ; foreword by Jabari Mahiri ; afterword by Edmund W. Gordon
       p. cm. — (Language and literacy series)
   Includes bibliographical references and index.
   ISBN 978-0-8077-5023-0 (pbk. : alk. paper) — ISBN 978-0-8077-5024-7 (hardcover : alk. paper)   1. Literacy—Social aspects—New York (State)—New York—Case studies.
2. Urban youth—Education—New York (State)—New York—Cases studies.   3. Urban youth—New York (State)—New York—Social conditions—Case studies.   4. Gentrification—New York (State)—New York—Case studies.   5. Blacks—Race identity—New York (State)—New York—Case studies.   6. Harlem (New York, N.Y.)—Social conditions—21st century.   I. Title.
   LC153.N48K56 2010
   302.2'244097471—dc22

                                                                            2009031105

ISBN 978-0-8077-5023-0 (paperback)
ISBN 978-0-8077-5024-7 (hardcover)

Printed on acid-free paper

Manufactured in the United States of America

17   16   15   14   13   12   11   10   8   7   6   5   4   3   2   1

I dedicate this book to Phillip and Khaleeq, two young men whose literacy lives are reflected—however much partial and incomplete—throughout this book. Their stories, lived experiences, and search for answers have greatly enhanced my understanding of literacy, community, and struggle. May this work honor their literacy experiences as their experiences have enriched my own life.

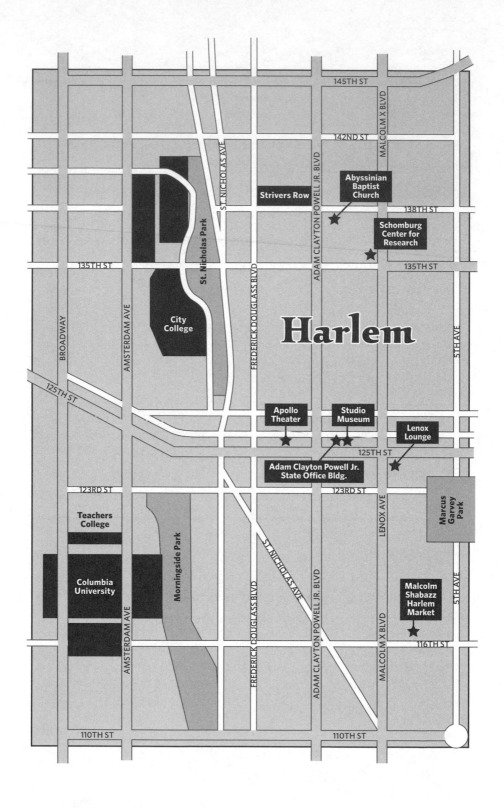

Contents

Foreword

Valerie Kinloch cogently proposes and demonstrates a "pedagogy of possibility" that motivates and supports young people in addressing and analyzing critical conditions in their lives through compelling narratives of community as well as other practices of literacy, both in and out of school. Kinloch's work centers on two African American young men, Phillip and Khaleeq, who collaborated with her for three years on a participatory research project to explore and document connections between literacy, community, and struggle. Khaleeq and Phillip were students at Harlem High School, where a pervasive critical condition facing their community still is the gentrification of Harlem mainly resulting from the extensive expansion of Columbia University's campus.

For Phillip, this "new" Harlem "don't include what we young people think about community and all the changes happening." According to Khaleeq, "nobody's trying to even figure out a plan or anything to save it from gentrification." Kinloch's systematic action research project engaged Khaleeq and Phillip as "critical doers" through their use of literacy narratives, dialogic journal writing, interviews and surveys of peers and community residents, presentations at neighborhood forums, community mapping, digital photography, and video walk-throughs to raise awareness and resistance to the remaking of Harlem.

These two young men are reminiscent of another pair of critical doers—LeAlan Jones and Lloyd Newman—who chronicled their experiences with life and death on the South Side of Chicago in the highly acclaimed book *Our America* (1997). Their journalistic activities were relevant models for how students can learn school subjects as well as about their local communities and the larger world. In the preface Cornel West's tribute to this duo is also apropos for Phillip and Khaleeq. "How rare it is to get behind the pervasive stereotypes of young black men and revel in their complex humanity. And how infrequent the chance to listen to the poignant and powerful voices of these fellow citizens" (p. xi).

An eminent value of Kinloch's work is its viable considerations for what teachers can do in and beyond classrooms to stimulate other poignant and powerful voices to reveal their complex humanity in a variety of textual media and communicative acts. For example, most chapters contain a number of concrete suggestions for ways to rethink and restructure activities of teaching and learning to help students make direct connections between literacy practices and their local communities. These suggestions work to transform "pedagogies of poverty" (Haberman, 2001) with their back-to-basics, test-driven orientations, and move toward critical pedagogies that enable students to use their learning and literacy activities to directly affect their lives and communities.

Although the stories of Khaleeq and Phillip are central, one of the many attributes of this book is the wide range of voices, perspectives, and literacy practices that are brought together to illuminate conditions of living and learning at the intersection of race and place. We hear the voices of their peers, their teachers, community members, and other researchers participating in the project that complicate and personally situate ways that gender, generations, and race are embodied and enacted in cultural and institutional places. In "Teacher Talk" (Chapter 6), for example, we hear conflicting and conflicted perspectives on gentrification from teachers who are White and Black, male and female, and residents and non-residents of Harlem. Rebekkah Hogan, a project participant, articulated the key question underlying these conflicts: "Is there a way for 'development,' 'progress,' and 'gentrification' to balance the past and future, while being inclusive of everyone regardless of class, race, or history?"

Based on the history of gentrification, the answer to this question is "no"! Harlem is in focus in this book, but it is merely a placeholder for similar activities taking place across the United States, from east to west and north to south. Yet, as a student named Kim asked while being interviewed by Phillip and Khaleeq, "[what has] all this got to do with writing?" This is the question that Kinloch's work in its entirety answers beautifully. Writing and other literacy practices ultimately are "situated" activities; they take place in a "place" that is delineated by tensions between distinctiveness and connectedness. These qualities are rooted in mutually held and mutually available cultural understandings. Gentrification is erasing both the cultural distinctiveness and cultural connectedness of Harlem for residents like Khaleeq and Phillip and so many others. *Harlem on Our Minds: Place, Race, and the Literacies of Urban Youth* portrays this community's struggle to write these qualities back.

Jabari Mahiri

Acknowledgments

This book came into being because of the openness, dedication, and active involvement of many people, some of whom I may overlook inadvertently in this acknowledgment. For such oversights, I offer my sincere apologies and accept full responsibility.

First, I must thank Phillip and Khaleeq, the two superstars of this project. For more than 3 years, Phillip and Khaleeq allowed me to ask questions, document their literacy practices in- and out-of-school, as well as observe and participate in their various literacy, language, and community encounters. Their brilliance, marked by their ongoing involvement in the community, resistance to traditional forms of education, sophisticated linguistic repertoire, and their concern for the preservation of historic African American communities, is not fully captured in the pages between the covers of this book. However, their brilliance has inspired me to write this book, to question my own literacy narratives, and to reconsider meanings of literacy, schooling, and struggle in relation to community change. I hope readers of this book will discover important lessons about literacy and community from Phillip and Khaleeq as well as from their peers. With admiration and sincerity, I thank you a million times, Phillip and Khaleeq. This "thank you" also extends to the respondents included in this book. In addition to Phillip and Khaleeq, they are Valerie Orridge, Rebekkah Hogan, Mimí Richardson, and Latoya Hardman. Your voices are important, and I am honored to include them in this form.

I would like to also thank the principal, teachers, staff, and students at Harlem High School in New York City for opening their school and offering their time to me. In particular, I thank, again, Latoya Hardman, Phillip and Khaleeq's English teacher and my dear friend and colleague who never shied away from critical conversations about teaching and urban youth, and who helped me to see the extended value in being committed to this project. In the acknowledgment to my book, *June Jordan: Her Life and Letters* (2006), is written: "And to Latoya Hardman: our journey began at the University of Houston, Downtown and has extended to New York City and the students at . . . [the] High School. I'm looking forward to the next chapter." Well, this is the next chapter, and I am look-ing forward to writing yet another chapter. My sincere thanks and appre-ciation to you!

To Ms. Cunningham, Mr. Walker, Ms. Brown, the countless other teachers, as well as the community members—you know who you are, even with pseudonyms—I offer my heartfelt appreciation for your can-didness during our interviews, follow-up conversations, and email and phone exchanges. I hope you will find this work as inspiring as I find you. Thank you.

I am also indebted to other individuals for providing assistance on this project: Ms. Hollman, the associate director of the Junior Scholars Program at the Schomburg Center; employees at Hue-Man Bookstore & Café and at the Studio Museum of Harlem for informal conversations; Professor Edmund Gordon for allowing me to use office space at the Teachers Col-lege Gordon Campus in Harlem; my former colleague Professor Pat Zum-hagen for inviting project participants to discuss gentrification with her graduate teacher education candidates; and my colleagues and friends Professors Beverly Moss, Janet Miller, and Marc Lamont Hill, for encour-aging me to continue this work. I thank Ken Lindblom, editor of *English Journal*, for inviting me to edit the journal's new "Innovative Writing Instruction" column, which published a piece on Phillip and Khaleeq and meanings of "writing in the midst of change" (September 2008). I ac-knowledge my professional colleagues Professors Maisha Fisher, Lalitha Vasudevan, David Kirkland, and Andrea Lunsford, who were contribu-tors to a special journal issue of *English Education* (July 2009) that I guest edited, aspects of which I have included in this book. I must also acknowl-edge Professor Michael Moore, editor of *English Education*, for supporting the special journal issue.

Additionally, I recognize the many archivists, reference librarians, interns, and volunteers at the following research institutions: the Donnell Branch of the New York Public Library, the Schomburg Center for Research on Black Culture, the library at Columbia University, and the Columbus Metropolitan Library in Ohio.

Aspects of this work have been presented at various meetings and conferences. I acknowledge conference organizers and audience members of the following: American Educational Research Association, Conference on College Composition and Communication, National Council of Teach-ers of English, University of Pennsylvania Ethnography Conference, and the Writing Across Borders Conference at the University of California at Santa Barbara. I thank Professor Cindy Selfe for inviting me to present aspects of this work at the Summer 2008 Digital Media and Composition (DMAC) Institute at The Ohio State University. Additionally, I thank Pro-

fessor Deborah Journet for inviting me to be a plenary speaker at the 2008
Thomas R. Watson Conference on Rhetoric and Composition at the University of Louisville.

I am grateful to Rebecca Kanfor-Martin and my wonderful colleagues
in the School of Teaching and Learning at The Ohio State University. Thank
you for supporting my release time and for providing a supportive environment while I was completing this project. Thank you for being such
great colleagues! I must acknowledge my colleagues Professors Elaine
Richardson and Adrienne Dixson, as well as one of our doctoral students,
Jamila Smith, for participating in our 2009 CCCC's panel session in San
Francisco, California, where aspects of this work were presented. Additionally, I am appreciative of important conversations with my current
graduate students at The Ohio State University and my former graduate
students at Teachers College. I must especially recognize Candace Thomas,
my former research and technology specialist, and Rebekkah Hogan, my
former research assistant and project participant, for tirelessly assisting me
with various aspects of this project such as collecting reference materials
and participating in project meetings and community sessions, among other
things. Without your assistance, this project would have been delayed for
years. I am also indebted to Kristin Lindquist, my fabulous research assistant at The Ohio State University, who assisted me with editing and revising the manuscript. I appreciate your meticulousness! I also thank Chasrah
Gomer for her friendship and fashion-forward sense of style. Keep doing
you! Also, I thank Charlie Ackley for engaging me in stimulating discussions on race, language, and gender. You are a true gem. To the countless
other students, teachers, and activists whom I have encountered, I am
inspired by your own commitment to expanding meanings of teaching and
literacy throughout the world.

I thank my wonderful, dedicated acquisitions editor, Meg Lemke, for
believing in this project and the significance of this book. Thank you, Meg,
for your expert editorial advice, responses to my many inquiries, and for
your encouragement throughout the process. I am also indebted to the
series editors, Dorothy S. Strickland, Celia Genishi, and Donna Alvermann,
as well as to my production editor, Aureliano Vázquez Jr., the Advisory
Board and the external reviewers for offering important feedback on this
work.

To my dear friend Maisha Fisher, I say thank you for your ongoing
encouragement of my ideas. You have listened to my ideas and frustrations, all the while offering insightful feedback. I am grateful. Thank you
for introducing me to your Emory University colleague, Kristen Buras,
whose work is both insightful and inspiring.

To my parents, Virginia and Louis, my brothers Wendell and Louis, my aunts, uncles, cousins, and other family members and friends, I say thank you for the continued support and encouragement.

To Tom, thank you for your patience, love, and critical feedback. Thanks for encouraging the work that I do and the goals that I have, especially the ones yet to be accomplished. You are an amazing man.

And to the readers of this book, thank you in advance for your comments and suggestions. I hope the various youth and adult literacy narratives included here are as inspiring to you as they are to me.

The Apollo, the Cotton Club, and a Lot of Blues

The Making of Harlem's New Literacies

It was not by accident that my high school students and I discovered New York City's Harlem, or that it discovered us. The first time I actually visited this historic community was in the summer of 1996. I had just graduated with a degree in English from Johnson C. Smith University in Charlotte, North Carolina, was preparing for graduate school in the fall, and was working as a youth program counselor for the Upward Bound and Bridge programs. That summer, the administrators of the Bridge Program in Charlotte had decided to take our graduating high school seniors to New York City. When the seniors were told the news, there was utter joy. Hearts pounded, smiles widened, and excitement filled the air. They were going to New York City and I was going to be a witness, an observer, and a participant in this first experience for them and for me. We were all over-joyed that the community we had read about in the Black Literature course that I had facilitated the year before was going to welcome us with a warm embrace. Even more, we were curious to leave our Southern dwellings behind, however temporarily, to be bombarded with what we considered to be Harlem's famous entertainment venues. These included the world-renowned Apollo Theater on West 125th Street and its amateur night performances, and the popular Cotton Club, which was originally located at 142nd Street and Lenox Avenue and named the Club Deluxe, but which has since been re-created on West 125th Street. At each entertainment venue, countless African American artists entertained audiences with their music of love, pain, and survival.

We were also eager to be present in the same spaces that poet Langston Hughes, activist Malcolm X, author Ralph Ellison, political leader Adam Clayton Powell Jr., and legions of other Harlemites—artists, educators, leaders, and local residents—called their first or second home. For all of us, we had finally arrived at the birthplace of the Harlem Renaissance and one of the hotbeds of the Civil Rights and Black Arts movements in the United States. I can still hear my high school student Lamar whispering in my ear the famously popular line, "It's show time at the Apollo," as beau-tiful Black women, men, and children waited in line to enter this historic emblem of Black pride, talent, and dreams. As soon as Lamar said that line, he looked at me with starry eyes: "We are in Harlem." Indeed, we were in Harlem, standing in line to enter the Apollo Theater that we had come to know and love from our 17- and 24-inch television sets. My students and I were in Harlem, and Harlem was in us. We walked 125th Street won-dering what life had been like when Malcolm X was a political force in this community. We wondered if Langston Hughes had fallen in love with Harlem as quickly as we had, and I wanted to know where Duke Ellington had walked on a Sunday afternoon or a Monday morning. Where in Harlem did Black jazz musicians perform? How did Louis Armstrong get his first Harlem debut? What and how were Paul Robeson's experiences with his White classmates at the Law School at Columbia University? We wanted to know about these experiences that had paved the way for us—young, Black Southerners wishing upon a star and falling into Harlem. We needed to know.

Years after this first visit to Harlem, I researched more deeply the many other lives that shaped this community into a mecca of Black life and cul-ture: W. E. B. DuBois, James Weldon Johnson, Marcus Garvey, Charles Mingus, Lena Horne, Arturo Schomburg, and Zora Neale Hurston. There were also Nella Larson, Claude McKay, Josephine Baker, Fats Waller, Richard Wright, James Baldwin, A. Philip Randolph, June Jordan, and many, many others. I can still recall entering, both as a high school student in Charleston, South Carolina, and later as a researcher in New York City's Harlem, various English language arts classes that had bulletin boards and walls decorated with pictures, quotes, and inspirational messages from Harlem greats: "the right to make my dreams come true" (Georgia Douglas Johnson); "hold fast to dreams" (Langston Hughes); "education is the passport to the future" (Malcolm X). I also became interested in the lives of local community members and activists with whom some of us may be unfamiliar: James H. Anderson, founder of *The New York Amsterdam News*; Benjamin J. Davis, editor of the *Negro Liberator* and city councilman who represented Harlem after Adam Clayton Powell Jr., successfully ran for a congressional seat; Geoffrey Canada, president and CEO of the Harlem Children's Zone; Valerie Orridge, president of a Harlem tenants' association; and Nellie Hester Bailey, cofounder of the Harlem Tenants Council. Who were these people and what were their Harlem stories? What could they teach the next generation of Black Americans, including Lamar and the students in my class?

I had no idea that in 7 years after I first visited Harlem I would become a professor at Teachers College, Columbia University; work with students in two different high schools in Harlem; live in Harlem; and conduct a multiyear research project on gentrification and Harlem youth. I had always thought of Harlem as a significant place, even in my own youth as I sat on the front porch of my parents' small house in South Carolina, and even as I sat in my middle and high school English classes. I dreamed then of becoming an educator, wishing to be a part of a larger community and so desperately wanting to walk the streets of 125th, Lenox, and Malcolm X avenues and Riverside Drive. I always wanted to know more; I needed my students to experience more.

As a teenager in South Carolina, I would get lost in the pictures of Harlem and of Harlem literary greats that filled the insides of books in the local library. I stayed indoors to read the books I borrowed on the lives of famous African American artists, writers, educators, and politicians, which served as my escape from the scorching summer heat in Charleston. I, like many others, fell so much in love with the poetry of Langston Hughes that I wanted to write my own version of "I, Too, Sing America." Many years later, after numerous failed attempts, I wrote a first draft at the age of 19. In my high school English classes, the Harlem Renaissance seemed far removed from the South Carolina that I called home. But, in fact, the two places are intertwined in important ways that speak to the lives, dreams, and ambitions of many African and African American people, among many other people of color, throughout the Diaspora.

In New York City's Harlem, much like in various communities in South Carolina, segregation, discrimination, and the fight for civil rights for people of color serve as hallmarks of local history. In both places, parents and community members deem education to be monumental. The presence of African and African American educators, principals, leaders, and active community members indicates a rich heritage and focus on education. Phillip, one of the Harlem youth you will meet in this book, penned a handwritten message on the cover of one of his notebooks that spoke to the significance of remembering this heritage in light of struggles. The message read: "Never forgetting our past and struggles!! Strength, power, Black people, Harlem." In many ways, this message echoed the sentiments of some of the students, residents, leaders, educators, and even family members with whom I have talked about the historical struggles and educational pursuits of African, African American, and other people of color. This message from Phillip's notebook and the sentiments from people with whom I have talked of hope—"We've come a long way" (Ms. L)—and perseverance—"The struggle is not over for us, so we'll continue fighting" (Orridge)—are essential to this book. What I did not know in 1996, when I first visited Harlem, was that we (the Bridge Program high school seniors, administrators, and myself) could never leave our Southern dwellings behind. New York City, and Harlem in particular, is overwhelmingly filled with Southern tendencies: from the Harlem residents who were either born in a Southern state or whose families still live there to the insignias on the sides of churches that denote a Southern presence in the community. However, those signs, along with many others, are being forgotten in public attempts to remake Harlem in what some refer to as "a second renaissance" and others call "gentrification." The struggle is indeed not over.

This book explores Harlem and its history and future through literacy research and sociocultural perspectives. I draw on the wisdom, literacy lives, and experiences of Harlem youth and adults who regularly question the meanings of community, civil rights, equal opportunity, and activism as they make sense of a new Harlem. This new Harlem, according to Phillip, the longtime youth participant described in this work, "don't include what we young people think about community and all the changes happening. Our voices are not in the conversation and we ain't talking about gentrification and struggle in school. See, our voices always go unheard. What's up with that?" Khaleeq, another youth participant, agreed. He insisted that the absence of youth perspectives on community and gentrification speaks to a larger, ongoing concern, "a complete conflict over what was here, and what is already coming here, and what residents— youth included—scared of. That's the possibility of being displaced from the only home some of us know."

Phillip's sentiments and Khaleeq's beliefs speak to an even larger concern with which I, as a teacher researcher and a person who deeply cares about Harlem, continue to grapple: how the lived experiences of youth—urban youth in particular—represent literacy stories, or narratives, about place, struggle, and identity. Many times, these stories are not part of the work that students do in schools. In fact, the lived experiences of youth are often absent from the conversations that we, adults, have with youth in and about the community. Phillip and Khaleeq's narratives also challenged my earlier memories of and encounters in Harlem. In 1996, I was not thinking about gentrification and community change. I was not considering the significance of creating "parallel universes," so to speak, between youth literacy experiences in schools and the surrounding communities. Even more, I was not questioning the meanings, representations, and misrepresentations of Harlem as a mecca of Black life and culture.

I was, without a doubt, blinded by the stars in my eyes. Since then, I have begun to see more clearly as a result of listening to and documenting the literacy and community narratives of people who actually have a direct, intricate connection to Harlem. They include youth and adult residents as well as longtime local business owners and educators. What is really going on in Harlem? Why are the voices, perspectives, and literacy narratives of local youths, to echo both Phillip and Khaleeq, absent from debates over the gentrification of community? In what ways, if any, can a focus on gentrification in Harlem stimulate additional concerns for the lives of youth in countless urban communities across the United States who walk through, in front of, and around visible changes on their way to school, work, recreational centers, or home? What about their literacy lives, lives that are all too familiar with the streets, buildings, and local events that represent a distinctively rich literary, artistic, and political history for many of us? Where shall this story really begin?

A SECOND BEGINNING

The chapters in this book take into account various factors that have made and continue to make Harlem a place of Black cultural practices. These factors, which I refer to as institutions, range from museums, storefronts and local theaters, community businesses, corner bodegas, churches, schools, and research libraries and centers to salons, barbershops, and afterschool and community daycare centers. They have always been and continue to be important markers in the community. Primarily occupied by people of African descent whose cultural and spiritual lives have transformed otherwise undesirable locations into cultural institutions, these spaces are invaluable aspects of the lived experiences and literacy lives of many people. By literacy lives, I am specifically referring to the ways in which Black people's lives are heavily connected to cultural practices, activism, and rights movements, as well as community forms of education that value the power of written and oral words.

With these things in mind, the chapters included here attempt to engage in a number of interrelated tasks, including the following:

- An examination of a longstanding social, political, and geographic concern—that of urban gentrification in a community of color and its impact on youth literacies. This examination has implications for youth literacy across settings that include not only urban communities, but also rural and suburban communities in both local and global contexts.
- A discussion of how a focus on place connects youth struggles and identities in schools with activism in communities. This connection supports Cushman's (1996) research on visible distances between schools/universities and surrounding local communities.
- An inquiry into how youth literacy practices are influenced by a politics of place that is connected to local histories, discourses, and lived experiences. This inquiry can lead to innovative approaches for pre- and in-service teachers as they explore youth literacies across spaces and within school curricula. Specific approaches will be highlighted to demonstrate ways for teachers and researchers to work with youth around topics of place, race, identity, and writing in school and nonschool contexts.

The chapters, collectively, investigate how the lives and literacies of African American youth in Harlem are affected by public attempts to gentrify the community. They also examine connections between race and place by discussing how Harlem youth, teachers, longtime Black residents, and new White residents in the area view their role within the gentrification process. Such goals take me back to my own familial background in South Carolina and to tensions that I often confronted as a researcher in New York City and as a professor at Teachers College witnessing the beginnings of Columbia University's expansion efforts into Harlem. This political situation raised many concerns for my work with Harlem youth and teachers. These included debates over spatial ownership/sense of belonging, racial and economic implications of power and privilege, and meanings of displacement for poor and working-class Harlem residents.

As a young, uncertified teacher long before my venture to Harlem in the summer of 1996, I was caught in a struggle to define literacy, to put a name to it, to assign specific practices to it, and to locate it within various cultural practices of people of color. The problem with this struggle, as I now see it, had everything to do with my limited approach to literacy, even in light of the multiple literacy experiences that were right in front of me. Living in South Carolina as the daughter of working-class parents—a retired truck driver (father) and a retired nurse (mother)—I was surrounded with multiple literacies. I sat with my father on the front porch as he read *The News and Courier* newspaper, examined local news pamphlets, and rewired a 12-inch-high and 10-inch-wide portable AM-FM radio that did not need to be rewired. I translated, when needed, his Southern Gullah-influenced talk to friends and strangers. I studied his expressive interactions with my mother, who methodically wrote her "to do lists" in the same 5- by 7-inch journal where she wrote out the household bills and grocery lists:

> Prepare for meeting and read the daily message and scriptures
> Pay bills: Sears and JCPenney's accounts
> Buy bread, eggs, vegetables, milk, juice, and detergent
> Call Ruth, Catherine, Annie, and check on Dorothy [her sisters]

Along with reading her lists, my mother read magazines, novels, and catalogs, paying attention to how ideas were phrased and how the images told stories. It was obvious, at least to me if to no one else, that she wanted to be a teacher—an unfulfilled dream that she rarely talks about today. At the time, I did not realize I was observing literacies—acts, practices, and events in context. In our community, I listened to conversations that my mother had with relatives that were filled with patterns of code-switching; she easily moved, or shifted, between mainstream English and African American Language. I noticed my mother and father's interactions, often unnamed and not discussed, in segregated public spaces. And I listened to their stories of being denied access to particular "public" spaces because of their skin color and low socioeconomic status: "That building your cousin's getting married in," according to my mother, "Black people could never go inside. If we did, it was at night through the back door to clean up." Their engagements in the world of South Carolina have always paralleled the struggle for access to safety, equity, and opportunity of other people of color throughout the United States. Thus, my familial community in general, and my parents' lives in particular, critically inform my interest in location, community change, and literacies.

In many ways, the lives of my parents speak to the lives of the youth with whom I worked as a young teacher in North Carolina and a researcher in New York. The youth you will meet in the following pages are outspoken, witty, and committed to protecting their New York City communities. They oppose gentrification if it means displacement of community residents, resources, and rituals. They curiously question gentrification if it means safer neighborhoods and more opportunities for local residents. As Phillip asked, "Why we have to have gentrification give us things we should already have based on the fact that we're human, we're people? Now come on, the answer for Harlem's gentrification? At whose expense?" Their conflict pointed to my own conflict with the gentrification of historically Black spaces—one that supports diverse public areas just as much as it supports the safeguarding of Black communities.

This conflict is often evident in my academic/professional lives. During my tenure as a professor at Teachers College, I felt caught between the local community's fight against gentrification and Columbia University's efforts to expand into Harlem, thus participating in its gentrification process. Often, I took the #1 train along Broadway Avenue from an uptown stop at either 207th or 145th Street. Every time the train left the underground tunnel at 135th Street and headed toward the outside platform at 125th Street, I would stare out the windows. Hanging from the Tuck-It-Away self-storage business on the westside of Broadway Avenue at 131st and 132nd Streets, and written in both English and Spanish, a large banner read, "Stop Columbia! We Won't Be Pushed Out!"

The president of Tuck-It-Away, Nicholas Sprayregen, has said that the storage business is the largest property in this West Harlem area known as Manhattanville, which is primarily occupied by Black and Hispanic residents. After a 4-year battle—and counting—against Columbia University, local businesses and residents have refused to move out in order for the university to expand further into Harlem, particularly into a 17-acre section of Manhattanville. Their refusal, in light of a past threat of eminent domain by the university, has caught the attention of local media (e.g., *The New York Daily News*, *The Post*, *The New York Times*, and *The New York Amsterdam News*). From banners that hang on the sides of businesses to organized rallies, marches, and demonstrations, local residents and business owners continue to voice their concerns about gentrification and the tensions between neighbors: Harlem and Manhattanville on the one hand with Morningside Heights and Columbia University on the other hand.

Together, these experiences—the train ride that exposed a message of "Stop Columbia," the voices of youth who questioned "the answer for Harlem's gentrification?", my parents' literacy practices, and my own conflicts over safeguarding Black communities—fuel the direction of this book. They speak to a need to account for the intersections of place, race, literacies, and community activism. They also speak to the ways in which I define literacy, which has moved from a quite narrow to a much more expansive conception: as acts of, practices in, and activities around reading, writing, and speaking. In my post-1996 experiences, I now believe that *literacies*, in addition to the aforementioned acts and practices, include a variety of media. These media—from oral language, multimodalities, to computer and visual literacies, and, among other things, performances—help us acquire voices and critical agencies. The recently released report from the James R. Squire Office of Policy Research (2007) titled "21st-Century Literacies: A Policy Research Brief" from the National Council of Teachers of English (NCTE) elaborates on this way of seeing literacy. The report is attentive to how literacy occurs in and is influenced by diverse contexts. It opens with the following:

> Global economies, new technologies, and exponential growth in information are transforming our society. . . . English/language arts teachers need to prepare students for this world with problem solving, collaboration, and analysis—as well as skills with word processing, hypertext, LCDs, Web cams, digital streaming podcasts, smartboards, and social networking software—central to individual and community success. New literacies are already becoming part of the educational landscape. (p. 1)

Although the increasing demands faced by English language arts teachers appear overwhelming, NCTE's report is significant. It insists that literacies, particularly in 21st-century contexts, can encourage people to have experiences with technology and multimedia texts, be connected to local and/or global communities, and work collaboratively with others to address defined problems. Twenty-first-century literacies can also encourage people to critically analyze, synthesize, and question information, and read, write, and critique words and the world (Freire, 1970/1997; Freire & Macedo, 1987).

This understanding of *literacies* is a wide and encompassing one. It relates well to the literacies of "old" and "new" Harlem that will be discussed in the youth stories of community presented in this book. With this definition, I am able to better understand the literacies that were always in front of me in South Carolina, that I observed while working with youth in the Harlem community and schools, and the literacies that contributed to the historical significance of Harlem and its cultural institutions.

A THIRD BEGINNING

As with any project, especially ones filled with stories and narratives, there are always possibilities for multiple introductions, varied beginnings. In my third attempt at an introduction for this book, I offer an outline of the chapters to follow as a way to invite you, my readers, into an exploration of youth literacies and urban gentrification. The stories to be told, the questions to be raised, the perspectives to be shared, and the theoretical and practical applications that I attempt to unfold are challenging ones for me. These challenges have everything to do with the ways I represent—even in light of constant data member checking sessions (Lincoln & Guba, 2000), in which I share data and my analyses of the data with participants for their feedback—the lived experiences of the youth with whom I have worked for more than 3 years. In attempting to represent the narratives provided to me from participants, it is important to note that I have consciously decided to honor their voices, and oftentimes my own voice, by using African American Language throughout the book. Doing so allows me to present their perspectives in honest, powerful, and important ways.

"Harlem on My Mind: Black Lives, Youth Literacies, and Urban Gentrification" is the first chapter in this book. It introduces the main superstars, Phillip and Khaleeq, African American youth who reside in New York City. Sparked by the ongoing gentrification within the Harlem community, Phillip and Khaleeq share a common passion for words and a curiosity regarding activism. As they question what is occurring, spatially, within the community, they also wonder about the effects of gentrification on their school and community lives. Their experiences are powerful, their questions are critical, and their literacy engagements far exceed their age. Through Phillip and Khaleeq's literacy narratives, as well as that of their English teacher, Ms. Latoya Hardman (aka Ms. L), the chapter examines *old* and *new* Harlem. The old is marked by Harlem's history with rights movements, literary traditions, and cultural practices. New businesses, gentrification, and new residents to the area—primarily White professionals—serve as signs of the new. This discussion leads into a description of how youth make sense of the old and new as they make meaning, create and contest stories about the world, and rely on multimodal forms (e.g., digital cameras; video interviews) to document community stories. After a brief description of the project's methods, the chapter concludes by asking how teachers and researchers can be attentive to community histories in literacy work with youth who live in gentrifying areas.

Following this first chapter is a brief response on gentrification and community written by Phillip. In his response, he talks about his feelings on community change and what he believes to be the two contributing factors that cause gentrification.

Chapter 2, "My Word's My Weapon: Literacy Learners, Soul Singers, and Street Survivors," explores gentrification, urban youth, and literacy by turning to examples from Phillip, Khaleeq, and two of their peers, Kim and Samantha. The chapter discusses how Phillip and Khaleeq, the two main warriors of the word, or youth who creatively and powerfully use words to theorize about the meanings of the changing community, understand gentrification by considering Harlem's relationship with race and place, or what Phillip and Khaleeq call "the White-ification of the 'hood." This discussion acknowledges the value of troubling race and racial perceptions when discussing gentrification. It recognizes, in the words of Phillip, how local history is "not even remembered in ongoing attempts to gentrify everything Black," from the soul singers and street survivors who love Harlem to the literacy learners who are committed to knowing as much as possible about the community in order to make a positive difference. Phillip, Khaleeq, and their peers' commitment to the community speaks volumes to how they draw on the power of production and product to create transformative literacy stories. While Khaleeq and Phillip struggle with conflicting representations of Harlem's legacy, Kim and Samantha discuss meanings of a community that is being challenged by White privilege. Their stories demonstrate the value of engaging youth in critical literacy opportunities that invite them to believe, as Khaleeq does, that "literacy is who I am . . . with literacy, my word's my weapon." What are emerging implications of this work for how teachers can think about youth as literacy learners, soul singers, and street survivors?

Following Chapter 2 is a brief response on gentrification written by Khaleeq. Here, Khaleeq talks about gentrification, the changes happening in the community, and the increasing rent that residents throughout New York City, including his mother, are forced to pay.

Chapter 3 picks up the conversation on street survivors by talking about "Dancing to Different Beats: Surveying a Community at the Crossroads." A local survey on gentrification created by youth explores how countless young people in and around Harlem, in addition to Phillip and Khaleeq, are concerned about the effects of gentrification on their community structures and familial network systems. They dance to different beats (lived experiences, perspectives, meanings of community) as a way to make sense of being at the crossroads of urban gentrification and preservation and to honor their struggles with community change. To document their reactions to the loss of community, this chapter analyzes data from a random selection of 155 surveys taken by youth attending Harlem High School as well as a local educational enrichment program. The survey represents an honest attempt to respect, listen to, and learn from youth in ways that can enhance literacy across contexts. The youth responses reveal a strong desire to be included in the decision-making process around gentrification within the larger community. It also reveals the many layers of Harlem: as home, as a space of survival, as a site of community practices and education, as an urban sanctuary, or cultural oasis, of Black life. Various voices, stories, and struggles of youth over Harlem at the crossroads are presented in a way that locates their perspectives in debates on gentrification. Phillip and Khaleeq's perspectives on literacy and community foreground the youth survey responses. How, then, can teachers and researchers find respectful ways to listen to young people and include their perspectives inside of literacy and community work?

Latoya Hardman (Ms. L) writes about gentrification and teaching in her brief response that follows Chapter 3. As Phillip and Khaleeq's former high school English teacher, she talks about teaching by considering the value of placing the local community center stage.

To talk of gentrification in a historic African American community is to talk of the increasing presence of White residents to the area. Chapter 4, "Singing in Multiple Keys: Literacy, Race, and the White-ification of Place," examines how Phillip, who resides in close proximity to Harlem's 125th Street, thinks about the White-ification of *his* Harlem by being aware of tensions between talk of newness (e.g., gentrification; new businesses; White residents) and oldness (e.g., history; corner bodegas; cultural institutions; Black residents). Phillip's discussion of White-ification foregrounds an examination of how he and others think about Harlem as a place of cultural events not represented in public debates on urban gentrification. To do this, the chapter establishes parallels between two unlikely sources: Phillip in Harlem and Jasmine, a sixth-grade African American female in a 2004 summer writing program in Egypt, Texas. Jasmine, like Phillip, turns to her community to create literacy stories of place. Phillip's and Jasmine's stories as well as interviews and perspectives from local White residents in Harlem will help readers question White-ification and contemplate meanings of Black-ification. What can teachers and researchers learn from Phillip, Jasmine, and local White residents as they explore conflicting perspectives about place, race, and belonging in their work with youth? How can we translate individual community encounters into classroom instruction that engages students in collective literacy experiences?

Rebekkah Hogan, my former research assistant and project member, discusses Harlem and gentrification in the brief response that follows this chapter. She describes the tensions she experiences and questions whether there can be a balance between gentrification and community preservation.

Chapter 5 brings us to "Crossing 125th Street: Youth Literacies in 21st-Century Contexts." Khaleeq and Phillip have been re-imagining their community from "in neglect" to a place where "art is in constant process" (Phillip). In an interview, Khaleeq remarked, "Harlem is . . . art. It has been for decades, although the community is now being gentrified to create a sense of art [Phillip interrupts, "A fake sense of art"]. If this new art . . . is going to improve our community, why's it displacing so many Black residents who've lived here for years?" Drawing on Khaleeq's sentiments, this chapter describes how Phillip and Khaleeq are critical doers, or community documenters. They use video interviews and photography to capture literate-artistic conditions in Harlem in the face of gentrification. As they do so, they reluctantly cross the physical and emotional borders of 125th Street to enter into a university setting that does not feel anything like home. This crossing leads them to rethink the idea of White-ification during their encounters with largely White female teacher education candidates at a local university. How can this work help teachers and researchers think about how youth cross borders to interrogate meanings of race and community literacies?

Following Chapter 5 is a brief response on adult activism written by Valerie Orridge, president of a local tenants' association in Harlem. She talks about the significance of community and adult activism.

In Chapter 6, "Teacher Talk: On Gentrification, Urban Youth, and Teaching as Survival," we meet three practicing teachers in Harlem: Ms. Cunningham, Mr. Walker, and Ms. Brown. Prompted by a series of interview questions from youth and adults at Harlem High School, the teachers' perspectives challenge previously held beliefs on race and place by Phillip and Khaleeq. Ms. Cunningham, a self-identified White middle-class woman, believes class is the major factor of gentrification. She openly shares her internal struggles with White guilt in relation to gentrification. Mr. Walker, a White male, struggles with being an outsider in Harlem in light of his own research on gentrification. Ms. Brown, an African American woman, discusses tensions with living in "new" Harlem. The process of breaking through power, race, class, and language barriers, as was evident in these open teacher interviews/discussions, fostered critical critiques of the world and one's place in it. This process also cultivated expanded understandings of race and place, and prompted conversations on creating collaborative, democratic learning environments. How can teachers and students engage in discussions across age and race? In what ways can multiple literacy stories on community, identity, and power transfer into classrooms?

Mimí Richardson, a former teacher education candidate in an urban high school in New York City and now a full-time teacher in a suburban middle school in New Jersey, writes the final brief response. In her response, she shares her thoughts on teaching, change, and youth.

We conclude in Chapter 7 with a discussion of "A New Literate Tradition: Classrooms as Communities of Engagement." While the aforementioned chapters examine specific events in the literacy lives of youth and adults who are concerned with urban gentrification, this chapter raises questions of application: What does "a new literate tradition" mean and why is it important for teachers and researchers who are committed to quality teaching? What are the specific implications for this work in classrooms? How can teachers and researchers discuss community (e.g., concerns; realities; histories) in their literacy work with youth? This closing chapter discusses ways for classrooms in Harlem and beyond to continue to be stimulating sites of engagement for youth and teachers by drawing on a pedagogy of possibility. It concludes with suggestions drawn from the literacy narratives of Phillip, Khaleeq, and the many other project participants on teaching, teachers, youth, and community change. I believe their suggestions can enhance educational practices, pedagogies, and policies.

I now enter into yet another beginning on which I hope you will join me, one that has "Harlem on my mind."

CHAPTER 1

Harlem on My Mind

Black Lives, Youth Literacies, and Urban Gentrification

I took the B/C subway or the M4 bus from an uptown stop on my way to Harlem High School. The ride became so familiar that I could have walked from my apartment to school if I had not been in such a rush to get there on time. In the subway car, much like the Harlem neighborhood where I temporarily lived, I encountered countless teenagers donning iPods, backpacks, and speaking a sophisticated combination of languages, from "school" English, African American Language, to Spanish, Spanglish, and, on occasion, French. Upon entering the high school, I noticed that the linguistic richness of the youth followed me across the threshold, to the security station where I signed in, up the stairs to the main office, and into the hallways and classrooms where I met with countless students and their teachers who were hurriedly changing classes for the next

academic period. The linguistic richness both encapsulated and mesmerized its listeners, from the school administrators to the teachers to me.

Before I knew it, I became not only an engaged listener, but also an active speaker of "school" English and African American Language, a position I have always proudly occupied. I noticed how the talk, or linguistic richness, of youth in school resonated with the histories within the local community—histories that, in many cases, are often left outside the school door. This absence, however, was not the case at Harlem High School, a school that sits in close proximity to City College (City University of New York) and Saint Nicholas Park in one direction and important cultural institutions in another direction. These institutions include the Schomburg Center for Research on Black Culture on Malcolm X Boulevard; Hotel Theresa, which is near the intersection of Adam Clayton Powell Jr. Boulevard and West 125th Street; the Studio Museum of Harlem on West 125th Street; and the Adam Clayton Powell Jr. State Building at West 125th Street and Adam Clayton Powell Jr. Boulevard. The blocks around the school are lined with historic churches and various public schools bearing the names of famous African American and Latino leaders. The school is surrounded by a legacy of social and political activism, civil rights movements, and literary and artistic renaissances.

Centrally located amid all of this history is Harlem High School of New York City (HHS of NYC), an open admissions school with 37 teachers and approximately 8 administrative staff. There are nearly 550 students in attendance at the school, in grades 9–12. Of the total students enrolled, 54% are Black/African American, 45% are Latino, 2% are White, and 1% are Asian. I must admit that I find it problematic that the racial and ethnic breakdown for Black/African American students is not divided into distinct categories of Black/African *and* Black/African American, given the increasing number of African students attending the school. In light of this racial and ethnic configuration, approximately 46.1% of the students are male and 53.9% of the students are female, many of whom qualify for the free lunch program (Hardman, 2006). According to Ms. L, the English language arts teacher in whose classes I worked, the school was originally designed as an elementary school. At the time of this research, the building housed three schools—two high schools and one junior high school. Although Harlem High does not share its governing unit (i.e., principal; assistant principals; teachers; support staff) with the other schools, it does share public spaces within the school, including the cafeteria, gymnasium, and stairwells (Kinloch, 2008). In the past, the school was faced with the threat of being shut down by the state of New York for its poor academic performance; it was once listed on the New York State's SINI list—Schools in Need of Improvement. The current principal, hired approximately

5 years ago, was determined to turn the school around and raise its academic standards. He, along with the teachers and parents, worked to accomplish important tasks: to have the school removed from the SINI list, to improve student attendance, and to increase staff development and teacher training. Probably more importantly, the school "has started to put together a school-wide curriculum in English; replaced the grade of 'D' with a policy allowing students to revise work until it is satisfactory; and brought technology into classrooms" (*Inside Schools Profile*, n.d.). These significant efforts have fortified in the school's ongoing dedication to the academic achievement of its students.

Making such achievements, however, incurs consequences. Having been removed from the SINI list means that the school no longer qualifies for the free tutoring program offered to "struggling" and "underperforming" schools. I do not use the terms *struggling* and *underperforming* lightly. In fact, I would prefer that these terms not be used to describe public schools, particularly in urban areas, given the rich literacies of students and teachers at the school as well as the history of the local community. However, recent data on academic performance at Harlem High indicate that many new students are not on grade level. This challenge is compounded by overcrowded spaces, a perennial concern in New York City public schools. For example, the freshmen class enrollment for the 2006 academic year at Harlem High had 100 more students than anticipated. While the district's support of tutoring has lessened, demands are still placed upon students to increase their scores on the Regents examination, a New York State requirement that tests students in English, science, mathematics, and social studies. Despite these realities, the principal and his staff have remained focused on student achievement and academic rigor. The school is committed to progressive forms of education that take seriously students with special needs, students who are considered "advanced," and students who are multilingual and bi-dialectical.

In recent years, Harlem High has become more interested in focusing on social justice and the arts in its work with students. While many of the teachers explicitly address social justice in their classes, the arts flourish in "after-school programs, where students can do drama, visual art, band, spoken word poetry, and martial arts" (*Inside School Profile*, n.d.). During an assembly for Black History Month (2006), it became obvious to me that students at the school responded enthusiastically to arts-based education. Among other things, the assembly showcased students across grade levels actively participating in spoken-word poetry performances and organized dance routines. Presentations were led by poet Abiodun Oyewole, a founding member of East Harlem's 1960s socially and politically active music group The Last Poets and highly regarded as a forefather of today's hip-hop and rap movement. Yet teachers continued to discuss tangible ways to bring the arts into their classrooms. According to Ms. L, "the arts, in whatever form we're talking about, can really motivate students academically" as well as help them improve their academic standing and interactions with literature and writing instruction.

It was Ms. L's sentiment—that the arts "can really motivate students"—that led me to collaborate on a number of arts-and-literacy-based projects in- and out-of-school with this book's two main youth participants, Phillip and Khaleeq. Phillip was outspoken about the importance of going to school, "even though it's like boring as hell sometimes"; his history of struggle, "believe me, life ain't easy"; and his disappointment with public perceptions that paint, according to Phillip, "Black males as dangerous" (see also Mahiri, 1998; Kirkland, 2008). His deep voice and bright smile quickly revealed a young man who was caring, passionate, and concerned about the reality that "school's so separated from the community. Take, for example, gentrification." On this point, Phillip continued: "You know, we're not talking about what's real in Harlem in school. Like the possibility that Black residents right here being put out [displaced] because of gentrification." Sharing Phillip's concern was Khaleeq, a soft-spoken and warm-hearted young man who was just as dismayed about public perceptions of Black males as he was with the possible displacement of Black residents from Harlem because of gentrification. According to Khaleeq, "we need to be looking at what gentrification's causing . . . we need to learn what we learning in school, but you saying we can't learn that by learning about our reality? It's right here . . . this gentrification thing we acting like it's all good."

During our initial conversation at the school on community struggle and gentrification, Phillip and Khaleeq expressed a lot of resentment toward, according to Khaleeq, "the way our neighborhood's like, is like changing and it seems like nobody's trying to even figure out a plan or anything to save it from gentrification." Phillip echoed these sentiments, asserting, "and that's the truth! It's important for us to know that like gentrification's real. It's happening right in our faces. So when you [Valerie] ask if I'm interested in what's going on, I'd be lying if I said I wasn't. This my home." When I later interviewed Phillip about his writing practices, he shared that school practices ignored his concerns: "I'm interested in the outside community and I want to write about my community in school. But there's never a real opportunity to do so."

I invited Phillip and Khaleeq to join me in an examination of youth representations of community change. We collaborated and engaged in talk for more than 3 years. Our conversations were documented in verbal, written, and digital forms, and contributed to the ways in which I collaborated with youth in school and nonschool spaces. Our work, as Phillip reflected, "began at the high school, which is why it's important, and is now happening in our communities, in the office [my university office], and just anywhere else we take it."

At the heart of our collaborations are questions we regularly contemplated: How do we individually and collectively define community? How are our definitions affected by gentrification? How do youth define their roles, involvements, and identities within a gentrifying urban community? In what ways can youth document their literacy experiences in Harlem and connect them to their literacy experiences in schools? And what can we (e.g., youth; teachers; community members; researchers) learn from gentrification in Harlem in terms of literacy work (e.g., practices; pedagogies; events; activities)? These questions ground this book's examination into how the literacy lives of Phillip and Khaleeq are affected by gentrification. When Khaleeq said, "nobody's trying to even figure out a plan or anything to save it [Harlem] from gentrification," he was indirectly saying that his school, writ large, did not provide such an experience or opportunity. Or, as Phillip so passionately claimed, "I want to write about my community in school. But there's never a real opportunity to do so." In this book, I explain how Phillip and Khaleeq questioned meanings of community, gentrification, and activism by defining literacy through multimodal forms, shared writings, and classroom and community presentations. With these questions in mind, let me more fully introduce you to Phillip and Khaleeq.

HARLEM IS HOME: INTRODUCING PHILLIP AND KHALEEQ

Phillip and Khaleeq are creative young men, as indicated by the smooth way they walked, the glances they gave me and exchanged between themselves, and by how they described the aesthetic value of community in relation to struggle. Phillip was known throughout his high school and Harlem community as a super sports player and enthusiast. He embraced any opportunity to talk about his struggles, dreams, and love for Harlem, USA. He knew about the sacrifices that his family went through and how he was often at the center of their sacrifices. In the second year of our work together, he confessed: "See, I know about struggle and being lost. I'm not even gon' lie . . . I gave my parents, especially my mom, a hard time. Not even a hard time, but like hell! At 13, I was locked up because of a lot of things, but really hanging with the wrong crowd that I thought were my homeboys. I've learned from my struggles. I'm dedicated to improving my lot in life. I want to be successful, and I can do that right here in Harlem. So, that's one reason why I'm serious about understanding gentrification." Phillip continued, "See, this might not make sense, but my struggles happened to me right here in this place I grew up in and I learned from my struggles right here in this same place I call home. This the only place I really know and taking that away from me is stabbing me, my struggles, my lessons, and even my moms in the heart. That just ain't right!"

Khaleeq, on the other hand, was not as popular as Phillip in his high school, but he was just as curious as Phillip to learn about gentrification. He wanted to understand gentrification and to help maintain Harlem's status as a Black community. He, too, knew about sacrifices and struggles. In one of his confessions to me, he talked about his mother's dedication to family: "She's a good person and takes care of it all. You know, we used to live in Brooklyn. But we moved into the projects [a housing development] not that far from here because my mom's the main one we rely on, and my sister [actually, his cousin] needs special care. She finds that in Harlem [access to caretaking facilities] and don't have to travel that far for work either. When I think about my family and mom, I think about community. It's given us a place to be together and try making it. That's a reality for Black and Spanish people here, and that's why I don't get why corporations gentrifying Harlem. That's a way to get us out 'cause who can afford to live here after gentrification takes over?"

Khaleeq and Phillip's confessions help me to better understand the struggles, questions, and concerns that many youth who reside in or near physically changing neighborhoods regularly ponder: hanging with the wrong crowds, understanding their family sacrifices and community lives, and trying to make sense of living "after gentrification takes over." Their confessions also speak to the idea that the lives of youth are greatly influenced by civic engagement and community affiliations.

Phillip and Khaleeq were high school peers. They self-identified as African American males who spoke African American Language, lived in or around Harlem, and were concerned with "the changes happening in the community" (Khaleeq). I met Khaleeq during his junior year (2004–2005) and Phillip during his senior year (2005–2006), both at Harlem High School and in the context of their English classes. I worked with them for the remainder of their high school years and into their first years of college. Upon my first encounter with Khaleeq, I noticed a sluggish demeanor that often concealed a bright smile, great personality, and attentiveness to detail, particularly details related to reading and writing assignments given to the class by the teacher, Ms. L. Over time, Khaleeq and I engaged in open discussions about his perceived difficulties with mastering the power of the written word. As Khaleeq confessed, "I don't know if I'm on grade level or nothing 'cause I don't seem to perform well when I'm writing for school." Khaleeq's dilemmas around perceptions of writing included recognizing "what the teacher want and what I want" and admitting "how

I think about writing in school's different from how I feel about it when I'm not in school." As Khaleeq and I worked to improve his writing, we also talked about larger topics: succeeding in school, being African Americans, family, not being a traitor to his community because of academic achievement (see Kinloch, 2010), and gentrification in Harlem.

All along, I was under the impression that Khaleeq *officially* lived in Harlem, not *around* Harlem. He talked about the community with a sense of belonging, ease, and familiarity, and when I would inquire into his thoughts about *his* community, Khaleeq often responded with the opening line, "right here in Harlem." It was not until much later that I learned that Khaleeq's actual street address fell outside of the defining physical boundaries of Harlem. Take the following two exchanges:

Exchange 1:
Valerie: How do you define community?
Khaleeq: A group of people sharing space. And it don't have to be
    private space, but public like what you see on 125 [W. 125th
    Street, which is the main thoroughfare in Harlem]. Or a group
    of people who have things in common, live in the same area,
    and maybe like share similar beliefs, but they could still
    disagree. Like the people who go to Abyssinian Baptist Church
    on 138th Street [in Harlem] could be a community just like
    the people at Harlem High is a community and the people who
    like, like interact on 125 make another kind of community.
Valerie: You have lots of examples of community in Harlem, I see.
Khaleeq: I do 'cause it's a community with little communities in it.
    That's right here, what I see all the time. Harlem.

Exchange 2:
Khaleeq: Here's the rhyme book [our shared journal] back. I
    answered your question about gentrification.
Valerie: What did you write?
Khaleeq: Okay, so, umh, I know you wanted me to think about
    gentrification just like on a large scale, but I keep thinking
    about Harlem 'cause that's home, you know, and these
    things happening right here. This is what I wrote: "I define
    gentrification as the displacing of groups or residents who live
    in the neighborhood to benefit the property value of the
    community. The new buildings that are being built up are for
    those who can afford it and who's in a higher class . . . it causes
    many of us to be put out, stranded, no place to live, or in a
    shelter . . . it puts pressure on those stores and residents who

still in the neighborhood struggling to pay the increasing rent. Just look all around Harlem. Everyone knows
gentrification's here and changing the community.

Valerie: I notice that every time I ask you about community or
gentrification or even struggles and pressures that young
people experience, you always bring it back to Harlem. You
have an affinity for Harlem. That's good.

Khaleeq: Yeah, I do, but these things all are here in front of us so
it's hard to talk about them without saying "Harlem, Harlem,
and Harlem." That's my community.

Then, I was surprised by a comment Khaleeq made when I was interviewing him, along with Phillip, during my second year at the school.
I asked for their opinions on Harlem's physical borders—where Harlem
started and stopped from the east to west and north to south. When Phillip
said, "110th Street to the south is the starting point," I glanced at Khaleeq
and uttered, "but you live below 110th Street, around 100th, right?" Looking at me with a "So, what's the big deal?" look, Khaleeq said, "Well, tech-
nically, I guess, that's where Harlem starts. And if that's so, I live on the
Upper West Side. Either way, I don't feel like I live there 'cause that part
of NYC is like where lots of White people with money live. [In his Response,
he confesses the Upper West Side has "a mixture of people from different
races and even backgrounds."] And I live in a housing development, you
know. Not just for that reason but lots more, I feel closer to Harlem than
what they call the Upper West Side." Ever since my "realization," Khaleeq
has taken me on a series of video walking tours of his community, has
described the literacy activities in which he engages there, and has begun
to make sense of his connection to Harlem, its gentrification, and his am-
bivalence with living on the Upper West Side.

Phillip, in juxtaposition with Khaleeq, was more outspoken and popular in various social circles. A local sports star in basketball and baseball, he
was a master of words and wit, both written and spoken. From one of our
initial interview sessions on writing in school, Phillip shared with me: "I don't
think I got many problems with writing. I said I don't think. I try to give
'em what they want since there's no room for creativity when everything's
all about standards." During one of our initial encounters, Phillip informed
me that he thought of writing in much the same way he thought of sports:
"You gotta always practice to get better. To be a better ball player, I gotta go
out there with the ball, my team, and my growing knowledge of the game."
When I asked him to explain the processes he used to become a better writer,
he hesitated before admitting that he did not know how to talk about his
writing practices and performances: "I don't know. I just do something,

sometimes without knowing how. That's kind of how I'd describe my writing." As a researcher and an educator, I accepted Phillip's hesitation as an invitation to work with him on using language to conceptualize processes of writing. As Phillip and I worked on his writing, we also talked about his personal struggles with friends, family, and school: "I done did my share of things, but I've learned from them. I know I wanna be successful in life. Without struggle, you know how it goes, there's no progress." Insofar as teaching is concerned, both Phillip and Khaleeq's confessions speak to the value of listening to students in order to learn about their lived experiences and dispositions toward school-sponsored reading and writing assignments. As teachers, we should not read their dispositions as grounded in "laziness" or "disengagement," given that some students fear that academic requirements disregard their community practices and familial identities.

Clearly, Phillip knew all too well about struggle. After his run-ins with the law at the age of 13, he decided to leave behind his "wrong friends" and focus on his education. He transferred schools and enrolled at Harlem High School, a place that has had its share of administrative turmoil. For Phillip, "It's been lots of changes. After my first year, lots of teachers left and the principal. Then Ms. L [his English teacher] got hired at the school." In one of his early video interviews, he elaborated on this point:

> My education here is . . . I can't really say that it's my fault, but for the first 2 years here, 9th and 10th grade, it's been kinda rocky because we have a lot of different teachers here in our, in my, 4 years here. None of my 9th-grade and 10th-grade teachers are here, ever since I made it to 12th grade. And I had about three or four different principals. But I can't really dwell on the past right now, I have to dwell on the future and so far the future's been good.

Unlike Khaleeq, Phillip *officially* resided in Harlem; he lived in an apartment with his mother and siblings just a few blocks from West 125th Street. Quite frequently, Phillip proclaimed that Harlem is "my home, my home. This is it! You know, we young kids don't really know how to appreciate it when we're young." On this same point, he continued, "You grow up, you realize this is home. I got love for Harlem. I gotta wonder how long this place gonna stay what it is, though." In one of his videotaped sessions in the community, Phillip was quick to point out various sites: the Police Athletic League (PAL) where "kids hang out to stay out of trouble and join in different activities they have. Sometimes sports and entertainment stars stop in." Eyeing the construction sites of newer buildings in the area, he then pointed to the recently opened and expensive drugstore to the right and the expensive high-rise condominiums being built to the left. As he took in this landscape, Phillip realized, "My apartment has a fire escape. A raggedy fire escape! These here [pointing to the new condos] have nice big balconies." A few seconds later, he continued, "I'm surrounded in a circle and I'm stuck in the middle." Every day when he left his apartment, he was amazed at "all the changes that's coming here when nobody wanted to live here before. Now you see all them White people on their bikes, walking the streets, thinking about which new apartment they want to buy. Life must be good for somebody."

Khaleeq and Phillip's definitions of Harlem as home were definitely different. On the one hand, Khaleeq claimed Harlem as *his* community, where he lived and through which he traveled. In fact, he did not live in Harlem with "Black people," but on the Upper West Side with "White residents." On the other hand, he attended school in Harlem and bonded with Phillip over how the reality of gentrification in the area affected them. Their lives, initially intersecting because of their enrollment at Harlem High, were heavily influenced by the Harlem community, a community where they attended school, engaged in out-of-school recreational activities, and questioned their sense of belonging: "I thought I knew who belonged here, but I guess I don't know" (Khaleeq); "if Black people belong in Harlem, no one gives a damn 'cause gentrification's forcing us out" (Phillip). Their concerns serve as the foundation of our examination into Harlem's gentrification and the literacy stories that youth tell about community change. In telling their stories, Phillip, Khaleeq, and their peers offer teachers insight into concerns they have in relation to community, culture, and identity. These insights range from how youth think about community, how they grapple with a sense of belonging in the midst of change, and how they use writing to tell stories and make sense of the world.

TEACHING IN HARLEM: INTRODUCING MS. L AS TEACHER

Ms. L is a really good teacher. She pushes her students so hard that I think it surprises them how much energy she has, and she does this pushing with a smile on her face. I'm honored to have had an opportunity to witness her teaching. She had been my own student when I taught undergraduate English classes in Houston, Texas. I had always hoped that she would go into education. Shortly after I moved to New York City, I got the phone call: "Dr. Kinloch, this is Ms. L. This might sound strange, but I'm wondering if you have any space at your apartment for me to stay as I look for my own place." She stayed with me for a while before moving into an apartment in New Jersey. With her undergraduate

degree in English, Ms. L was starting her transfer job at a major bank head-
quartered in New York City while taking evening graduate level classes at NYU.
I figured that it was only a matter of time before she would decide that teaching,
and not banking, was where she needed to be. She figured it out at just the right
time. It's amazing how things worked out: I was her professor. I watched as she
weighed her career choices. I saw the excited expression on her face when she
went into teaching. And I saw how her excitement caught on with her new high
school students.

Ms. L started teaching at Harlem High School in September 2004 after completing a few courses in an interdisciplinary program at New York University. That same summer, she was accepted into the New York City Teaching Fellows program and began taking graduate courses in English education at City College (City University of New York). One could say that the fellows program, which is local to New York City, is similar to the nationally publicized program Teach for America. Both attempt to "recruit and prepare high-quality, dedicated individuals to become teachers who raise student achievement" (see New York City Teaching Fellows: http://www.nycteachingfellows.org) by taking its fellows through a quick approach into teaching. Programs like the New York City Teaching Fellows and Teach for America are often criticized for their fast-track approach into education. They are also criticized for recruiting college graduates who, for the most part, do not have an academic background in education and who are assigned to teach in "low-performing" and "disadvantaged" schools.

Ms. L herself has also talked about the struggles she experienced with the Fellows program, from its fast approach to immerse prospective teachers in the practices of classroom instruction, to pushing fellows into the classroom, full-time, by the end of their first summer as they continue to take graduate courses. However, Ms. L successfully completed the program, earned a master's degree in education, and taught at Harlem High School for almost 3 years. In January 2007, she decided to move back home to Houston, Texas, for a teaching position at the same high school from which she herself graduated years before.

Ms. L taught a combination of students at Harlem High: "In my classes, I had students who had already passed the Regents exam and students who had yet to pass the exam." On this point, she continued: "This created some issues in my classes, because I could not focus on Regents prep, but I could not completely ignore the students who needed this assistance, especially since they had failed the exam once already." Her approach to teaching was to create flexible but rigorous lessons that would meet student needs. She incorporated "many of the Regents-based skills into many of the lessons without putting emphasis on the fact that they were Regents-based skills. I don't teach to the tests; I teach with and for my students." From our many conversations and interview sessions, I noted in my journal that Ms. L "is all for her students," "is always thinking about her students' reading and writing," and "has been thinking lots about voice." In an assignment completed for a graduate course at City College, Ms. L wrote that she wanted to "help students become better readers, writers, speakers, listeners, and thinkers. . . . [I have to] encourage my students to find their own voice in their learning and have confidence to demonstrate their understanding through their own voice."

One way to do this, according to Ms. L, is by encouraging students to explore their identities within the local community. In this way, her teaching choices responded to the kind of questions that Phillip and Khaleeq asked about Harlem. Teaching books by Assata Shakur, June Jordan, Elie Wiesel, and Frederick Douglass, among others, she asked students to make connections to themselves: "How would you respond to the dilemma raised in this book?" This connection was then paired with how students saw their community: "Now, imagine that something like this or similar happened in Harlem. What would it mean? How would it change what you know about the community?" These questions motivated students to re-read the texts and think about their local context—New York City's Harlem. At the same time, it encouraged them to rethink definitions of community through the stories, lived experiences, and historical events of others.

Ms. L's strategies moved Phillip and Khaleeq to think deeply about Harlem's past, present, and future. When she asked them to make connections to their community, Phillip hesitated before asking: "Any connections? If I said I don't get why Harlem's changing so fast, I could go with that, tell you what changes? Relate it to what we read here [in class]? Or what?" Over time, Ms. L encouraged his explorations. She admitted to me her awareness that Phillip's caution to explore his community came from mixed messages received in school about what did and did not constitute academic learning. She knew that many of his teachers were not invested in his discussions of community concerns inside the classroom, which created further distance between Phillip's understanding of "academic" and "community" literacies and the places in which they allegedly occur. Ms. L remarked, "Along with you, he has his teacher [Ms. L] telling him to go out there and do it and it's probably the first time he remembers a teacher saying it. To do this in his community, no strings attached." I asked Phillip to also explain his hesitation, and he confirmed, "I don't know where some teachers come from. They want you to do this, not that. You just never know."

THE OLD AND THE NEW: INTRODUCING HARLEM
WITH MS. L, PHILLIP, AND KHALEEQ

Freeman's (2006) *"There Goes the 'Hood": Views of Gentrification from the Ground up,* examines the impact of gentrification on indigenous residents in two Black urban communities: Harlem in New York City and Clinton Hill in Brooklyn, New York. Through historical research, interviews with residents, and observations of residents' perceptions of gentrification, Freeman asks: "How do people feel when gentrification comes to the 'hood" (p. 1)? His question provides a framework for talking about Phillip and Khaleeq's understanding of gentrification as "a way to get rid of the old and bring in new" (Phillip).

In some ways, I agree with Phillip's sentiments that new practices in Harlem have replaced many of the old ones. This is what happens when a community is being remade and revitalized. For instance, Copeland's, a well-known soul food establishment in the community for 50 years, closed its landmark restaurant in the summer of 2007. Copeland's experienced a changing clientele, increases associated with cooking costs, and the demands of rent and other business-related bills. Copeland's restaurant is not the only "old" having to adjust to the "new" community changes. There are countless other popular restaurants that have had to adjust:

- Dating back to 1938, Wells Supper Club Site, which closed its doors on Adam Clayton Powell Jr. Boulevard in 1999, was known as one of the first establishments to serve waffles with fried chicken.
- Singleton's Restaurant, located at West 136th Street and Lenox Avenue, was known for its stew.
- 22 West Restaurant and Lounge at West 135th Street near Malcolm X Boulevard served many soul food dishes, including smothered chicken and barbecued ribs. Civil rights leader Malcolm X frequented this restaurant.
- The now closed Wilson's Restaurant and Bakery, which was located at West 158th Street and Amsterdam Avenue, was known for its famous breakfast, including salmon croquettes, grits, and biscuits.
- With a 30-year presence in Harlem, Pan Pan Restaurant on Lenox Avenue was known for many of its dishes, including waffles with fried chicken and oxtail stew. Located across from the Schomburg Center for Research in Black Culture, the restaurant was gutted by fire in 2004.
- Wimp's Southern Style Bakery on West 125th Street was known for many dishes, particularly its homemade desserts, such as red velvet cake. It closed in December 2007.

Newspaper headlines read, "Harlem Mainstay Survived Riots, but Falls to Renewal" (*New York Times*, June 23, 2007); "Sikhulu Shange speaks on Harlem Gentrification" (*Amsterdam News*, August 10, 2006); "In Changing Harlem, Soul Food Struggles" (*New York Times*, August 5, 2008); and "Poverty in New York City" (*Amsterdam News*, July 17, 2008). Additional headlines read, "Tensions of gentrification lead a U.S. City to Dialogue" (*Herald Tribune*) and "At Housing Project, Both Fear and Renewal" (*New York Times*, March 18, 2007). Countless Weblogs post farewell messages to Copeland's restaurant as well as to other local businesses in the area. Change is not on its way; it is already here. What do these changes and these old and new practices mean for youth literacy lives and stories? Thinking about this question leads me to Phillip's journal entry, dated April 24, 2005, in which he reminisces about community rituals as a way to write against public narratives that portray Harlem as dangerous or as "jungle" (see Haymes, 1995). Phillip writes:

> There are a lot of rituals in my community. People show each other love. We have Father's Day basketball tournaments, Mother's Day races in Central Park, block parties on 116th, 117th, and 118th streets during the summertime. . . . everyone shows emotions when something good or bad happens. All these rituals are beginning to fade because of gentrification talking place. It's getting rid of Black and Spanish people and replacing us with Whites. This is hurting the community in Harlem because we cannot afford these buildings. That's why we need to stop this before it goes too far. And the young people my age have to talk up about this, too.

In an interview session with Khaleeq, he talked about some of the same points raised by Phillip—community rituals, public narratives of urban decay—but in a way that located literacy in the discussion:

> Yeah, we got lots of rituals here, like Phil be talking about. People always have something to do, which is fun. That's why this is a community. I learn from the rituals, become a better person. I listen to stories people tell. I want my stories to pass down one day. I listen to what they say and make sense of it. I think about writing stories about what's here and how these things not gonna be here. I should write more, keep them memories 'cause this is one way to talk against the stereotypes people have of H-town.

In his comments, Phillip focused on "tournaments," "races," "block parties," "emotions," and how "these rituals are beginning to fade because of gentrification." Khaleeq attempted to capture Phillip's attention to changes in Harlem by confessing, "these things not gonna be here." This point is profound because instead of simply accepting the changes and the public narratives of Harlem as dangerous, Khaleeq came to terms with wanting to write about local stories. Both Khaleeq and Phillip, in their growing interests in the community, initially situated gentrification between the community's old and new in an effort to understand, as R&B songwriter Luther Vandross declared, what's "here and now." Yet in their understanding of old versus new, Black life in Harlem versus current efforts toward gentrification, they slowly realized that the most powerful response they can create comes in the form of writing and storytelling: community journals, videotaped sessions in the community, designing maps, and authoring their Harlem stories at tenants' association meetings. I realized this during one of our data member checking sessions (Lincoln & Guba, 2000) when I asked Khaleeq about his desire to write stories and where this desire came from. He replied, "from this project 'cause we always talking, sharing stories, writing about Harlem, what we see, what we know, what we think of the change." His response encouraged me to revisit the research methods that guided our inquiries into gentrification in Harlem. Revisiting the research methods and processes behind this project, which I do below, connects to the ways in which we—Phillip, Khaleeq, and I—publicly questioned our understandings of and writings on community change.

HARLEM ON MY MIND: A BRIEF DISCUSSION OF RESEARCH METHODS

With Phillip and Khaleeq at her side, Rebekkah, my former research assistant and a former graduate student in anthropology and education, described our project to an English education class of teacher education graduate students at Teachers College. She explained, "We've been researching and interviewing people . . . about a lot of different topics: gentrification and what that means, the relationships between gentrification and community involvement, and whether gentrification means whitening, improvement, etc." Then, Rebekkah talked about some of the various articles and books on gentrification that we have been reading, including There Goes the 'Hood *by Lance Freeman, who "raises some interesting questions about the impact of gentrification on the community." Explaining how my work centers around students and how they feel about the changes going on in their community, Rebekkah pointed to Phillip and indicated that he was "one of the first students" to participate in the project. Quite eagerly, she described her observations of "students feel[ing] empowered to discuss*

*gentrification in order to educate themselves and their communities on these
changes."*

How did this participatory action research actually begin? In introducing this research, I have alluded to the timeline and guiding inquiry questions, yet I believe it is important to provide more clarity for my readers. I
started visiting classes and talking with students and teachers at Harlem High
School during the 2003–2004 academic year. The following year, 2004–2005,
I began regularly participating in Ms. L's English language arts classes. During this time, I spent 3 days a week assisting Ms. L with writing workshops,
brainstorming lesson plans, and talking with students about various topics:
writing, testing, community literacy, Harlem, White teachers teaching students of color, and youth language practices. Then, during the 2005–2006
academic year, I began to engage in extensive conversations with Phillip
and Khaleeq, to observe them more frequently in classes, and to engage in
follow-up discussions with them outside of class time. Many of our conversations extended into afterschool meetings.

As a participant observer, I documented my observations in an eth-
nographic journal and participated in audio- and video-recorded sessions
with youth in the community. Participants and I exchanged rhyme books,
or writing journals, in which we posed and openly responded to a series
of self-designed questions related to schooling, community, and literacy.
I formally interviewed 27 participants ranging from students to teachers
and created an interview protocol for each group. However, I welcomed a
diversion from format in order for participants to openly share their perspectives on a variety of topics, including writing, identity, school, gentrification, and place. Interviews ranged anywhere from 30 minutes to 1½
hours. They took place at the high school, in my university office, or in
the community. It was not unusual for me to interview someone during
teacher-planning periods, lunch breaks, after school, or during summer
vacation. I tried to arrange interview sessions around the interviewees'
availabilities. Surveys on Harlem and gentrification were distributed to
approximately 168 students in grades 9–12 in a total of seven English teachers' classes. Students, both those participating and not participating, were
encouraged to visit community institutions and write about their observations. These institutions included the Schomburg Center, the Studio
Museum of Harlem, the Museum of Modern Art, the Apollo Theater, the
Harlem Theater, recreational facilities, and afterschool educational programs. Students were also encouraged to interview family and community members and to document their participation in the community sites
they frequented. Over time, students at the school introduced me to friends
who were interested in talking about community and gentrification.

Phillip, Khaleeq, and I attended tenants' association meetings and rallies in protest of the Columbia University–Manhattanville Expansion Plan, which seeks to expand the university's physical presence into Harlem despite the opposition of many local businesses in the area. The project proposes to create new academic buildings for various schools at Columbia University (e.g., School of the Arts, Business School, Science Center, and a magnet public school) as well as new buildings for interdisciplinary studies and graduate student housing. We also talked about our work with others: community members, new White residents in the area, and teacher education candidates at a local university. Even after Phillip and Khaleeq graduated from Harlem High in 2006 and began their first year of undergraduate studies at local colleges the following fall, we continued to talk about Harlem's gentrification. Armed with their rhyme books and digital cameras, Phillip and Khaleeq took to the streets to document well-known sites (See Table 1.1).

Overall, my data sources range from researcher field notes, taped interviews, shared journals, mapping activities, responses to a number of surveys and questionnaires, and handouts from open houses held at Columbia University in reference to the Manhattanville Expansion Project, to classroom observations, digital photographs of community sites and videotaped community walk-through sessions. The latter—community walk-through sessions—is when a youth invites project members into his/her community for a tour of the area. Generally during the session, another student does the videotaping while I, the researcher, take a "back seat," and become a learner and not a facilitator. For example, Phillip's walk-through began in front of the apartment building where he and his family lived and included the areas in his community where he socialized, shopped, studied, or simply passed by on a daily basis. It also included the places he wanted us (Khaleeq, me, and others who joined his walk-through) to understand as we considered the various stories of change and struggle that formed his literacy response to gentrification.

In my phases of analysis, I coded and digitized data for recurring themes of community, struggle, and resistance. Participants were instrumental in collaboratively designing survey questions and engaging in extensive data member checking sessions (Lincoln & Guba, 2000). They analyzed data for relative meaning and participated in follow-up discussion sessions, which proved helpful in overcoming their resistance to being "studied." In my journal, I noted that Phillip and Khaleeq were invested in "remaining loyal members of the community that has always protected them from the watching eyes of outsiders" (Researcher Field Notes; see also Kinloch, 2009). This became a major theme in my ongoing research with youth in the community.

Table 1.1. Selected Harlem Sites, Photographed in 2006 by Project Participants

Sites to Photograph	Location	Something to Know
The Apollo Theater	253 West 125th Street	Before becoming a theater, it was known as the Apollo Hall and catered to mainly White audiences. Later, the Apollo Theater became known as the place "where stars are born and legends are made." James Brown, Ella Fitzgerald, Billie Holiday, Diana Ross & the Supremes, The Jackson 5, Patti Labelle, and Gladys Knight & the Pips performed at the Apollo Theater.
Adam Clayton Powell Jr. State Building	163 West 125th Street (east of Adam Clayton Powell Jr. Boulevard)	Built in 1973, this building is named after Adam Clayton Powell Jr., the first African American state congressman of New York. It is home to agency offices, cultural groups, and city and state elected officials representing Harlem.
The Studio Museum of Harlem	144 West 125th Street (near Adam Clayton Powell Jr. Boulevard)	A local museum that sponsors exhibits, readings, films, lectures, a series of workshops, tours, and other cultural activities. The museum store sells posters, books, postcards, gifts, and other items.
The Schomburg Center for Research in Black Culture	515 Malcolm X Boulevard	A national research library that houses collections of research materials on the history, lives, and legacies of African people throughout the Diaspora.
Audubon Ballroom	3940 Broadway (between 165th and 166th Streets)	Built in 1912, it is known as the site where Malcolm X was assassinated on February 21, 1965. Malcolm X conducted weekly meetings of the Organization of Afro-American Unity (OAAU) at the Audubon. The ballroom served as a meeting hall, a vaudeville house, and a movie theater.
Hamilton Grange National Memorial	287 Convent Avenue (moving to a Saint Nicholas Park site)	National memorial site where Alexander Hamilton, the first U.S. secretary of treasury and a political philosopher, lived in from 1802 to 1804.
Abyssinian Baptist Church	132 Odell Clark Place (also known as West 138th Street)	A well-known church, Abyssinian Baptist was founded in 1808 by African Americans and Ethiopian merchants.
Harlem YMCA	181 West 135th Street	A community service organization that relocated to Harlem in 1913 from its West 63rd Street site that opened in 1905 where it rented rooms. It offers educational and enrichment programs.

(continued)

Table 1.1. (continued)

Sites to Photograph	Location	Something to Know
Hotel Theresa	2090 Adam Clayton Powell Jr. Boulevard (at 125th Street)	Opened in 1913, it was the tallest building in Harlem and the heart of Black life in the community until the Adam Clayton Powell Jr. State Building was erected. Once it began to allow African Americans to stay in it, its clientele included Jimi Hendrix, Muhammad Ali, Duke Ellington, Josephine Baker, and Ray Charles. Fidel Castro stayed at the hotel in the 1960s. Malcolm X's Organization of Afro-American Unity was housed there. In 1971, Hotel Theresa became, for the most part, office space.
Marcus Garvey Park	East 124th Street (between Mount Morris Park West and Malcolm X Boulevard)	The park was renamed from Mount Morris Park to Marcus Garvey Park in honor of the Jamaican-born activist who promoted the "Back to Africa Movement."
Duke Ellington Statue	East 110th Street and 5th Avenue	Designed by artist Robert Graham, the monument portrays Ellington positioned in front of a grand piano that is lifted over the heads of ladies.
Riverbank State Park	Enter at 145th Street and Riverbank Drive	This is a 28-acre park that overlooks the Hudson River and has facilities such as an outdoor pool, an indoor Olympic-size pool, basketball and tennis courts, and ice and roller-skating rinks.
Riverside Church	490 Riverside Drive (at 120th Street)	A well-known interdenominational, international, and interracial church that was built in 1927. Dr. Martin Luther King Jr., Marian Wright Edelman, Nelson Mandela, and others have spoken at this church.
The Cotton Club	656 West 125th Street	Originally named the Cotton Deluxe and located at 142nd Street and Lenox Avenue, it attracted a "White only" audience and African American performers. Now, people of color perform at and patronize the business.
Striver's Row	West 138th and 139th Streets (between Adam Clayton Powell Jr. Boulevard and Douglass Boulevard)	These two streetscapes contain some of the most beautiful row houses and apartment buildings built by David King Jr. in the 1890s. Famous Harlemites called Striver's Row home.
Renaissance Ballroom	West 137th Street and Adam Clayton Powell Jr. Boulevard	This site was the mecca of nightlife in Harlem in the 1930s. Often referred to as "The Renny," it had cabaret acts, live bands, and dancing.

LOCAL COMMUNITIES AND LITERACY WORK:
EMERGING LESSONS FOR TEACHERS AND RESEARCHERS

Writing scholar Reynolds (2007) studies relationships between theories of writing and the physical, spatial, and visual locations where people interact. We—teachers, teacher educators, researchers, parents, policymakers, community leaders—in classrooms and communities from New York City's Harlem, New Orleans, San Francisco, and Chicago, to Detroit, the Sea Islands of South Carolina and Georgia, as well as other places, must take seriously the lives, literacies, and struggles within communities that are undergoing gentrification and spatial reappropriation. Students at Harlem High School have taught me that youth involvement in the community can help teachers create curricula that invite students to participate actively in their ongoing learning. Phillip and Khaleeq's creation of poster-sized maps of Harlem, which they presented at a tenants' association meeting, encouraged Ms. L to create assignments in which students mapped and visited local sites referred to in the poems, essays, and novels by literary authors such as Langston Hughes, June Jordan, and Assata Shakur.

Some teachers might resist "getting too personal" with students. Yet we speak of classrooms as sites of literacy learning and democratic engagements (Kinloch, 2005a; 2005c) where students and teachers take risks, exchange experiences, critique positions, and question perspectives. Therefore, inviting students to discuss their critiques of literacy within classrooms can encourage them to be responsible for their learning as they critically engage in writing, reading, thinking, and speaking activities. Simultaneously, it can ease the hesitation that some teachers have with getting to know their students. This can be accomplished in a number of ways, including:

- Inviting students to journal about how they define their identities in relation to the classroom, the school, the local community, and the larger world.
- Asking students to make critical connections between texts and lived experiences. In this way, they could establish various texts-to-self connections that they can interrogate throughout the span of the academic year and across the study of various literary authors.
- Collaborating with students to identify community concerns such as gentrification, violence, youth voting rights, or a city-sanctioned curfew. Together, students and teachers can read related articles, create arguments and counternarratives, and present position papers

that assert their various viewpoints. Then, they could invite local community leaders to class to exchange perspectives.

There are many other ways for teachers to get to know their students through literacy encounters in the classroom while encouraging them to take responsibility for their literacy lives. In the next chapter, I discuss the literacy stories of Phillip and Khaleeq as well as two of their peers, Kim and Samantha, to demonstrate how youth can assume ownership over their identities as literacy learners, soul singers, and street survivors in the midst of a changing, rapidly gentrifying community. As with the youth whom I describe, I have "Harlem on my mind."

On Gentrification and Community

By Phillip Reece Jr., Harlem Resident

Dear Readers,

Have you ever wondered: What is gentrification and why are so many minorities, or people of color, and their family and friends affected by it? Well, in response to the first chapter, I would like to discuss with you the ways gentrification affects the Harlem community in New York City, especially since gentrification also has major effects throughout the United States of America. There are two important points that I feel you should be aware of in relation to gentrification. The first has to do with the definition of gentrification, what it means and what I think it includes. The second point has to do with the remodeling of old buildings into brand new homes that have excessively high rent and ownership costs, and the possibility that more homelessness might happen where gentrification and housing changes are occurring. I want to tell you what is happening right in front of our eyes.

Some of you reading this response might not be faced with the realities and effects of gentrification. However, you just might know friends, family members, neighbors, or associates who are suffering or may eventually suffer from living in a community that is becoming gentrified. You might say to yourself, "How does this affect me?" Well, I believe that even if where you live is not being gentrified, or even if you can afford the cost of gentrification and you welcome its presence, you should really consider what it involves. Try to understand how gentrification affects people like poor and working people, from what they might not be able to afford to pay in rent increases to how they fear being displaced from the place they call home. It's hard to think that these things can happen, but we know they do.

So, let me start with the definition of *gentrification*. The *Merriam-Webster Online Dictionary* identifies *gentrification* as a noun and defines it as "the process of renewal and rebuilding accompanying the influx of middle-class or affluent people into deteriorating areas that often displaces poorer residents." The *Webster's Online Dictionary* defines *gentrification* as "the restoration of run-down urban areas by the middle class (resulting in the displacement of lower-income people)." Then, the *Columbia Online Encyclopedia,* sixth edition, defines *gentrification* as "the rehabilitation and settlement of decaying urban areas by middle- and high-income people. Beginning in the 1970s and 80s," according to this encyclopedia, "higher-income professionals, drawn by low-cost housing and easier access to downtown business areas, renovated deteriorating buildings in many cities, reversing what had been an outmigration of upper-income families and individuals from many urban areas."

Two contributing factors that cause gentrification are: remodeling of old buildings into brand new homes and the excessive rent increases that result. The new condominiums that are being built look like great buildings, but some of those new buildings are replacing things that were already there, things that were important to many people for a long time. Baseball fields, homes and apartments, and meeting places that were there are now gone. We are now seeing displacement of many family and friends. According to some of the people who owned buildings or even the landlords who manage them, the average price of rent in some of the buildings in Harlem comes to more than $1,500 a month, and that doesn't even include electricity and other household expenses. This is the average cost to rent a very small apartment that you do not even own or have the right to change or remodel yourself. This is more money than most people who've been living in the area for a long time make and can afford. So, I ask: What are they to do? How are they supposed to survive without worrying about being displaced or becoming homeless? What about their children and other family members? And how are young people supposed to concentrate on schoolwork and achievement when they know their families are struggling to stay above water? You tell me.

Beyond the concern of individual families, gentrification is greatly affecting our society and country. It's a word and reality that's come to symbolize wealthy White newcomers to a particular community. While that's a reality, the other reality is that it causes the displacement of poor Blacks and Latinos. Changes in the community can take many forms. Some of those forms include wealthier people displacing poorer people. And don't get me wrong: I am aware there are some wealthier Black people in Harlem who are benefiting from gentrification as well. When I am walking down the street, though, it's really visible that more and more White people are moving into the area, buying into gentrification, and enjoying an area that many of them ignored before. So, while wealthier Black and White people are moving into gentrified Harlem, one of the tensions I feel comes from being ignored by the new White residents. I try to talk to them and at least acknowledge them as neighbors, but they seem so uncomfortable. Why would anyone be uncomfortable in a place where they choose to live unless they have feelings of guilt? I wonder.

Gentrification is a reality that does cross race and class boundaries. The unnecessary displacements, homelessness, and excessively high rent are just a few ways gentrification is affecting a lot of families and friends. It is also affecting the sense of community and the feeling of belonging all throughout this country. Readers, I have discussed some of the realities that I associate with gentrification. I believe it is up to us to make wise decisions on how we live, where we live, and how we live with other people in mind. Do we accept gentrification if it causes displacement of groups and groups of people, or do we stand up and seek other solutions?

Thank you for reading this response.

—Phillip

CHAPTER 2

"My Word's My Weapon"

Literacy Learners, Soul Singers, and Street Survivors

Valerie: When I asked you to introduce yourself on the tape you
said your name and where you're from and that you live
in Harlem. So I'm just curious, what do you think of your
community?

Phillip: Well, now you talkin' about where I live at, or just community in general?

Valerie: Your immediate community, where you live, where you
might hang out.

Phillip: Well, where I live, my community where I live is trying
hard to make it better for people. Like where I live at I live
across the street from the Harlem PAL [Police Athletic League]
that's where I've been working for years now. You seen it on
my video walk-through. Anyway, I mean the PAL it helps out

39

a lot, it attracts attention but around where I live at there's a lot of gentrification. Like there's a lot of buildings when I was 6, 7 years old that were abandoned or, from what I was told, were crack houses and all that. And they're rebuilding these buildings now at a higher cost, most likely a lot of minorities can't afford these buildings around where I live at. Like there's a Rite Aid like a block from where I live, there was never a Rite Aid. All 17 years of living there, there was never a Rite Aid! I mean I think it's funny and hilarious and I joke with my mother all the time about how "I love gentrification 'cause now we got a Rite Aid right up the block where I can get my medicine and all that. Never had that before." But for real, all these people that I see, like basically it's nothing but White people coming in around here right now. Like they walk their dogs, they pay a lot of rent for these nice buildings but . . .

Valerie: How do you feel about that?

Phillip: I mean I feel, I can't really say I feel bad about it. I can't really say I feel good about it 'cause I don't! I'm trying to figure it out. I'm kinda in the middle because it looks good because it gets people a place to live. People do need a place to live, but the people getting the nice places don't look like me or you, know what I'm saying? These White people, they coming in and probably worked hard in school, probably got a nice job, and they want what they think they should have. But people right here in Harlem, we work hard, too. I guess I can't blame them [White people] for that, but I can blame them for not recognizing the community that's already here before they decided to move on in. Take it over. That ain't right! Like that man, Maurrasse, say in one of them books, let's talk equity. (From March 14, 2006, Videotaped Session, Transcribed Excerpt of Frame #16)

Phillip's feelings about gentrification in Harlem were complicated. On the one hand, he jokingly described gentrification as bringing the convenience of a newly opened drugstore to the area. Yet he questioned the newness that results from gentrification—renovated buildings, White people, higher rent prices—while positioning himself "in the middle." This positioning gave Phillip multiple perspectives by which to critique the changing community that seemingly is getting resources it did not have before (i.e., new stores; renovated apartment buildings; financial capital from wealthier new residents; public attention). Nevertheless, Phillip readily admitted that although he cannot blame White people for wanting to have affordable rent—affordable in comparison to other parts of New York City— he can "blame them for not recognizing the community that's already here before they decided to move on in." As Phillip saw it, White people are not just moving in at full speed, but taking over Harlem. This raised significant issues for both Phillip and Khaleeq, issues that are often addressed in literacy research: concerns over equity and fairness, debates over spatial power and a sense of belonging, and questions over representation. Whose stories are told, privileged, honored, and valued in- and out-of-school and in relation to a gentrifying community?

This chapter explores these issues by turning directly to the literacy stories (e.g., writings, conversations, and multimodal forms of communication) of Phillip, Khaleeq, and two of their high school peers, Kim and Samantha. Because literacy was central to Phillip and Khaleeq's community lives, this chapter explores how these two youth, to whom I also refer as warriors of the word, defined and made sense of gentrification by considering Harlem's rich history. According to Khaleeq, this history "ain't even remembered in gentrifying all things Black," which affects Harlem's longtime Black residents who are committed to community preservation. Although I examine relationships between race and place, or what Phillip and Khaleeq called "the White-ification of the hood," more extensively in Chapter 4, this chapter will unpack Khaleeq's sentiments that "literacy is who I am, what Harlem is, what big G [gentrification] taking [a]way. But with literacy, my word's my weapon." In unpacking the lessons within Khaleeq's confession, this chapter will conclude by discussing the emerging implications of this work for teachers. When we think of urban youth as literacy learners, soul singers, and street survivors, we open the door for their creative expressions to take center stage in our classrooms, which, in turn, can stimulate students to experiment with expanded definitions of literacy within their communities.

LITERACY LEARNERS

When Phillip made the comment, "Like that man, Maurrasse, say in one of them books, let's talk equity," he was referring to David J. Maurrasse, the author of *Listening to Harlem: Gentrification, Community, and Business* (2006). Participants and I read selected chapters from this book and were captivated by Maurrasse's assessment of the economic changes caused by gentrification in Harlem. Drawing on data from historical research, current demographics, real estate statistics, and interviews with residents, business owners, and community organizations, Maurrasse defines issues of equity/inequity in initiatives aimed at improving urban communities.

He seeks more equitable options to bring resources into urban areas without adversely affecting longtime residents of color, many of whom are poor and working-class. For Phillip, Maurrasse "gets me thinking about the place, like this community, what we ain't got, never had, what we got coming in now." He continued: "Like that Rite Aid. Some people laugh and say, 'What's the big deal?' The deal is these businesses never thought Blacks were worth having nice things here before 'cause we ain't never had a Rite Aid 'til gentrification and White people started looking at Harlem saying, 'Yeah, I can afford that rent.'"

As an educator, the big deal, as inspired by Maurrasse, is that both Phillip and Khaleeq were beginning to create their own literacy narratives of the community. Their written narratives took into consideration the history of Harlem as a major site of Black artistic, intellectual, and political action that spanned from the Harlem Renaissance, the Great Southern Migration, the Civil Rights Movement, to the Black Arts Movement, and the open admissions policy at City College on West 138th Street and Convent Avenue. In light of this history, Phillip questioned the increasing presence of new White residents in the area against the backdrop of middle-class Black residents who were returning to Harlem. The following exchanges between Phillip and me attest to how Phillip drew on Harlem's history to narrate stories:

> *From Phillip's journal:* I got stories to tell about Harlem. I'll say the kinds of struggles I see in my community is Blacks fighting each other 'cause we don't know what to do about gentrification that's here. Gentrification taking place in my community. It's bad enough Black people struggling with job security and rent. Now we struggling for place, for our community to stay ours.
>
> *My response:* You talk often about struggles you see in Harlem. When I interviewed you early on, you mentioned gentrification is bringing these new and different types of struggles that have always been here, but are more in your face now. Do these new struggles take something away from Harlem? Can you use literacy to explain this? Remember, you want to think about a literacy story about Harlem.
>
> *Phillip's response:* I could create a response by using literacy. I guess you can call it a literacy story, narrative, whatever. The simple fact that we listening to each other and sharing ideas without you having to tell me what to do or agreeing with me and me with you, that's like literacy. We gotta first listen and find ways to use our language to get points across. That's the beginning point of making a literacy response to anything, especially gentrification,

listening and talking. Then we go away, write what we think without feeling pressured.

Phillip's resistance to being pressured into creating a literacy narrative about Harlem paralleled his resistance to engage in school-sponsored writings that are timed, forced, and neatly structured into five paragraphs. He was a careful listener and a conscientious thinker who engaged in critical reflection on his community and school. He voiced the pain he experienced following a set structure that "don't let students be creative and color outside the coloring book lines." In many ways, he proved that students can "color outside" the lines of the formulaic essays that they are regularly assigned. Phillip gravitated toward the theme of struggle in his writings about Harlem. He advocated listening and talking about the "gentrification taking place." Over time, I noticed how acts of listening, talking, writing, and not feeling pressured found their way into Phillip's school life: He listened more to his teacher and battled less with the academic requirements that were "imposing on my creativity, man."

Khaleeq also started his literacy story concerned about struggle, displacement, and policing in Harlem. He writes:

> *From Khaleeq's journal:* I still see gentrification as displacing groups of residents from the neighborhood. I can start there. With how I live around lots of White people. How more policing in the projects now than before. I might start with something like that.
> *My response:* Can you go with that more? What do you mean . . . more White people, policing?
> *From Khaleeq's response:* Like Phil been saying, more Whites moving in buying up things, like new apartments. With this you get more cops in the area, like on *1-2-5* [West 125th Street]. This could be a literacy story. I can take pictures of new things, new fixed apartments, White people hanging out on the streets when they never used to. I could put the pictures with my reflections like of, I don't know, like how these things changing Harlem. I can research how life was like here 5, 10 years ago and how now's different from before.
> *My response:* That's a great idea. You got . . . photos, reflections, history . . . and you could include something about your own identity and how you see the world. Correct me if I got you wrong here.
> *From Khaleeq:* What you wrote me back, you ain' wrong. You got what I'm saying.

Khaleeq's literacy narrative had everything to do with how he personally saw and experienced Harlem. Although he did not officially live in Harlem, but around Harlem—on its outskirts—as I described in Chapter 1, Khaleeq refused to disassociate himself from the community, though we debated this issue for some time. Khaleeq's approach to a literacy narrative was multiple and multilayered: He was a visual person, which came through in his desire to "take pictures," "put the pictures with my reflections," and "research how life was like" in the community. As he wrote about the images he wanted to capture with the video camera, Khaleeq had already started to create a literacy narrative without realizing it. Through our writing exchanges, he was able to imagine, in the words of Phillip, how to "be creative and color outside the coloring book lines." Khaleeq, like Phillip, questioned the purpose of constantly having to produce the formulaic essays assigned in his English classes, believing that when he was required to write on demand (Gere, Christenbury, & Sassi, 2005; Pike-Baky & Fleming, 2005; Lunsford & Ruszkiewicz, 2006), it "suffocate[d] me, not letting me express what I want how I want to." Khaleeq resisted this pressure by redefining literacy as "expressions about myself, my beliefs through words, images, opinions and they can be written or spoken or like digital or what you see [visual], but they give a feeling of power, like feelings of knowing or something." He shared, "Maybe I feel like that [suffocation] in here [classroom] 'cause I don't think I got power. You think I do?"

As my relationship with Phillip and Khaleeq developed, we discussed how writing serves many purposes: to exchange ideas, explain positions, critique perspectives, question values, establish points of view, and reflect on beliefs that may contradict other people's beliefs. By exchanging journals, we learned together how writing also offered us a space to continue to think about Harlem and gentrification even when we were not meeting or talking face-to-face. The paper became our meeting place and writing in our journals was not censored. We had collaboratively decided on our topic—gentrification, and our site—Harlem. Through writing, we were able to ask one another follow-up questions that we may not have asked in person because of time constraints or the current paths of our streams of consciousness. Additionally, with writing, we were able to do what Fishman, Lunsford, McGregor, and Otuteye (2005) describe as performing writing. Drawing on Heath's (1999; see also Heath & McLaughlin, 1993; Heath & Smyth, 1999) years of research in the arts and literacy, Fishman and coauthors write: "when young people perform writing they perform literacy, and their activities . . . exemplify the self-conscious, multimodal communication that distinguishes literate interactions today" (p. 225). Elaborating on the idea of performance, they insist that it "often refers to demonstrable mastery over skills or knowledge, and in writing programs we tend to treat student performance like something we can measure and assess using rubrics . . . our students compelled us to pay attention to the live, scripted, and embodied activities they stage outside the classroom" (p. 226).

In many ways, Fishman and coauthors' point connects with Fisher's (2007) description of the "read and feed" process that she documented in a literacy class at University Heights High School in the Bronx, New York, a process that engaged students in writing, responding to, rewriting, and performing their poetry and spoken-word pieces. Though not public, our "read and feed" process—that is, the process in which Phillip, Khaleeq, and I participated—was performed by writing our ideas and engaging in a constant feeding of those ideas through ongoing writing exchanges. Our feedings eventually influenced the ways we thought about literacy in- and out-of-school: as transformative, reciprocal, and emerging.

Our writing exchanges also served as reference points during face-to-face discussions, interviews, and video walk-through sessions in the community. With writing at the core, we enhanced our thinking about literacy and community as we created group and individually authored literacy narratives about Harlem. Our videotaped walk-through sessions were attempts at creating visual narratives grounded in Khaleeq's definition of literacy: "expressions about myself, my beliefs through words, images, opinions and they can be written or spoken or like digital or what you see, but they give a feeling of power, like a feeling of knowing or something." As literacy learners, Phillip and Khaleeq took charge of the writing they produced, the ideas they exchanged, and the questions they posed about gentrification: "Why's it happening in Harlem?" "What can young people do?" "Why aren't we talking about this more in our school, it's located right in the center of all this anyway?" Indeed, they were actively redefining literacy outside the context of traditional schooling and in the context of their immediate communities. As they addressed gentrification, they were, as poet Adrienne Rich (1993) describes it, "writing as if their lives depended on it."

SOUL SINGERS

It was a hot day outside, and inside Harlem High School was not much better. Along with students, I climbed the stairwell to the third floor on my way to Ms. L's English language arts class. On this day, her seniors were in the middle phase of creating a multigenre paper in which they had to either prove or disprove the use of caricatures in modern-day African American sitcoms. They used Spike Lee's (2000) movie *Bamboozled* as one of their guiding texts. Although he was intrigued with the idea of connecting a popular culture text to history, this was a difficult assignment for Khaleeq, not because he struggled with creating a multigenre paper, but because he found it difficult to research caricatures in relation to African Americans. According to *The New Oxford American Dictionary*, edited by Jewell and Abate (2001), *caricature* is defined as "a picture, description, or imitation of a person or thing in which certain striking characteristics are exaggerated in order to create a comic or grotesque effect." The definition of caricature and the lesson being taught were difficult for Khaleeq to grasp. As he learned about aspects of history, he battled with the hurtful acts of racism (grotesque depictions of African Americans) from the past in his present moment as a student seeking to understand the overt racism in the gentrification process.

Khaleeq was interested in history and he always asked detailed questions about historical events. He wanted to know about the struggles of African Americans prior to the 1970s and, as he learned more, he made connections between historical events and contemporary struggles. Yet it was hard for him to face the reality that African Americans throughout the Diaspora were depicted in such exaggerated ways. He often remarked: "This is bad"; "Really, they thought of us like that"; "We don't look nothing like that"; and "How racist." Even with his discomfort, he made larger connections to history, representation, and community. I often think about Khaleeq's initial discomfort with examining caricatures and how it stirred up an emotional reaction about the ways in which African Americans have been (and, often, still are) misrepresented in society. This misrepresentation speaks to historical struggles around belonging and identity as much as it points to battles over place-making (i.e., creating and sustaining safe spaces) and civil rights for people of color. Hence, Khaleeq was not just struggling with those offensive images, but with issues of belonging and ownership. According to Khaleeq, "If we been seen that way [as caricatures; grotesque] back before, who's to say we're not now?

He wanted to belong to a community and he wanted other people of color to have ownership of the spaces and places they called home. Khaleeq rejected caricatures much as he rejected gentrification—with energy and with multiple questions. His thinking about caricatures (e.g., "We don't look nothing like that"; "How racist") related to his initial thinking about gentrification (e.g., "displacing groups of people from their neighborhood"; "thinking we don't exist like we not important") in terms of the misrepresentation of Black people in public narratives of community. His emotional reactions spoke to his desire to take action. He did this by writing about and questioning the meanings of images that portrayed Black people as grotesque. In his disagreement with popular culture's negative depictions of Black people, Khaleeq turned to the local community to search for meanings of Black identity, pride, and solidarity. In his search, he discovered a community that has been greatly influenced by the Harlem Renaissance and its literary artists as much as a community that rallied around its local political leaders. As he contested negative depictions of Black people as caricatures, Khaleeq made references to community protests and rallies as well as to the creation of Black-owned businesses and educational sites outside the traditional space (and limitations) of schools.

In one of our community writing assignments, I asked both Khaleeq and Phillip to think about their understanding of certain words and to write down whatever came to mind. Khaleeq responded:

1. *Harlem:* history, landmark, African culture, comfort, struggle, resisting racism, ownership
2. *Art:* writing, poetry, drawing, dancing, and singing; freedom not fear or judgment
3. *Urban:* crowded, noisy, more stores, traffic, people, language, more apartment buildings, community, belonging
4. *Community:* culture, a mini village, home, social area, language, place to be free from racism.

The central idea of resistance is obvious from his word choices: *resisting racism, freedom not fear, belonging,* and *to be free from racism.* Here, much like in discussions within his English class, Khaleeq passionately and powerfully resisted gentrification, racism, and stereotypes of African Americans. He relied on forms of literacy to enact resistance: "I was gonna write how with art, Harlem got fancy architectural designs like the buildings. That's part of art, urban, and community . . . that could go with what I wrote on Harlem. The more I write about all this, I realize what's around me. History."

As Khaleeq expanded his literacy narrative during the course of our work together, writing became not only an activity that he performed at school; it became an activity that allowed him to express difficult ideas and emotions in and about the community. In an interview session, Khaleeq talked about not being on grade level and needing to improve his writing, especially his vocabulary and grammar. After a brief pause, he continued, "I'm seeing writing now as more than something to do for grades. It's . . . part of who I am, how I think things. Maybe it's not that I ain't on grade level 'cause I ain't never understood all the purposes, like value, of writing before." Khaleeq's increasing literacy involvements in school and the local community helped him to identify the power (i.e., act, activities, purposes, and functions) of writing to connect to larger themes in his lived experiences: "I could write on Harlem history;" "somebody could do poetry about Harlem;" "like that multigenre paper for English [class], somebody could do one on Harlem or community."

Literacy scholars Hull and Schultz (2002) explore ways to bridge the divide between school and community by encouraging researchers "to test the boundaries between out-of-school and in-school literacy and to draw attention to tensions, complementarity, overlap, and possible divisions of labor" (p. 4). Khaleeq relied on Hull and Schultz's insistence when he studied caricatures by establishing connections across topics such as the history of stereotypes and the present reality of gentrification in Harlem. He also sought the power of literacy to create counternarratives of African Americans in popular culture and community contexts.

Phillip, Khaleeq, Damen (one of their peers who joined our group in its later stages), and I had a conversation about the ways community people leave legacies behind for us to build on. We called these people "Harlem soul singers." To be a soul singer is to be an active participant in the community, to take up issues that affect the community, and to sing—write, work, talk, and organize—for positive change. There are many soul singers who worked for change in Harlem and throughout the Diaspora. Their strategies for dealing with community issues locally and/or globally such as racism, discrimination, and exclusion from public institutions were plentiful. They included writing literature (e.g., Langston Hughes; Nella Larson; Claude McKay; Zora Neale Hurston), performing music (e.g., Eubie Blake; Bessie Smith; Louis Armstrong), and supporting arts and politics (e.g., W.E.B. DuBois; Paul Robeson; James Weldon Johnson). They also included participating in visual culture (e.g., Josephine Baker; Romare Bearden; Aaron Douglas; Jacob Lawrence) and engaging in rights movements (e.g., Civil Rights; Black Arts), among others. I believe the legacies of these soul singers greatly influenced Khaleeq and Phillip's sense of belonging and ownership in the space of Harlem. Although they believed they belonged in this space, it (the space) was increasingly excluding them because of gentrification. They learned to deal with this exclusion by turning to literacy to create counternarratives. They became soul singers who sang back to exclusionary measures brought about by the gentrification of historic Black spaces.

Reiterating Hull and Schultz's (2002) position on bridging the divides between in-school and out-of-school literacy, Khaleeq and Phillip eventually brought their singing from the community into their school. Khaleeq's interest in learning about caricature, however hesitant, intersected with his desire to learn about gentrification. The two topics connected around larger themes: struggle, belonging, representation. His interest in learning about his immediate community (officially known as the Upper West Side and *not* Harlem) increased when I asked him to explain why his apartment building was named Frederick Douglass. When he could not answer, even after Phillip's probing, he researched Douglass and made a connection between the name of his building and an English class unit that Ms. L had taught on Douglass's (1995 reprint) autobiographical memoir, *Narrative of the Life of Frederick Douglass, An American Slave*. With pride and enthusiasm, Khaleeq later expressed, "I don't know if they named it in honor of Mr. Douglass, but I'm proud to know the name of my building is the same name of this great Black abolitionist." His soft voice and warm presence could not be mistaken, for he was singing the lyrics of his newfound knowledge to Phillip and me. He was a literacy learner who was confronting the difficulties of talking about "touchy" topics (e.g., caricature; gentrification; struggle) and a soul singer who was embracing his newfound love of Frederick Douglass—both the place where he lived and the ex-slave turned abolitionist.

STREET SURVIVORS

Phillip interviewed Kim and Samantha, two of his senior peers at Harlem High School, about writing, struggle, and gentrification. The interview occurred after school in a teacher's office space. Word was already spreading about "Phillip and that video camera," and when he approached Kim and Samantha, they agreed to the interview only if they could do it together. I considered Kim and Samantha to be street survivors, not because they have to survive on the streets—they don't—but because they have a sophisticated awareness about the community, its history, and street codes (e.g., language; dispositions; appearance; popular venues/spots like the Apollo). After I secured official and appropriate permissions, Phillip videotaped and facilitated the interview discussion.

Almost 12 minutes into the interview, Phillip directed the session away from discussions on academic writing and skills by asking, "How do you guys feel about your community?" Both Kim and Samantha paused as if to let the question sink in before Samantha replied, "I don't know, like, I don't know. I think they waste their time on stuff that . . . on buildings and condos and stuff like that and they need to be working more on schools." At the time of this interview, Samantha was 17 years old and was preparing for life after high school graduation, which was only a month and a half away. When she said, "they waste their time," she gave me a quick "schoolgirl glance" as if to say, "You know who I'm talking about." Nevertheless, I asked, "Who's 'they'?" Samantha responded, "I don't know, like . . ." Kim interrupted with "the government, the government," which, in this context, I read as code for White people, particularly given Khaleeq's earlier reference to "they" as "corporations."

In our examinations of gentrification in the community by way of onsite observations and census data, it was obvious that more White people were moving into the area. However, as Taylor (2002) describes in her book *Harlem: Between Heaven and Hell,* there is also a growing group of middle-class African American residents—some new to the community, others longtime residents. Their decisions to remain in or move to Harlem, according to Taylor, are affected by politics, economics, and cultural legacies. The "new faces" of Harlem, then, are not all White (see Taylor, 2002; Freeman, 2006; Maurrasse, 2006). For Phillip, Khaleeq, Kim, and Samantha, many but not all middle-class African Americans "blend in with the vibe of Harlem" (Kim) and are not trying to rewrite "the Harlem we got based on race. They participate in the community, ain't scared to talk to us, be part of Harlem. That's the difference" (Phillip) between White- and Black-ification in urban communities like Harlem (see Chapter 4).

Samantha's focus on putting money into new buildings and condos and not schools served as a segue into Kim's feelings about community. First, Kim elaborated on the need to invest in urban schools: "This school don't have benefits. So instead of them building a condo across the street from the school, why not give us money to make our school better?" Then, she agreed with Samantha, who added, "They make condominiums that people can't even live in. People from Harlem can't live in no condos or stuff because a lot of people can't afford that." Phillip quickly and excitedly asked: "So do you think this has to do with White privilege?" This was followed by a long pause, broken by Phillip's explanation of White privilege: "Well, White privilege is basically White people getting whatever they want. For example, us minorities can't get into a certain school and a White person can get into that school . . . somebody donates money to that school, a White person particularly, and they get accepted to that school. You think that has to do with privilege, having certain rights that we ain' got?" Listening to Phillip's emerging understanding of White privilege, I recalled that in one of his interview sessions with me months before, he grappled with what he referred to as "the rights new White residents seem to have." I mentioned the phrase *White privilege* to him and he filed it away and never mentioned it, until now. From his expanded definition to Kim and Samantha, it was apparent that he had deeply considered the term and tried to understand the meanings of Whiteness and White privilege.

Samantha responded: "Yeah, it does cause it. . . . I don't understand why they make buildings in a community that is mostly filled with minorities. Y'all making buildings for White people to live in and a lot of minorities around here don't have a lot of money like that to be living in no condos." The following conversation between Kim and Samantha offers more insight into their feelings about gentrification:

> *Samantha:* . . . If there were no condos, no White people would be living over here. No White people would be living in no Harlem. They would be living in Long Island, Staten Island . . .
>
> *Kim:* They don't want to live with the drug dealers on the corner 'cause there's a condo on 145th and Edgecombe [Avenue] and there's drug dealers that's on 145th and Saint Nic [St. Nicholas runs parallel to Edgecombe and is one block over]. Now, if it was just a regular building, you think they'd [White people] be living here?
>
> *Samantha:* Hell, naw!
>
> *Kim:* No, 'cause it has security and because it's clean and because it's nice and the apartments are very nice that they living in. Lots of security!

This conversation echoed points that Khaleeq made when discussing ideas for a literacy narrative (see this chapter's section "Literacy Learners"). There, Khaleeq talked about the increased "policing in the projects now than before." He associated this with gentrification: new White residents, new businesses, new apartments, and higher rent costs. Increased security, or policing, in Harlem was a topic that came up in many of the interview sessions with students and teachers. The security was not perceived to help minority residents, but instead to increase their struggle. For Kim, "they don't want to help lower-class people. They don't [Samantha whispered, "We know who they is"]. They'd rather for us to struggle than to help us."

Kim's powerful sentiments summarized debates on struggle that Khaleeq, Phillip, and I had been having for months. Recognizing our own ideas and positions on gentrification, we talked extensively about struggle —its definitions, our personal relationships with it, and our community perspectives on group struggle. We wrote in our journals about the topic, spent time in interview and rap sessions sharing examples of struggle, and discussed the idea during community video walk-through meetings. Also, I observed countless students at Harlem High School either talk about or perform (embody, demonstrate, and critique) struggle in their interactions with teachers and peers. Unfortunately, and too often, many of us— researchers, teachers, and administrators—misunderstand struggle as laziness and disinterest. When students miss a class session, it might have to do with their assuming increased familial demands and/or adult responsibilities, which is an indicator of familial and/or community responsibility rather than student failure. I believe we must critique our own assumptions about students and student performance in relation to lived experiences and cultural practices.

When Samantha said, "They'd rather for us to struggle," Phillip looked at me and said, "Where's my journal? See, I told you. I told you." I was taken by surprise, replying, "Wow! Well, Phil and I have this journal where we write back and forth to each other and I think that's one of the questions I wrote to him to answer this week about struggle. . . . I'm trying to understand when you say struggle, 'They want us to struggle,' but why? So, first of all, so Harlem, okay, wait! How do you describe Harlem in two words?" Samantha blurted out, "Ghet toe," and the room erupted with laughter. She then said, "No, for real. Harlem, I think it shows our culture, what Black people about." Kim agreed that Harlem represents the cultures of "Blacks and Hispanics" and is a visible indication of a historical place in the United States where people have formed and sustained a rich community. As Kim described, Harlem is "our place of freedom," even in the midst of a variety of personal and public struggles.

Again, students discussed how this "place of freedom" is filled with historical legacies: "Malcolm X Boulevard, Malcolm X was there, preached there" (Kim); "Apollo" (Samantha); "Adam Clayton Powell" (Kim); and "Frederick Douglass Boulevard" (Samantha). For Kim and Samantha, Harlem is an important place for people of color. One hundred twenty-fifth Street is the heart of Harlem because it is "where everybody got their fame at" (Kim). Samantha and Kim continued talking about gentrification, White people, struggle, and Harlem fame—such as the well-known artists, activists, and politicians from the community—even after Phillip turned off the camera and said, "It's a wrap." When Kim asked, "All this got to do with writing?", Samantha added, "Why y'all sharing journals? What's a literacy narrative? We been *talking* gentrification."

Indeed, what does this have to do with literacy? For one thing, both Kim and Samantha were sharing stories about gentrification, place, and race that they did not share during the course of their schooling, but that had an impact on their out-of-school lived experiences. These stories allowed them to exchange ideas on community change while considering Harlem's cultural significance and its public perceptions. They used accessible language to describe their struggles and successes with writing, to analyze the increasing presence of White residents in the community, and to question the purpose of building new condominiums that are too expensive for the majority of the local residents to afford. This reasoning through arguments is essential to communicating literacy narratives about community and sense of belonging. Additionally, Phillip's facilitation of the interview session served as a model for Kim and Samantha to witness and eventually imitate during class presentations and facilitated discussions. Phillip did not have a set script or an interview protocol, but decided to start the interview by asking questions about writing—struggles and successes. This disrupted Kim and Samantha's expectations for the interview because, as they indicated, they assumed that I would be "in charge and asking all sorts of questions." Instead, Phillip "was in charge." He performed acts of literacy that encouraged Kim and Samantha to ask: "How do you know all that about Harlem" (Kim)? "When did you learn to use a video recorder" (Samantha)? "How you know what to ask people? You're good at that" (Samantha). Phillip's explanation of White privilege also impressed Kim and Samantha.

After the interview, they asked him where he obtained his knowledge about White privilege. He said, "You gotta read and write. This ain't just about gentrification; it's about reading and writing, figuring out what's going on." Philip had a growing desire to know "what's going on," and he employed literacy practices to fulfill this desire. The video camera was his pen and paper, and the interviewees were his references, or sources of information. Together, they provided him with opportunities to pose questions and learn alternative or shared perspectives that helped him to critique gentrification further. Indeed, he was not only asserting a powerful voice, but reclaiming *his* community from popular narratives of decline and decay. Phillip believed, "You gotta know what they know." After he said this to Kim and Samantha, he turned to me and said, "What's that phrase you got written on one of our journals?" I answered, "reading the word and the world" (See Freire & Macedo, 1987).

MY WORD'S MY WEAPON

Phillip, Khaleeq, Kim, Samantha, Ms. L, and other youth and adults whom you will meet in the following chapters are literacy learners, soul singers, and street survivors. They all have their own perspectives on gentrification in Harlem, and they began to consider how their perspectives could be enhanced through reading, writing, listening, questioning, and performing in the course of our work together. Kim's question, "All this got to do with writing?", is my question as well. Researchers working at the intersection of literacy and context from sociocultural perspectives (Street, 2005; Dyson, 2003; Kinloch, 2009) argue that literacy serves various functions across "socially and historically situated, fluid, multiple" contexts (McCarty, 2005, pp. vii–xviii). This was definitely the case in my engagements with Phillip and Khaleeq in their school and community. In turn, this was the case with Phillip's engagements with Kim and Samantha during and after the interview session. As Phillip responded to them, "You gotta read and write. This ain't just about gentrification." Our work addresses more than gentrification. It was about examining a local community through the lens of literacy. We also identified arguments both pro and con around gentrification by engaging in shared readings of articles, books, and news stories. Then, we returned to the school to present, share, and collaboratively critique these narratives. We conducted interviews with other youth and with teachers, and made connections between school and community literacies. We questioned other people's beliefs as we questioned our own. To do these things, we agreed to be honest and to engage in self-reflection even when our observations about the community were multiple and led to different interpretations. These lessons materialized inside of Khaleeq and Phillip's literacy experiences in their English language arts classes. They also found themselves in some of the teachers' curricular choices in the classrooms and literacy conversations with students and colleagues in the hallways, stairwells, and school lounge.

I truly believe that as teachers and researchers, we have an obligation to encourage youth to sing their songs and to tell their stories without making them feel as if some stories are valued over others or as if we all have the same stories. We don't. Yet there is the reality that some stories are more "difficult" or "different" to hear. I tell my teacher education candidates and doctoral students all the time that to embrace the idea of multiple perspectives is to practice it. One cannot insist on the value of multiple perspectives without modeling it and believing in its worth. To encourage students to adopt different perspectives in their writings or class discussions requires us to invite them into the curriculum as participants and not as observers on the sidelines. Youth should be given opportunities to co-create their learning experiences and to share in the work of critical literacy—that is, to take responsibility for their learning by being active listeners, participants, and doers. In so doing, youth can begin to envision their civic roles and duties within a larger, democratic society.

This type of learning, which is participatory and democratic in nature, occurred all the time in my work with youth in Harlem. Whether I was observing at Harlem High School, working with youth in their local community, or teaching a mandatory senior English class at Perennial, an East Harlem high school (2007), I witnessed how youth engaged in learning that was cyclic and reciprocal. We wrote literacy narratives, questioned the purposes of traditional schooling, and wondered aloud about community change. These experiences—with students at Harlem High School, Perennial High School, and throughout the Harlem community—pushed me in critical ways and encouraged me to seriously consider the voices of youth whose realities are often far removed from the curriculum. As I continue to be pushed and challenged, I extend an invitation to you, teachers and researchers, to think about the songs that youth already know how to sing in ways that invite them and us to sing more loudly and think more deeply.

There are a lot of methods and resources to help us think about our students' literacy engagements. I recommend the following classroom practices:

- Reading and discussion sessions of texts (e.g., books; news articles; Web sites; Weblog stories; novels) on their local community and on current community issues that they identify, can research, and can co-lead, with the teacher and/or another peer, a class session on. From here, they can work to create connections across local and global contexts in a variety of forms: print, oral, and digital.
- Writing sessions where students learn to pose inquiry questions instead of always being given the questions by us. They can be encouraged to revisit and revise their inquiry questions in order to turn them into researchable essay questions/prompts.
- Peer feedback and detailed critiques of one another's writings or expressed positions.
- Active listening to the perspectives of one another, themselves, and the adult members of their school (see Schultz, 2003) and within local and global communities.
- Classroom presentations that are creative and that students design and facilitate (reading circles, writing workshops, PowerPoint presentations, and multimodal demonstrations) as they make explicit connections to the assignments' essential questions, guiding objectives, and overarching goals.
- Community presentations at sites they frequent (e.g., recreational sites; church; museums; local meetings) and research assignments on community sites and historical landmarks.
- Classroom visits with local community members, activists, leaders, artists, and writers.

Now, consider Khaleeq's confession, "literacy is who I am, what Harlem is, what big G [gentrification] taking away. But with literacy, my word's my weapon." With this in mind, I invite you to reflect on ways to use language that is accessible, open, honest, and critical in our ongoing work with youth.

Whether Phillip, Khaleeq, and I were using what Smitherman (1977; 2006) refers to as the "language of wider communication" or whether we were code-switching to African American English (Kinloch, forthcoming, 2010), we agreed to suspend judgment of one anothers' language capacities. This way, we were engaging in acts of talking as well as practicing ways of listening (Schultz, 2003). Doing these things allowed us to document the languages of Harlem, from the musical sensations that pulsate throughout West 125th Street to the ways people use language as a tool for civic participation and an indicator of belonging. Our language use, which could change as quickly as we blinked our eyes, was essential to investigations into urban gentrification. Placing language center stage encouraged us to willingly negotiate "who we are, the languages we speak, and the codes we use only if this negotiation is embraced . . . as 'negotiation' and not 'abandonment'" (Kinloch, 2005b, p. 99). In discussions and subsequent analyses of community conditions (e.g., gentrification; shifting demographics; housing and employment concerns; social and political events), we discovered the difficulties with not using language that is at times personal, intimate, and familial. Hence, we embraced our various linguistic patterns and, in turn, learned to embrace the linguistic varieties of people in the community, students in the schoolhouse, and canonical and contemporary authors of textbooks.

In consideration of these things, I invite you to reflect on the following questions:

- In what ways do I invite students to employ various languages and dialects in the classroom as I model for them specific ways to create academic texts?
- Do I provide opportunities for my students to experiment with language as they define for themselves what literacy is and what it means in their lives? If so, then how can I juxtapose their definitions with other definitions (i.e., academic; communal) of literacy? If not, then how can I structure the classroom and our work around discussions that produce multiple meanings of literacy?
- What are literacy narratives, and how can I invite students to create them? How can we talk about creating literacy narratives by collaboratively exploring connections among writing, multimodality, and open yet concrete critiques? In what ways can literacy narratives help us read texts about and discuss positions on race, class, gender, language, and community identities?
- Are there artifacts from the local community that my students and I can bring into the classroom that will enhance our involvement with the curricular materials? How can these artifacts serve as signs and symbols of writing? In what ways can we learn to draw on various literacy stories and make meaning from them?
- What would a unit on place/space and local community issues look like? How can I create a unit around the theme of community by drawing on literary works by Gloria Naylor, Toni Morrison, Pat Mora, Walt Whitman, Ann Petry, George Orwell, and so on?

- How can I use popular culture in the classroom to stimulate student involvement with community issues such as gentrification and with shifting meanings of power and belonging?

As Phillip insisted, our work "ain't just about gentrification; it's about reading and writing, figuring out what's going on." I invite you to make your work not just about academic literacy, but also about the lives, literacies, and languages of our youth in the out-of-school communities that they call home, frequent on a daily basis, and travel in, through, and across on their way to and from school. Doing so can give expanded meanings to and additional recognition of our students' critical capacities to learn and to act. Maybe we can all begin to see how youth are literacy learners, soul singers, and street survivors.

On Gentrification and Change

By Khaleeq Middleton

My name is Khaleeq Middleton and, yes, I live in the Frederick Douglass Houses on the Upper West Side of New York City. I attended school in Harlem. Since the time I moved there in 1999, the areas around the Douglass Houses have changed tremendously. Before I can talk about the specific changes that happened in my area, I have to say the whole neighborhood has really changed since gentrification has been taking over. I recognize that there were places and small businesses that were closed down in an effort to improve the image of the area. This point is debatable because so many people have their own ideas about what improvement means. Moving to the Douglass Houses was my first experience living in a public housing development. It was also the first time I lived with people from ethnicities other than my own. I was always used to living in neighborhoods that were predominantly Black, well, almost exclusively Black. I have always seen people of other races and ethnicities such as Spanish, White, and Chinese, but I never had the experience of living in the same neighborhood with them. Living in the Douglass Houses also exposes me to a lot of different types of stores in the area such as Chinese stores, bodegas and other deli stores, a hardware store, a discount store, game stores, an Indian restaurant, C-Town Grocery Store, and The Wiz technology and appliance store. I mention these places because I was not familiar with the convenience and location of so many places before moving to where I live now.

The Upper West Side does have a mixture of people from different races and even backgrounds; however, at the time I moved in people just stayed to themselves. For example, White people would walk all the way around the development and not through it. The only time I would see White people close to the projects or even in the projects is if they are walking on the sidewalk or waiting for the bus. This distance was strange for me to witness. It was like White people were visibly separated from Blacks and Puerto Ricans and the other people who live in the projects. Black and Puerto Rican people would go into a lot of the stores that I've mentioned such as the bodegas. It is rare for me to find a White person going into the bodegas to buy products. I've always wondered about this. They did not go into the bodegas, as far as I can tell, but would go into the local grocery and discount stores owned by chains and corporations. This is one of the observations I've made about people in this area.

I've also observed stores have closed down. The Wiz was one of the first stores that I can remember closing. It sold things like televisions, computers, music CDs, software, and a lot of electronic equipment at a reasonable price, except for their DVDs, which I thought were a bit expensive. I remember wanting to buy a lot of stuff from this store because it reminded me of a small Best Buy. I believe The Wiz closed in 2003 or 2004. The store that took its place was a Grestides store, an overpriced, never any good stuff, cramped spaced store that was hard to maneuver inside. However, some people in the area think it is a decent store and that it's better to have something than to have nothing. I think the residents in the area should have a better and less expensive grocery store to go to, but that's my opinion.

Another store I've noticed closed down was the hardware store, where I would go to buy screws, screwdrivers, and copy keys. The store is no longer there, and last time I looked, the lot was vacant. I believe a condominium development might take its place, but I will wait to see what they build there. Other stores that have been shut down are the Cyber Games and Game Station. The Game Station store was a good place to buy animation movies such as Dragon Ball Z/GT and Street Fighters as well as toys. I never bought anything from that store because things were always overpriced. It closed in 2004; however, nothing has replaced it. Cyber Game was one of my favorite hangout spots. The store had arcades and video systems such as the Playstation, PS2, Xbox, Nintendo 64, and Dreamcast. The manager of Cyber Games wasn't a good businessman because he kept kicking people out of the store, which caused people to not feel welcomed. The store eventually closed down, and I am not sure why. I assume that the cost of having the store was going up and costing too much, something that seems to happen to a lot of small businesses here. That's unfortunate.

Now, the last thing I will talk about is the rent where I live. Well, I can say that the rent has become so expensive. I've also heard that the Frederick Douglass Houses where I live with my family is going to be turned into condominiums. I've heard stories about people being paid $30,000 to move out. I see this as a problem. For example, my mother is one of the only people that I know of who is paying a lot of rent, more than the average rent is going for in the building. Her rent is over a thousand dollars and this does not include the cost of heating, which seems to always be changing from one month to the next. She would often get upset, which she has right to, when people complain about a certain amount of rent that they don't pay or when they complain about rent that's a lot less than what my mother has to pay. I don't think it's fair that landlords can decide the price of rent without considering people's struggles and their history of always being good tenants. Now that the economy is bad, a lot of people cannot afford to spend money on lots of things. Some people cannot afford to pay the bill to heat their homes and apartments because of financial burdens. This is unfortunate, but true. I hope things improve in the economy everywhere and in New York City for the poor and working people who are suffering the most because of changing times and because of gentrification. We can't forget people's struggles.

CHAPTER 3

Dancing to Different Beats

Surveying a Community at the Crossroads

"This is what I ask . . . that we immerse ourselves in looking closely at the transactions we make across cultures; that we think about these classrooms in the shower as we prepare for work, in the car on our way there, and in our sleep, long after we have closed the classroom door; that we wonder aloud and silently, alone and with colleagues, early and late, with students and because of students; that we see the work of learners and teachers as something infinitely worthy of all this close examination . . . that we come to respect the intellect of every child and every teacher by expecting them to transact within rather than just occupy space." (Bob Fecho, 2004, p. 157)

"Starbucks has arrived in Harlem." (Monique Taylor, 2002, p. ix)

Kim and Samantha (see Chapter 2) are definitely soul singers and street survivors who "wonder aloud and silently" (Fecho, 2004, p. 157). They talk about gentrification in Harlem and how "no Black people can afford those condos." This statement was an inquiry into the reasons for building expensive condos in a historically working-class African American community. Their comments speak to issues of race, class, and place in a community dealing with the realities of an old history and a new beginning. Kim and Samantha were "transact[ing] within rather than just occupy[ing] space" (Fecho, p. 157).

In his book *"Is This English?" Race, Language, and Culture in the Classroom*, Fecho (2004) examines relationships among culture, literacy, language, and race within the space of his English classroom at Simon Gratz High School in Philadelphia, Pennsylvania. He uses critical inquiry pedagogy to engage his students in meaning-making activities around transactions with texts and with people. Fecho's work helps me recognize gaps in the ways literacy research critiques youth interactions across school and nonschool spaces. These gaps, in my opinion, are exasperated by many things, including academic standards, testing drills, and routine assignments that often limit students' creative prowess and restrict their experimentation with multiple voices and perspectives. As I observed Phillip, Khaleeq, and their peers' interactions within the space of their school and local communities, I began to wonder about the transactions of other youth within the space of Harlem: How did they make meaning of the space? How did they use literacy, if at all, to respond to gentrification? In fact, what were their feelings about gentrification in the community? I wanted to know their thoughts on community change as I attempted to better understand Phillip and Khaleeq's, Kim and Samantha's perspectives, which, at times, differed from my own because of my lived experiences (see the Introduction) and my positioning as a teacher and researcher in Harlem as opposed to a native resident.

It is this latter point with which I regularly struggled to come to terms. In one sense, I identified with Phillip and Khaleeq's resistance to embrace gentrification and White-ification with open arms, believing that Harlem's cultural legacy and well-documented status as a Black community were under fire. Although Phillip and Khaleeq resisted my claim that middle-class White *and* Black people were taking up residency in the community, it was indeed a visible reality. Nevertheless, I wondered if the movement of White and Black people into Harlem carried the same spatial and cultural implications, especially as I considered the possibility of loss. This loss, at least for me, related to "minority"-owned businesses, cultural forms, as well as literary and political histories. I pondered meanings of diversity and multiculturalism in relation to urban communities that have been home to many people of color, often at the rejection of White people, many of whom could afford to move away from the core city district. Such tensions—preserving Black spaces verses remaking these spaces into racially and economically diverse areas—are at the forefront of this chapter's investigations into youth reactions to gentrification.

Through a local survey on Harlem gentrification created by project participants, we discovered countless youth in Harlem who are concerned about the effects of gentrification on the community. This chapter takes its argument from a random selection of 155 surveys completed by youth attending an out-of-school program at the Schomburg Center for Research in Black Culture and other youth attending Harlem High School. Their responses reveal a strong desire to be included in the decision-making processes around gentrification within the community. They also reveal the many layers of Harlem—from Harlem as home, as a space of survival, community practices, and education, to Harlem as urban sanctuary, or cultural oasis, of Black life and activism. Various voices, stories, and struggles of youth over Harlem at the crossroads are presented in a way that situates, and does not ignore, youth perspectives in debates over gentrification. These same voices, while often ignored and/or undervalued in debates on community change, offer unique perspectives that should be considered if we are to heed Fecho's advice: "to respect the intellect of every child" (p. 157).

In respecting the intellect, opinions, and lived experiences as well as honoring the creativity of youth, this chapter is organized into four sections: Dancing, The Drums, The Beats, and At the Crossroads. Dancing refers to people's movements through and across social contexts in ways that do not ignore the collective struggles of historically marginalized people. The Drums represent the passionate anger that students express through their responses to community change. As students contemplate meanings of gentrification, they are authoring The Beats, or new ways of seeing and describing the world. Taken together, Dancing, The Drums, and The Beats situate students At the Crossroads, where they question gentrification through critiques of literacy and the production of narratives in the spaces of schools, changing communities, and local educational programs.

DANCING

He disliked the buildings in the area. Not all of them, but some of them. I asked him why, and in response to this question, Khaleeq glanced at me and concluded that when the buildings are not maintained or cleaned, when there's a lot of drug dealers selling and/or using drugs, then there becomes a lack of pride because of the condition of the buildings. So, why would anyone like them at all? What's the point, he continued, when we who live here know that the new constructions going up and owned by a corporate group aren't for us? What's the point when we know that, soon enough, the projects will be eliminated and probably converted into condos? What's the point when "the low-income, Section 8 buildings" that people call home and that those looking from the outside call "being on welfare," "being poor," "elderly," "minority," and/or "simply unfortunate" . . . when those buildings will be taken away from us? He pointed to a high school located in the midst of the housing community where he lived. He told Phil and me that the school was just a place for "educational outcasts, and that's bad to say, but true." Khaleeq claimed that the school district doesn't care about them—the students and teachers at the school—and doesn't care what they do there. He believed that's why the school is the way it is. This bothered him just as much as the changes in his Upper West Side community and in Harlem bothered him. He believed that no one's really "listening to us, asking our opinions." Instead, everyone is just dancing around, or moving through, the world in ways that ignore the collective struggles and pains of people who have been and continue to be historically marginalized because of race, language, and cultural identities. Thus, "dancing" refers to the varied, uncoordinated physical movements, travels, and actions of people across socially constructed spaces. Such spaces have served as homes and safe havens for many "disenfranchised" people of color throughout the Diaspora, but in recent years, they have been under attack by processes involving gentrification. In light of such uncoordinated dancing, Khaleeq wonders, "So you think I should still be caring?"

There are a lot of other young people who agreed with Khaleeq. Damen, a youth from a different high school in the area who eventually joined the project, lived on the borders of West and East Harlem, what Phil names "Black and Spanish Harlem." He claimed that he did not really understand what's going on because "no one's talking to me." What his confessions told me, made me think about, were truths that we, educators, already know about neighborhood changes and the impact that such changes can have on students. However raw, real, or painful, these truths are in our faces. Unfortunately, many of us may ignore or forget to consider them as we get caught up in the demands of our own lives. That is, young people have their own voices, perspectives, and experiences that are highly ignored in schools, in local communities, and in larger sociopolitical debates. As Kim and Samantha proclaimed, "Youth can protest and speak out to the changes. Yeah, we can." Youth can dance to the same beats as they attempt to understand gentrification. They are ready and willing to dance and to be heard.

We sat in a lounge space—Phillip, Khaleeq, Ms. L, four other teachers, and I—at Harlem High School talking about what to eat for lunch: "Should we walk around the corner to Frederick Douglass Boulevard and get something from Quiznos?" "Does anyone want pizza?" "Oh, you brought your lunch today? Oh, okay, I see how you are." Ms. L and I decided against going out for lunch—she wanted to grade papers during her break and I wanted to talk with Phillip and Khaleeq about our work and their academic progress. "What are y'all doing here? You want something," Ms. L jokingly asked Phillip and Khaleeq. "We're meeting Ms. Valerie," Phillip responded.

Ms. L, Phillip, Khaleeq, and I briefly talked about school until the topic of gentrification came up. We told Ms. L our latest idea for the project—to interview local business owners about how they are dealing with the effects of gentrification. She asked us to consider talking with other youth first. In this way, Phillip and Khaleeq would "get other ideas on the topic from people in your age group to hear what they think" (Ms. L). Her interactions with Khaleeq and Phillip, and hence, their exchanges with one another, led to Phillip and Khaleeq's peer interactions. That is, learning in this nonclassroom space was predicated upon the youth's consideration of Ms. L's idea to talk with other youth about gentrification before interviewing local business owners. Once they decided to take Ms. L's suggestion, Phillip and Khaleeq's peer interactions included devising an approach, formulating questions, and engaging in meaning-making activities (e.g., brainstorming multiple definitions of *gentrification*; debating ways to gather student opinions). We were aware, as Phillip indicated, that "this could get bigger than we thinking 'cause young kids got a lot to say and all. So how we gon' do this?" Khaleeq suggested that we get tape recorders and go around the school and community stopping people to "see if they'd want to tell us their thoughts." Phillip chimed in, "We just gone stop people just like that? I don't know . . . [but] I'd do it. I just don't know how they gone feel." At this point, I suggested that we think about creating a short survey, and Ms. L interrupted, "Good idea. That way, you could just distribute them and have them fill it out either right then or return them to you later." Questions followed: "You trust them to return them" (Phillip)? "Where they gone fill 'em out at? If they take 'em, suppose they don't give 'em back" (Khaleeq)? "You trust kids gon' remember? Let me see, would I remember . . . I don't think so. Hahaha" (Phillip)!

Over the next 3 days, we decided in favor of the survey and in favor of asking teachers at Harlem High School to distribute them to their students either as a do-now at the beginning of class, as ungraded homework, or as ungraded work to be completed over lunch and returned later in the day or the next day. We explained that completing the survey was completely voluntary and that teachers could refuse to have their students participate. We agreed that the purpose of the survey would be to understand how other young people at the high school felt about gentrification in Harlem or, if they did not live in Harlem, in their own community. Collaboratively, Phillip, Khaleeq, and I developed the eight questions included in the survey, which were adapted from other interview questions we developed for teachers and local community members, and we identified teachers to invite to participate: Ms. L, who was their English teacher; Ms. Nelson, a literacy coach; Ms. Brown, an English and special education teacher; and English teachers Ms. Cunningham, Mr. Walker, and Ms. Ali. By March 2007, we had collected a total of 95 surveys completed by students enrolled in English and special education courses at Harlem High School.

Eventually, we expanded our outreach to Harlem community organizations: the Jazz Museum in Harlem, a cultural institution that sponsors programs including Harlem Speaks Education Initiative, Jazz for Curious Listeners, and Jazz for Curious Readers, among others; the H.E.L.P. Harlem group, a not-for-profit literacy and tutoring program; and Julia De Burgos Cultural Arts Center, which offers workshops and programs on the development of East Harlem's social, economic, and cultural presence. We found a partner for our project in the Schomburg Center Junior Scholars Program, a Saturday institute that provides youth between the ages of 11 and 18 with knowledge of African Diaspora history and information about entrepreneurship. The associate director of the Junior Scholars Program at the Schomburg Center, Ms. Hollman, returned approximately 60 completed surveys to us.

Altogether, we collected 155 surveys from youth to enlighten our discussions on gentrification in Harlem. Youth from the two groups that responded—those from the Junior Scholars Program and those at Harlem High School—admitted that Harlem is undergoing a lot of changes. Most respondents noted "the expensive and new" housing developments (i.e., condominiums) as a major change. An analysis of findings from the surveys indicates that youth, as young as 11 and as old as 18, have wondered what the changes will mean for the Harlem they have known and loved, the Harlem, as one youth from the high school wrote, "that's been here forever, and like my family and friends."

What do these changes mean for the youth, changes that include the development of "brand-spanking-new" condominiums, new stores, increased rent, as well as more White residents (i.e., White-ification) and middle-class Black residents (i.e., Black-ification)? How can a short survey serve as a tool that engages youth in discussing gentrification just as much as it engages them in exploring their reactions through practices in literacy (e.g., responding by writing; discussing by sharing; reading by responding)? In the next section, I present youth responses to the survey in two groups: responses from the Junior Scholars Program and from Harlem High School. This section is subtitled The Drums because of the passionate anger and emotions, reminiscent of the sounds of beating drums, that the students express in their responses to gentrification. In their responses is a sense of urgency, a call to action for conscious-minded people to preserve the historical legacies of Harlem for future generations. The passion, anger, and seriousness in the youth responses bring to mind the sounds of the drum calls that are felt when one reads the poetry of Gil Scott-Heron ("The Revolution Will Not Be Televised"), Amari Baraka ("SOS"), and June Jordan ("Calling on All Silent Minorities"). In what follows, I hope to show how the responses, or the drum calls, point to the value of listening to youth in order to enhance our literacy work with them across highly contested spatial contexts.

THE DRUMS

Out of the 60 youth respondents from the Junior Scholars Program at the Schomburg Center, 17 lived in Harlem. Other respondents wrote that they lived in Upstate New York, in one of the city boroughs, or in New Jersey or Connecticut (see Table 3.1). There were 35 respondents who identified themselves as African American, and the rest identified themselves as Jamaican, Caribbean, Black and Puerto Rican, Black and Indian, among others (see Table 3.2). Additionally, of the total amount of respondents, 28 identified themselves as females, 21 males, and 11 people did not identify their gender (see Table 3.3). Most wrote that they were aware of changes happening in New York City, from Harlem to the Bronx, Brooklyn to Queens, and beyond. Most notable were the changes with the physical appearance of communities and, according to a 12-year-old Harlem male identifying himself as "African (un)American," with how "the new buildings make Harlem look nicer." This same youth went on to admit, "but I think most of the changes are negative. Especially running people out of their apartments. . . . I think it is cruel."

This youth was not alone in his belief. A 13-year-old African American male respondent living in New Jersey wrote: "No, I don't support this [changes in the community] because they are closing a lot of stores, bringing them out of business, just to have new apartments and people. Increase in rent prices will be bad because the people here won't be able to afford that price." The various changes that are occurring in Harlem, according

Table 3.1. Respondents' Area of Residence (Schomburg)

Current Area of Residence	
Harlem	17
Manhattan (not Harlem)	6
Brooklyn	6
Bronx	5
Queens	5
Staten Island	1
Upstate New York	6
New Jersey	6
Connecticut	1
Unknown	7

to this same youth, are "unfair because people are doing what they are suppose to and the payback they get for that is higher rent prices. My grandmother owns an apartment on Convent Avenue and lived there for like 40 years . . . but other people don't have that advantage."

As with others who took the survey, these two youth were concerned about the cost of living in Harlem. They acknowledged how they "feel bad that Harlem had so many changes. First it's a majority of Black people, then you know it, the Caucasian people are invading it again." This quote led to provocative discussions on class divisions, access, race, and the politics of place in a historically African American community.

Browsing through *Harlem Lost and Found* by Adams and Rocheleau (2002), I am confronted with images of old Harlem: the Mount Morris Park Fire Tower, built in 1855; the Madame C. J. Walker House, built in 1915; William Renwick's Roman Catholic Church on West 132nd Street, built in 1904; and the Harlem Courthouse on East 121st Street, completed in 1893. These images tell stories of history, change, and architectural diversity. They also tell a story of Harlem as "iconic, mythic, larger than life, known throughout the world. It is the home of jazz and black culture. It is feared as an impoverished, crime-ridden ghetto. However . . . Harlem is attracting scores of new inhabitants" (p. 15). In the midst of this rich yet complicated history are stories of change and struggle: "Violence, drug dealing, unnecessary deaths," according to a 15-year-old African American male respondent from Harlem. For a 16-year-old African American female from Harlem, "expensive buildings around my blocks [are] made

Table 3.2. Respondents' Self-Identified Racial Groupings (Schomburg)

Racial Identification	Number Identifying with Group
African American	35
Black/Jamaican	1
Jamaican (born)	1
Caribbean (born)	1
Biracial (Black & White)	1
Black & Puerto Rican	2
Black & Honduran	1
Asian & Caribbean	1
Black & Italian	1
Black Aruban	1
Black & Indian	2
Black Guatemalan & British	1
Black, White, & Indian	1
Black Canadian	1
Black Cherokee	1
Native American & Antiguan	1
No identifying info included	8

for White people." The reality is that gentrification is not just coming to Harlem, but is already there.

While 95% of youth respondents wrote extensively on what they believed to be the negative effects of gentrification, such as "increased rent" and "White people moving in," others wrote about positive effects. For one 17-year-old African American and Honduran female living in Harlem, "the changes being made in Harlem are good because it brings diversity, making NYC less segregated when it comes to the communities in which people live." Nevertheless, this same youth indicated, "it's not fair [increase in rent] because rent should not increase unless the person's income has increased, so other than that it should remain the same. Lots of people here don't get increases in income." Youth in the Junior Scholars Program seemed to echo many of the sentiments expressed by Phillip, Khaleeq, Kim, and Samantha in terms of affordability in Harlem and the relevance of the

Table 3.3. Respondents' Self-Identified Characteristics (Schomburg)

Gender		Grade		Age Group	
Females	28	Elementary	1	10–12	11
Males	21	Junior High	26	13–15	26
Unknown	11	High School	23	16–17	13
		Unknown	10	Unknown	10

"new stuff" to their own realities. They all had a strong awareness of community change, even if they did not live in Harlem. As one youth who lived in Brooklyn wrote: "Positive—neighborhood becomes nicer and tends to look more like the suburbs; negative—many people are being thrown out of their buildings who don't deserve it and have nowhere to go."

When Phillip read the latter response, he focused on the phrase "look more like the suburbs." He was bothered by this response and questioned me: "Who wants to look like the suburbs? See, if that's the case, go live in the suburbs." Phillip, already on fire and full of energy, continued: "Harlem's not that, it's a community with its own vibes and can't be duplicated or made into an area it's not. People trying to do that. Expensive cafés, little delis and grocery stores, condos, but this ain' no suburb. That's what I'd say to the person who gave that response." The person to whom he was referring—the Brooklyn youth who alluded to Harlem as looking like the suburbs—also wrote the following: "It's unfair [rent increases] because some people don't have the money sometimes to even pay for the rent they may have . . . so if an increase in rent were to happen it will be worse for them." This comment reiterated Khaleeq's belief, expressed in one of his video interviews, that the reality of rent increase was one that "puts people in a bad situation" because it already costs a lot to live in New York City, and "if you got a family, you trying to make the ends meet. People wanting all this new, new, new don't care about that."

Phillip and Khaleeq engaged in a "read and feed" (Fisher, 2007) of the other survey responses and concluded, "They got a lot to say. That's good" (Khaleeq), and "I might not agree with everything like the suburb-talk but that's okay. We gotta still listen to what kids say" (Phillip). Khaleeq, Phillip, and many of the youth in the Junior Scholars Program shared a strong sense of justice and injustice. They were not afraid to write about "how Black people being threatened out of Harlem" on the same page that they explained, "all these Caucasians coming in to take our place." They understood the link between economic change and community change, as referenced by a 17-year-old African American and Caribbean female from Crown Heights in Brooklyn: "Recently, the new management has changed the buildings, attempting to clean it up, make it all better, and I have noticed more people of Southeast Asian descent and White people moving in, but the result of this, rent prices have gone up." Her reading of the racial dynamics emphasized the cultural diversity that can result from newness: "The different people of different cultures moving in doesn't bother me as much, as long as they try to add to the culture within the neighborhood instead of taking away."

Other youth also referred to a sense of loss, or feeling as if something is being taken away from them. A 13-year-old female who lived in Harlem and identified herself as African American and American Indian responded, "It is *so frustrating* to see all this happening and know there's nothing we can *really* do about it, times change. I feel as if Harlem I've known all my life is being thrown out of my grasp and written out of history. Will I be the last generation to remember it" (her emphasis)? Her response paralleled that of a 13-year-old African American female from the Bronx who ended her survey with, "It's basically going through a lot of gentrification, which is forcing the people of Harlem out of Harlem, which is killing its history." Over 70% of the youth respondents echoed a similar sentiment.

Phillip read this response and offered some suggestions that arose from our work to create literacy narratives as responses to gentrification: fight for ongoing rent stabilization for longtime Harlem residents who simply cannot afford the increasing rent; organize youth and adult members of the community to strategize and present ideas to community housing boards; write letters to the mayor; create a video about Harlem that reflects our "Renaissance period and Black leaders and what's happening here now." Khaleeq, during a separate meeting, suggested that people should talk from their own perspectives and that together these perspectives could show how Harlem is many things to many people. Their plans for literacy narratives about the concerns of the survey participants seemed to be influenced by the multigenre paper that Ms. L assigned students in her senior-level English classes at Harlem High School (see Chapter 2). She had insisted that the paper be "multi: genre, voice, perspectives" and that students "take it all in."

Indeed, the youth were taking it all in; the surveys confirmed a daunting list of the consequences of urban gentrification on their lives and those of their family members. While the youth heavily critiqued racial dynamics —White people moving in; Black, Latino/a, and Puerto Rican people being displaced—they were confronting real-life issues. These included feeling wronged because "the world does not work in their favor because of race and class" (Maurrasse, 2006, p. 129); believing that they do not have a place in the world, given the looming threat of an eviction notice; and working to reject characterizations of their struggles as never-ending and their poor and working-class status as dispensable and substandard. In light of these issues, the youth attempted to make sense of community change by using writing and language to advance personal opinions that, like all opinions, could be contested.

Today's youth are voicing concerns that can be traced back to beliefs articulated by famous African American literary writers. In his essay "Harlem Ghetto," James Baldwin (1948) writes, "Harlem wears to the casual observer a casual face" (p. 57), and underneath the casual look are complicated issues. For example, this community has served as a home to countless African and African American literary artists at the same time that, historically, it has been widely perceived as a place of urban decay. Harlem has been (and still is) known as the "Black capital of the world." In this capital community, recent statistics claim that Harlem's unemployment rate is normally double the rate for the rest of New York City. In December 2008, the New York State Department of Labor (www.labor .state.ny.us) estimated that the unemployment rate for New York City was 7.4%, making the rate for Harlem nearly 14.8%. The youth respondents were aware of these complicated relationships and, in some ways, consciously or unconsciously, they alluded to both the struggles in Harlem and to Baldwin's literary legacy as they created their own literacy stories. Just as the youth respondents wrote openly and honestly about gentrification, Baldwin, too, wrote powerfully about the difficulties in and with Harlem: "all over Harlem now there is felt the same bitter expectancy with which, in my childhood, we awaited winter: it is coming and it will be hard; there is nothing anyone can do about it" (p. 57). Although "there is nothing" one can do to prevent the coming of winter, youth respondents are hopeful that through the attainment of a quality educational experience— school- and/or community-based—they can eventually do something to stop the adverse effects of gentrification in their respective communities.

THE BEATS

The Schomburg Center for Research in Black Culture, the cultural institution that sponsors the Junior Scholars Program among many others, is centrally located in Harlem. It is not far from Harlem High School, historical buildings, well-known restaurants, and busy 125th Street. The Junior Scholars Program and other educational programs in the community share a common concern: to educate youth about the cultural, social, economic, political, artistic, and literary realities within Harlem and throughout the

African Diaspora. The success of this educational vision became clear when I began to categorize, analyze, and compare the responses of survey participants across the two youth groups from Junior Scholars and Harlem High School. For both groups, by and large, themes of struggle, place, race, history, culture, and affordability surfaced. Clearly, youth were concerned about their changing community space: 95% of youth in the scholars program wrote about gentrification's negative effects in comparison with 92% of youth from the high school. Based on their responses, both groups possessed a growing awareness of current issues occurring in the community.

The youth drew on their emerging understandings of history and culture, whether referenced in their schools or learned in their educational enrichment programs, to articulate their positions on gentrification. Such acts are significant because they demonstrate young people's critical capacities to make meaning of and from the local community in ways that connect to their knowledge of history, culture, and place. In making meaning, they were orchestrating, or authoring, new beats—steps, approaches, ways of seeing the world, songs of survival, passionate responses—as a way to voice their concerns with gentrification in Harlem. They were also testing out these new beats in community-based educational programs. I believe that schools and local educational programs should work collaboratively to develop curriculum, learning goals, and literacy activities that better integrate historical and contemporary aspects of the community into students' academic lives. Thus, the ways youth authored new beats are representative of their interactions with literacy in multiple educational settings.

The youth surveys from Harlem High closely paralleled the arguments expressed by young people in the Junior Scholars Program; however, the responses were more diverse in terms of youth racial identification (see Table 3.4). Of the 95 respondents ranging in age from 14 to 18 (see Table 3.5), 56 lived in Harlem (see Table 3.6) and 27 were classified as African American while 13 were classified as Dominican and another 13 were classified as Latino/a or Hispanic. Table 3.6 provides additional information on respondents' area of residence. One student, a 15-year-old male identifying himself as multiracial and living in the Bronx, wrote that gentrification is about race just as much as it is about class, but "people scared to mention race. I guess 'cause it's all up in their faces." In response to the question, "How do you feel about Harlem and the changes taking place here?", he wrote, "Harlem's nice, but with too much White people." He is not alone in seeing that White people are increasingly moving to Harlem.

While the responses from the Junior Scholars Program focused heavily on rent increases, most youth respondents at Harlem High School focused on their dislike of the racial shift in the community. The youth

Table 3.4. Respondents' Self-Identified Racial Groupings (HHS)

Racial Identification	Number Identifying with Group
African American	27
Black & Dominican	4
Dominican	13
Latino/a or Hispanic	13
Puerto Rican	3
Black & Puerto Rican	2
Biracial (Black & White)	1
Haitian	2
Jamaican & Chinese	1
Guatemalan	1
Black & Indian	1
West Indian	1
Multiracial (details not offered)	2
No identifying info included	24

who complained about Harlem having "too much White people" went on to offer a list of the positives and negatives he saw with gentrification: "Positives: new housing, more 'new' people, more businesses; negatives: high rent, no place to live, more 'new' people who don't care about our place." In his description of the positives and negatives, this youth was aware of how "new" people can either contribute to or take away from the community, depending on their motivations and reasons for moving

Table 3.5. Respondents' Self-Identified Characteristics (HHS)

Gender		Grade		Age Group	
Females	46	9th Grade	28	14–15	27
Males	25	10th Grade	0	16–18	41
Unknown	24	11th Grade	13	Unknown	27
		12th Grade	29		
		Unknown	25		

Table 3.6. Respondents' Area of Residence (HHS)

Current Area of Residence	
Harlem	56
Manhattan (not Harlem)	7
Brooklyn	3
Bronx	12
Washington Heights	11
Inwood	1
Unknown	5

in. He also understood that "new" people bring additional businesses and improved housing, which can be positive factors.

His concern was about belonging and ownership of these improvements: "I believe that it's very unfair that this is going on in Harlem. The reason is because just because 'new' people can move in and afford the rent does not mean everyone else can. I feel that they should move everyone who has been living in the community for a while into the newer homes and let the others live in what we had." This youth appeared to be torn between "support[ing] the changes, it's good that the community is being built up," and fearing the changes because "people here are getting hitched out of their own homes." One solution, as stated in this youth's response, was to have "them" move into what "we" had so "we" can move "into the newer homes." When I shared this response with Khaleeq, he told me that it was true, that "these people coming in, they can help or hurt. They can try knowing about us and the community, or walk in and act like they own it and us." "New" people can potentially undermine the rituals, traditions, and practices of a community "if they don't care about our place."

A 16-year-old female from the school who only described herself as a resident of "the Lincoln Projects" wrote about similar themes. Expressing her disappointment that rent prices are rising throughout Harlem, she commented, "The increase of the rent just went up. I don't support that because people these days don't make a lot of money and the government is being selfish because all they want is money. We have single parents who living in the projects struggle to pay rent. Now they [landlords; government] want more money. How are minority people suppose to take care of their kids and pay that rent?" Phillip read this response and said to me, "You know who she talking 'bout. 'Member what Kim and Samantha said?" In this case, Phillip was referring to the belief that the government equals White people (see Chapter 2), which is a controversial claim. The survey respondent then elaborated on her disapproval of rent increases by demanding: "It's unfair . . . pay close to a thousand dollars to live somewhere that is not a mansion or a palace!! For that they should make the apartments bigger and better or something. Give us more rooms, more bathrooms, closets, or something. Come on! Or help us get better jobs that give us more money. You want what you want, but what about what we want?" Phillip shook his head in agreement and blurted out, "Instead of bringing expensive condos, bring quality job opps. Level the playing field."

A 17-year-old Puerto Rican male from Harlem described one way for youth to participate in the process of leveling the playing field—that is, by using their education to protect the community from the devastating effects of gentrification. He suggested, "be dedicated to our education, get as much of it 'cause that's gone help us make cases to save the community. People don't listen if we don't have good enough arguments." Nearly 51% of the respondents from Harlem High School mentioned the need to get an education, which they view as an individual responsibility as well as a community obligation. This is an important point, given the fact that young people are often portrayed as disinterested and disengaged from learning by mass media, in popular culture, and even in some literacy studies that employ deficit thinking. For the youth whom I have interviewed and/or surveyed, receiving an education—acquiring higher-order thinking skills, generating knowledge, having critical experiences with texts and people—serves as the foundation by which one can later challenge inequitable systems, institutions, and practices.

One youth, a 16-year-old Dominican female who lived in Manhattan, wrote about lessons learned in one her classes in relation to the nature of changing communities. According to this respondent, "Honestly, Harlem is starting to look new and even more sophisticated. But I think that this is just taking away what it used to be back in the days, but we learn in our history class that communities change. I guess this was gone happen in Harlem one day, but these major changes unfair, though." Her knowledge that communities do change was gained from lessons taught in a high school history class and, according to her, from the "extra readings I do on my own so I can understand what's happening around me. See, we don't get all the information in school, just a glimpse." Education, for most of the youth respondents, was a fundamental responsibility in becoming informed citizens, especially in the midst of a rapidly gentrifying community that they did not ask for, desire, or see themselves and their families in.

The aforementioned respondent's sentiments, "but I think that this is just taking away what it used to be back in the days, but we learn in our history class that communities change," not only raise questions about education (receiving information), but also about making sense of change. Her reference to "back in the days" encouraged me to examine elements of Harlem's newness as I pondered additional opportunities for youth to produce community literacy narratives. For instance, "back in the days," the community did not have a Starbucks coffeeshop. Now, there is one located on West 125th Street near Lenox Avenue. According to countless online news stories two additional Starbucks have opened in Harlem within the last year: one along 118th Street and Frederick Douglass Boulevard and the other on 125th Street near Adam Clayton Powell, Jr. Boulevard. A few years ago, Old Navy, Harlem USA Shopping Mall, the Body Shop, Aerosoles Shoe Store, the now defunct HMV Music Store, Magic Johnson Theatre, and even billboards for the Gap were not yet a part of Harlem's landscape. Now they are, and their presence creates conflicting feelings for many of the youth who were surveyed. A 16-year-old Guatemalan youth who lived between Brooklyn and Harlem expressed surprise that "all of a sudden, Harlem gets this and that almost overnight. I remember when there was a Disney Store. I wasn't shocked it closed. A Disney Store. Do we need a Disney Store in Harlem?"

Youth are aware of the changes in Harlem. They walk down their streets and see signs announcing the closing of local stores and know that "new businesses coming in." They walk by street vendors who sell jewelry, incense, greeting cards, novels, and magazines and realize that soon, they may be distant memories: "What we know as Harlem going away." The tall, distinguished African woman who sets up her jewelry booth on the corner of St. Nicholas Avenue and West 125th Street may no longer be permitted to operate there because of new zoning laws and the Columbia University Expansion Plan. According to youth participants, ". . . when wealthy people, and I'm saying White people, too, move in, our practices . . . you know, our sense of community, just forced out the backdoor without question." The local businesses in Harlem—and especially in the Manhattanville section of Harlem—may, in fact, be displaced after years of protesting gentrification and expansion. Even more, local legacies in Harlem—the Hueman Bookstore and Café on Frederick Douglass Boulevard, the Studio Museum of Harlem on West 125th Street, in addition to others—may be taken over by corporate entities. Or they may follow businesses such as the Harlem Record Shack on West 125th Street and Bobby's Happy House music store on Frederick Douglass Boulevard near West 125th Street and be forced to close. Then, there are the local churches, the educational enrichment programs, and the men dressed in Sunday suits who stand on soapboxes, emblematic of Malcolm X, preaching Black Nationalist messages of "power to the people, hope, and love." For Phillip and Khaleeq, Kim and Samantha, Damen, and countless youth at Harlem High School and in the Junior Scholars Program, "these things we know we see on the regular might be gone tomorrow, next week, next month. Who really knows" (Phillip)? Undoubtedly, their belief that things "might be gone" is grounded in the physical and visual changes that are occurring through-out Harlem as well as throughout other major cities in the United States: the closing of longtime community businesses, the construction of expen-sive condominiums that local residents cannot afford to live in, and the relocation of new residents to the area.

Youth are not making excuses for those they consider responsible for the changes caused by gentrification that affect their own lives as well as the lives of their family and friends. Here are some of their thoughts:

> My mother seemed . . . more stressed about money and rent
>   (16-year-old Black Latina)
> Columbia students are starting to move in
>   (16-year-old African American female)
> Sooner or later my family will be evicted
>   (17-year-old Dominican female)
> High rent prices . . . not affordable
>   (18-year-old African American male)
> Improvements happening, but not for us
>   (18-year-old African American male)
> Will people have to live on the streets?
>   (17-year-old Puerto Rican female)
> Columbia trying to kick the people in my neighborhood out and bring
>   theirs in (16-year-old African American female)
> We do need some more integration but what cost is it gonna be?
>   (15-year-old Latino)
> New buildings we cannot afford
>   (17-year-old African American female)

Youth walk into their schools and wonder how the changes will affect them in that space, a space that serves as a second home for some, a safety zone for many, and a place of conflict and surveillance for others. One youth wrote, "Gentrification might take all our stuff. The community, churches, schools. I dunno [don't know]." In his introduction to *Harlem on the Verge* by Alice Attie (2003), Robin D. G. Kelley asks, "So, will the black working-class hold on to Harlem? Did they ever have it to begin with? With all the congratula-tory talk of Harlem's 'empowerment' and rebirth, one would think we are witnessing the beginning of black Harlem's greatest moment" (p. 16).

Kelley argues, "the beauty and power of a community that refuses to disappear" are "documents of daily life" that can serve as artifacts of the past or calls for current-day action and activism against "the Disney-fication of Harlem" (pp. 16–17). I believe that in these "documents of daily life," we cannot forget about the voices, perspectives, and literacy experiences of youth (as well as adults) who reside in, attend school or teach in, and/or travel through Harlem. The quotes from youth respondents are powerful reminders that the history of struggle for civil rights, housing rights, educational equity, and fair treatment for people of color in the United States and throughout the Diaspora is not over. This might be a hard, even painful, reality for some educators (including progressive White liberals) to accept because it requires that we acknowledge our students' struggles and anger with inequitable situations by engaging in conversations on race, racism, and struggle. To do otherwise is to ignore the opinions and lived experiences of many of the students who walk in and out of our classrooms on a daily basis.

Youth are more than aware of the consequences of gentrification in the community. They want to be included in the decision-making processes by talking, questioning, and collaborating with members of city council, legislative boards, the housing authority, and even leaders behind the Columbia University Expansion Plan. Doing so could reveal more equitable approaches to addressing urban gentrification, the redefinition of community, and the possible displacement of youth and adults. My work has made me realize that youth want to be asked their opinions, and they need to be provided with more specific reasons for gentrification than "that's how it is." Additionally, they must be given opportunities to read, write, and respond to community change. Their lives depend on knowing, particularly as they attempt to bridge the divides among school, community, and governmental practices and as they seek ways to become productive, active citizens in this democratic society.

AT THE CROSSROADS

> Maybe before we didn't know,
> That Corey is afraid to go
> To school, the store, to roller skate.
> He cries a lot for a boy of eight.
> But now we know each day it's true
> That other girls and boys cry too.
> They cry for us to lend a hand.
> Time for us to take a stand.
> (Geoffrey Canada, president of
> Harlem Children's Zone,
> from *Take a Stand* 1996)

Every day, teachers and researchers work with youth around practices in reading, writing, inquiring, and knowing as youth learn to become
leaders in their schools and eventually in their communities. The issues
adolescents face include gaining a sense of responsibility and ownership,
confronting identity issues of becoming versus being, struggling with ways
to express oneself, interacting with others, questioning sex and sexuality,
and developing one's own set of beliefs and values. I believe, as do other
researchers, that we could better work with youth—and the literacy and
lived experiences they bring from their communities into schools—if we
truly engaged with them in collaborative, reciprocal teaching. Collaborative literacy learning involves asking youth to make self-to-self, self-to-
text, and self-to-world connections. More important, it invites youth to
critically consider their responses to literature, current events, local and
global community issues, and their peers' perspectives as they enhance
their own critical capacities (e.g., Democratic Engagement).

I want youth to make connections to texts and ideas freely, but I also
want them to be comfortable making disconnections. By this, I mean that
students should be encouraged to explore the purposes of counternarratives and oppositional stances, participate in debates and close textual
readings, and learn to acknowledge and negotiate multiple perspectives,
positions, and viewpoints. Learning to oppose a dominant voice or ideol-
ogy can enhance students' own unique voices—or help them see that they
do, in fact, have voices—as they situate and resituate themselves in literacy conversations within school and the larger world. First, teachers
should hear students. Then, they could debate Khaleeq's insistence that
"these people coming in, they can help or hurt. They can try knowing about
us and the community, or walk in and act like they own it and us." Inviting students to take critical approaches could parallel literacy experiences
that ask them to publicly question acts of "coming in" (see Charlton-
Trujillo's novel, *Feels Like Home*), having the ability to "help or hurt" (see
Fleischman's *Breakout*), "knowing about us and our community" (see
Naylor's *The Women of Brewster Place;* Hurston's *Their Eyes Were Watching
God*), and "walk[ing] in and act[ing] like they own it and us" (see Ellison's
Invisible Man; Wright's *Black Boy*). Additionally, Khaleeq's sentiments can
be paired with themes of struggle, place, and confronting the past as presented in Fitzgerald's classic novel *The Great Gatsby*. Such pairing can serve
as a way to investigate meanings of the American Dream and positions of
outsider-insider from at least two distinct perspectives: an African American youth living near Harlem and a White male author writing about
aspects of life in New York. In this way, educators can ask students to participate in the requirements, standards, and creativity that come with
school-sponsored learning in ways that draw forth critical text-to-self-to-

world connections on the one hand, and that stimulate rigorous conversations about struggle, change, and belonging on the other. I firmly believe that this approach can support our collective inquiries into how students conceptualize learning and understand multiple constructions of self, texts, and the world across sociopolitical contexts.

Whether youth are studying aspects of their communities, themes of place in the writings of Walt Whitman and Langston Hughes, or the related language practices in the literary works of William Shakespeare and Toni Morrison, we can encourage them to engage in the following tasks:

- Document, discuss, and debate their reactions to texts and current events by engaging in critical reading and writing within the space of our classrooms. As teachers and researchers, we can regularly survey students to gather their feelings about (and their understandings of) curricular choices, reading materials, discussions, and writing assignments. This could occur at the beginning, middle, and/or end of the marking period or academic year.
- Work with us (educators) to co-create assignments in which they survey other people at the school, in their local community, or even in their family about current events, literary debates, and issues in popular culture that relate to the literacy work they are doing in our classes. Their surveys can take multiple forms: written questions and answers, oral presentations, and visual representations.
- Conduct oral histories with their family members, friends, neighbors, and leaders in their communities. Students can learn various interviewing techniques, practice transcribing their collected data, and experience creating written arguments from their engagement with qualitative forms of inquiry. Indeed, students can become literacy learners and soul singers, like Kim, Samantha, Phillip, and Khaleeq.

Surveying a community at the crossroads by paying attention to youth reactions to gentrification has taught me valuable lessons, which I will further describe in subsequent chapters. These include listening to multiple perspectives even if they differ from my own, asking youth to be critical doers by providing opportunities for them to be just that, and expanding my own understanding of literacy as acts, practices, and events that happen everywhere—in schools, in communities, and in literacy enrichment programs, among the many other places where literacy lives. It has also shown me that young people, when given the opportunity, can draw on their perspectives about the outside world inside of our classrooms. Clearly, literacy incorporates reading, writing, and performing, but it also includes listening, questioning, critiquing power relations, and grappling with our sense of agency as we engage in meaning-making activities in our classrooms and in the larger world. Doing these things would allow us to critique being at the crossroads—schools, changing communities, local educational programs, newness, oldness—as we "wonder aloud and silently" (Fecho, 2004, p. 157).

Teaching in the Midst
of a Gentrifying Community

By Latoya Hardman (Ms. L), High School English Teacher

Since I have been a teacher, the "buzz" I have heard in my professional development and graduate courses has been on cross-curricular or interdisciplinary instruction. This becomes every teacher's challenge, as we are often held accountable for linking other subjects into our discipline. In addition to incorporating other content areas, we are also encouraged to take our instruction outside the classroom, a point that is evident in comments made to teachers from administrators. These comments include: "Relate your teaching to the real world;" "Make the lessons interesting;" "If they [students] do not come to school, it is partially your fault because they are bored." As a teacher, I interpreted these statements to mean that I had to be an entertainer. How else could I compete with advanced technology, MySpace, and other modes of entertainment central to the lives of our youth? I must admit that as an English teacher, I find ease with making my instruction and classroom experiences interdisciplinary. I am able to delve into other disciplines because they lend themselves to studies in English. However, the "entertainer" role is one I have not mastered. Over time, I have realized that I do not have to know how to play video games, register with MySpace, or broaden my musical interests to match those of my students. In fact, doing so may not necessarily make me a "better" teacher. Instead, I attempt to make my teaching relatable by turning to students' local communities. Their communities help *us* understand the texts we read and often help us to better understand ourselves. Even if there is not an obvious, direct relationship between the community and the texts being studied, I still ask students to make connections with the texts and the world in which we live.

While this may sound easy, it was difficult for me to do when I first started teaching because I was trying to understand a new community—an unchartered territory. I had never really given much thought to the idea of gentrification prior to moving to Harlem. I was raised in the suburbs of Houston, Texas, where new buildings were built from the ground up and not by tearing down livable buildings and displacing residents. I had trouble thinking of ways I could make connections between class texts and a local community I really did not yet understand or feel at home in. Eventually, I came to terms with my new community and my role there. As I accepted my responsibilities, I wondered: How would I teach students who were raised in a gentrified community when I was just beginning to question it myself? This is when I decided that my classroom would be a learning community where different perspectives on learning and community were welcomed. I encouraged students to examine their opinions and experiences through the texts and people I invited into class. In approaching learning in this way, my hope was that my students and I would learn more about the local community as we questioned the ways we fit, or did not fit, into it.

I must admit the difficulty of being inundated with academic policies and procedures, let alone facing the pressure of creating new curricula from scratch. I assumed that inviting the community into my classroom would require too much time. However, after teaching for only a few short weeks, I realized the value of both the space of and literacies within the local community. Gentrification was teaching my students many myths, such as old equals bad, new equals good. Some students started to believe that to be displaced meant that one was not worthy of the new. Although they did not readily recognize it, these myths caused students to have negative self-images. I needed to help my students recognize their feelings while engaging them in discussions on gentrification, being worthy, and acknowledging the old and new.

Embarking on this journey presented a few firsts for my students. For the first time, some students came face-to-face with the "other" America, which was a racial one. The entire time I taught in Harlem, I did not have one White student in my classes. As I described in my master's thesis, the student population at the high school in Harlem where I taught was comprised mainly of two groups: Black/African American (approximately 54%) and Latino (approximately 45%), with a small percentage of White (2%) and Asian (1%) students. The only White people many of my students knew were their teachers, and even this knowing was limited. Their understanding of the "other" was simply that all Whites were in positions of power and/or had money. Although some students did not know any White people, they did notice more and more White people entering the community and moving into "newer"-looking buildings. They began to question the financial divide between their new White neighbors and themselves.

There was yet another "other" my students had to face. In a school where over 76% of students qualified for free and reduced lunch, this "other" America was the America of money. The students saw the effects of millions of dollars being spent on new condominiums, knew stories about displaced residents, and knew of people who shared a two-bedroom apartment with seven other people because of financial restrictions. They were aware of the limited resources in their own schools. Students noticed an economic disparity, and for the first time, they began to question this disparity publicly within the classroom space.

The reality of gentrification seemed to be magnifying students' fears of displacement. This fear was not surprising. What was shocking was my realization that, despite living in the "mecca" of the United States, many of my students had not traveled beyond 106th Street. Museums, theaters, and parks beyond their local community were off-limits. Perhaps they were uncomfortable in those areas or just scared of what was out there, or maybe my students did not believe they belonged anywhere else. What happens, then, to students who might be displaced, but do not feel they belong anywhere else? Where can they feel wanted? I grappled with these questions when I created lesson plans. I wanted to employ teaching strategies and readings that would help students survive in a local community from which they could be displaced and a larger community where they did not feel they belonged. I wanted students to see what was going on around them so as to not become immune to the sounds of bulldozers and visions of debris. I wanted them to question the world and their place in it.

To do this, I brought in texts that were set in New York. Novels such as *Assata: An Autobiography* and short stories like "The Lesson" by Bambara allowed my students to see a different Harlem. At the same time, such texts encouraged them to ask questions about community differences. I invited people from the community to class to reinforce issues in the texts we were reading or to introduce students to new ideas. Bringing the community into my teaching helped raise my students' confidence level. Students who rarely spoke looked for opportunities where their voices could be heard.

Acknowledging that their changing community was a part of who they are, students began to embrace their cultures, identities, and literate practices. As I reflect on the articulate, intelligent, "teaching" voices of my students and recall their faces, I realize that my efforts in bringing the outside in was the most valuable tool I ever could have given my students. They learned more than English. They questioned the changing community as they discovered their roles as informed citizens within it.

CHAPTER 4

Singing in Multiple Keys

Literacy, Race, and the White-ification of Place

Whenever I look back at the data I have collected; when I reflect on the official and unofficial conversations I have shared with Phillip, Khaleeq, their peers, and Ms. L; and when I think of the historical significance of a community like Harlem, I am reminded of Phillip's passionate feelings about gentrification. His passion was always present and could always be felt; it energized Khaleeq as much as it energized me. At the time, I am sure that Phillip did not think that his passion and interest in community could turn into activism. In time, he came to understand what activism entails as well as how youth can be activists in their local and global communities. During a presentation to a group of my teacher education graduate students one summer in New York City, he confessed, "Maybe I'm an activist. . . . I'm thinking so. Maybe?" He continues to wrestle with that idea as his determination to tell his story about Harlem increases.

I remember it like it was yesterday: Phillip talking about using literacy (e.g., writing; multimodal forms of communication) to "tell my story because we young kids need to talk up." He made this declaration everywhere and all the time, even as he and I debated the purposes of community change—"who's benefiting from gentrification, again" (Phillip to Khaleeq and Valerie)—and the need to assert an active voice—"if you don't take a stand, do you expect others to? And if they do, will their stand be what you want it to be? Take your own stand" (Valerie to Phillip). Our different perspectives reflected our differing lived experiences. Phillip had become accustomed to local government and political groups enforcing change throughout the community without question. I, however, was used to resisting and speaking against changes if they appeared to negatively affect the cultural practices and lives of longtime residents in a community. I threatened to write letters, call elected officials, and to publicly express my disagreement with actions I deemed unfair. I recognized that my own actions stemmed from a collection of lived experiences from a variety of diverse and multicultural contexts, while Phillip's actions were still emerging and influenced by his specific African American community. These differences, Phillip's interactions with Khaleeq, and the powerful conversations I had with them guide this chapter on race and the White-ification of place.

During one of our later interview sessions, Phillip shared: "Whose story [about Harlem, writ large] is going to be told? I see this [regularly]—how this Black community is changing from how it was back in the day, how Black folks being pushed to the edge, and from the edge to being completely pushed out of Harlem. Who can afford the cost of gentrification? Who can say, 'I'll pay that high rent with no problems, so long as you increase police presence and clean up the 'hood? Oh, and get better grocery stores and restaurants.' Not my family and not my friends' family, and we've been living here like forever. I call this process the White-ification of the 'hood." Phillip's confessions include major themes that he and Khaleeq often talked about in the community and in our various interview and rap sessions, especially in regard to race (White-ification = White people and White privilege in Black spaces; Black-ification = Black people and Black cultural practices in historically Black spaces). For Khaleeq and Phillip, White-ification meant the increasing presence of White people and White privilege in communities traditionally thought of as African American and minority. They did not associate Native Americans and Dutch settlers with Harlem space. For them, Harlem is a historic Black community with Black cultural institutions, businesses, families, and traditions, which, in some ways, contribute to Black-ification across socioeconomic groupings.

What does it mean to talk about gentrification by talking about the increasing presence of White residents in the area? What can teachers and researchers learn from Phillip's story as they explore multiple perspectives about place, race, and belonging in their work with youth? To examine these questions, this chapter describes how Phillip documented the gentrifying urban landscape of Harlem and critiqued the increasing presence of Whiteness in the area to argue that Harlem should remain an educative place of Black cultural events. Then, the chapter establishes parallels between two unlikely sources: the story of Phillip in Harlem and that of Jasmine, a sixth-grade African American female participant with whom I worked in a 2004 summer writing program in the rural community of Egypt, Texas. The intersecting discussion of Phillip and Jasmine's community literacy experiences sets the stage for a more detailed exploration of the idea of White-ification as documented in interviews with local residents, primarily White professionals, who live in Harlem. With these discussions, I argue for additional explorations of race, place, and identity in ways that privilege youth stories.

I can still see Phillip and Khaleeq standing on a busy Harlem street corner talking with me about gentrification, videotaping their visual stories of Harlem, and asking me, "You see this? All these changes, these new people we ain't never seen here before. You know Harlem's not gonna be the same, right?" Indeed, Harlem is "not gonna be the same," much like other communities—urban and rural—that are undergoing massive spatial changes. In the midst of these changes, it is necessary to include the perspectives of various people, including White residents and Black youth.

In countless cities across America—including Chicago, Cleveland, Detroit, Houston, New York, and San Francisco—conflicts over the gentrification of urban communities, what Freeman (2006) describes as "there goes the 'hood" and Phillip names "White-ification," are increasing. News images of abandonment, decline, poverty, and strife are too quickly and often stereotypically grounded into the spatial landscape of urban life. Such images often pair decline with renewal, collapse with gentrification, and fortification with efforts at improving, or making safe, "urban" and "inner-city" spaces (even if they are already safe). These images tell contradictory stories about existing conditions within urban communities by ignoring the stories local residents have about their community. They also overlook how residents understand relationships between power and politics, access and opportunity, and the ways in which they, especially youth, are now forced to interact across spatial, racial, and cultural differences on a daily basis whereas previously they did not have to (see Hardman Response).

According to Ms. L, such images "paint the area so negatively that people have their own feelings about urban communities that are unfounded. Look at Harlem! What's wrong with Harlem? Why do people talk about Harlem like they've been here when many have never even stepped foot in?" As a teacher and former resident of Harlem, Ms. L's sentiments challenged perceptions of Harlem, as well as other urban communities, as unsafe, dangerous, and criminal. To create a counternarrative for students, Ms. L relied on descriptions of Harlem that are positive, culturally rich, and participatory. Doing so allowed her and her students to understand how community stories (e.g., truths; memories; lived experiences; cultural events) can serve as responses to the negative images often portrayed in popular culture about urban areas.

Some stories of urban communities are made more public and are privileged over others. How does this affect urban youth? When urban communities, which are primarily occupied by people of color, get gentrified, then racialized narratives (e.g., "Black community"; "Spanish Harlem"; "White-ification of the 'hood") and power dynamics (e.g., middle class and rich versus poor and working class; recently displaced longtime residents; new businesses) emerge. These affect the lives of youth in- and out-of-school. They also have influences on their sense of identity, ownership, belonging, and feelings of familiarity versus feelings of strangeness in their familial communities. The following exchange serves as an example:

Phillip: You already know that gentrification gon' bring displacement even if people don't want us to believe that.

Valerie: Who are these "people?"

Khaleeq: Government [both Phillip and Khaleeq laugh at this]. I mean corporations [more laughter] making decisions. They don't be looking like us!

Phillip: Where does that leave us? Remember what you said about where residents going?

Valerie: He's talking about what you said in the video walk. You remember, Khaleeq?

Khaleeq: I said people gonna have to move out of Harlem and the Upper West Side, go to the Bronx, Queens, Washington Heights, Inwood [New York City boroughs and Manhattan communities]. Maybe even move down south [i.e., Southern USA]. I know people who did.

Phillip: Why don't they look like us, I mean the people in charge? That just another way of keeping us in our place? You can't keep us in our place, we been through too much to know that.

Khaleeq: We have. Look at history. Full of struggle. That makes us stronger.

Phillip: So what about us? People want to gentrify Harlem, they don't care that this our home, what we know? Lots of us been here all our lives and you telling me somebody's gonna up and

> take it all away from our reach? Our home, neighbors, parks, even schools! This our home, where we belong.
>
> *Khaleeq:* We belong, our identities wrapped up in our place. That's messed up people could take it away 'cause of gentrification. That might happen.

As discussed in previous chapters, Phillip and Khaleeq were aware of the changes occurring in Harlem just as much as they were aware of the possible consequences of those changes: rental increases, closing of local businesses, and displacement. When I suggested that all communities undergo changes associated with economic influences, shifting demographics, and land development, and that Harlem is only one example of a gentrifying area, they resisted my argument by stating: "You're from down South, right?" (Khaleeq) and "Everywhere changes, but are people trying to figure out how to take care of the people living in the area before they come in making the changes? I don't think so" (Phillip). Phillip in Harlem and Jasmine in Egypt, Texas, have lived experiences that, as Khaleeq so eloquently stated in an interview session, represent "a complete conflict over what was here, and what is already coming here." By traveling between communities in New York and Texas, we return to the central concern of this book: how the lived experiences of youth embody ways of telling stories about place, struggle, and identity that are often not part of the literacy work students do, or perform, in schools.

To use the words of Phillip, this telling of stories includes "figuring out how we can get people to see how we have something to say about our community and what's happening to it. But nobody's asking our opinions, like we don't exist." Phillip wanted people to know that youth should be heard. Their stories are not represented in debates over gentrification, and too often are not recognized in "schools, 'cause we students just sit there and take what teachers tell us without saying how we feel. We don't get to talk about what's happening in our world. It's the same thing. It's like that word you [Valerie] be using, *performing*. It's all performance. We students don't get to perform what *we* want to." In our work together, the youth in Harlem and in Egypt were encouraged to perform literacy narratives about their community that *they* wanted to perform. This included a critical discussion of race and the value of place on one's identity development. For Phillip, this meant exploring "how Harlem is going from Black to White residents, from a Black 'hood with culture to a gentrified place." Phillip documented community changes by engaging in onsite observations of Harlem and unpacking stereotypical images of his "'hood." He recalled an old Harlem that stands in opposition to a new Harlem and performed narratives about place and identity. One could say that Phillip is really not performing anything, but I argue that his questions, observations, body language, and verbal expressions are performances that helped him tell a story about power and politics in Harlem. Thus, youth performing literacy narratives about community through videotaping, mapping (designing poster-size visuals of Harlem's geographical boundaries and sites), and writing can offer a response to gentrification and can speak to how they authored identities of location and self.

"YOU GOTTA KNOW WHAT I MEAN BY WHITE-IFICATION": PHILLIP AND *HIS* HARLEM

Phillip talked about his understanding of Harlem as a "mecca of Black life like nobody ever seen before, that's being changed because of gentrification and White-ification." In this discussion, he described Harlem as "once a place where well-off Whites used to live" that eventually became a community where Black people "from all over settled in and made action happen. Now, they [White people] want it back." As he talked about *his* Harlem, he paced the floor in my office. When I asked him, "So, what do you mean by White-ification?", he paused in mid-sentence and then wiped a smirk off his face. His voice grew more intense, and he seemed unsettled, bothered by my question.

Phillip opened my office door to see if anyone was lingering around, and looked at me before saying, "You know what I mean. They want the rest of Harlem to look just like this university [Columbia]. Like everything and everybody around you, without signs that Blacks or even Latinos and other minorities was here. They already think this university ain' in Harlem." He continued, "That's step #1: when the community where the university is located is given a different name from the actual community. Man, that's like, real White-ification. Fo' real, though."

For Phillip, White-ificaton paralleled White privilege (McIntosh, 1988), and in other conversations and in his journals, he freely described how this privilege extended from "the local public schools to the colored folks' community," all the while never wanting to say, "White people." His comments echoed arguments on gentrification, Whiteness, and class issues expressed by Mr. Walker, a White teacher at Harlem High School, during his teacher interview (see Chapter 6). In highlighting the challenges of being a White male in Harlem, Mr. Walker expressed ambivalent feelings about residing in the community at the height of its gentrification process: "It was a hard decision for me, but what was I going to do? Yes, I'm seen as an outsider." In revisiting his sentiments that "the community where the university is located is given a different name from the actual community" in relation to his talk of White privilege, Phillip offered a grim, stereotypical picture of people's perceptions of urban life and landscapes:

> See, White privilege, when we talking about urban places like Harlem, would have you believe Harlem's dirty, dangerous, lots of crime, criminals, poor Blacks on welfare, people not caring about where they live, schools on lockdown. That always get plastered on the news and people think, "Harlem is so dangerous. I can't go to Harlem 'cause it's a jungle." It's not that. It's almost like the opposite. We have love for our 'hood. You see that when you walk down any street in Harlem or go to any cultural center or speak to the people who live here. Because so many folks think these negative things, they think we need *them* to clean *us* up . . . to gentrify *our* community. Get real. [Phillip's emphasis]

In our work together, Phillip learned to critically theorize meanings and assumptions associated with "urban," and his increasing awareness of Whiteness and White privilege became a central factor in his community literacy narrative. His definition of community, his recognition of the conflicting perspectives of urban communities, and his performances of literacy helped him develop an emerging theory of place that resisted negative depictions of Harlem. As I described in Chapter 2, he began to publicly question whether White privilege was the guiding force behind gentrification and economic power, especially in Harlem. When Phillip asked Kim and Samantha if they thought White privilege explained the presence of new White residents living in new, expensive developments in the area that, to use Samantha's words, "a lot of people here can't afford," he was attempting to theorize specific reasons (e.g., racial, economic) for spatial change. Phillip was trying to critique meanings of privilege as a way to include it in a literacy narrative.

To do this, he either explicitly or implicitly made references to terms such as *access, getting whatever they want, more opportunities, certain rights,* and *money*. His references, paired with his question—"So, do you think this has to do with White privilege?"—represented, however partially and incomplete, his emerging theorization of the boundaries and limitations of privilege for many urban residents—in this case, people of color in Harlem. Such youth theorizations in regard to place are essential for literacy education and educators because they demonstrate critical engagements with sociopolitical issues that impact youth acts of re-imagining their own lives and literacies. Such theorizations also prove that youth have sophisticated methods—which often go untapped in classrooms—by which they make sense of the way they are situated in the world and with others. At the backdrop of this theorization, Phillip was also naming and questioning various stereotypes that some people continue to have of Harlem space and its racial landscape. These stereotypes range from Harlem as "dirty" and "dangerous" to Harlem as "a jungle."

It is important, I believe, for educators and researchers to encourage students to theorize concepts of place and race in direct relation to access and belonging. While I struggled (and often sat on the fence of indecision) with Phillip's insistence that White-ification was *the* motivating factor behind gentrification, I openly embraced his critiques of spatial (urban) stereotypes. I also welcomed his critiques of the association between race and place, an association that has historically cultivated Black people's cultural practices, sense of self, and feelings of belonging in a racist world. Indeed, Harlem is becoming increasingly White. Yet it is also re-emerging as a Black middle-class "gentry" (see Taylor, 2002). In both ways, Harlem's continued gentrification will be impacted by the presence of race (i.e., White- and Black-ification) and class. It will have implications for the long-time poor and working-class residents who have resisted spatial change as well as negative depictions of Harlem.

To support Phillip's critical thinking, I asked him to unpack stereo-typical images of Harlem as being "dangerous" and having "lots of crime," "criminals," and "schools on lockdown" (i.e., where do stereotypes come from, how do they infringe upon identities and sense of self, and what do you mean by "almost like the opposite?"). I also asked him to further explain White-ification by indicating what he meant by "them/people" and "us/our:"

> *Phillip:* You know me by now. You know I'm ah speak my mind and tell my truth, Valerie, and the way I see things around here is quite simple: They coming in and taking over by using privilege to get what they want. What's difficult about seeing that?
>
> *Valerie:* Again, who you talking 'bout when you say "they?" Seems like you ain' comfortable giving a description for this "they." And what are they taking over?
>
> *Phillip:* My Harlem, your Harlem, you know, Black people's Harlem. I'm talking about White people, but you already know that. And I'm not just talking about White people, but like I said, White privilege. So, I've been fortunate to live in Harlem all my life and I've had to make do with what is here, but now that they want to gentrify this, gentrify that, I'm suppose to just sit back and smile. This my home. I might be a teenager,

> but I got a right to this place, and my right runs deeper than
> theirs.
> *Valerie:* Why's that the case? This thing about your rights running
> deeper?
> *Phillip:* From when I can remember from living here, I ain' never
> seen so many White people in Harlem walking the streets,
> moving into the 'hood, you know. And when I'm talking with
> folks in the 'hood, like residents who been living there forever,
> it's like we don't know what's going on. Nobody talks to us;
> they [White people] just walk by. Then before you know it,
> with new folks come new businesses. The Old Navy and
> Aerosoles, the corner cafés. That's not my Harlem. Mine's
> Black people on the streets, the Apollo when it was cheap
> enough for Black people to go to a show at, and the attitude
> that everybody looks out for everybody else. My rights run
> deep, but gentrification's coming, and with it goes my rights.
> It's complicated.

Beyond his attention to the changing space of Harlem—"the new
folks," "new businesses," and "the corner cafés"—Phillip was performing
a story of belonging. "My rights run deep," he claimed, and these rights
were being threatened by the White face of gentrification, as "they just
walk by." His story was grounded in a language of resistance, a grounding
that encouraged him both to tell and perform it to me, an African American woman originally from the South who was a part of his Harlem, "my
Harlem, your Harlem, you know." This Harlem, for Phillip, was Black
people's Harlem, a universal and historic Black space in contemporary
times that represented struggle, belonging, hard work, and civic engagement and served as a "homeplace" (see hooks, 1990). This point solidified
his position that gentrification heavily influences racial demographics and
cultural traditions. In many ways, his passionate stance supported arguments posited by Haymes (1995) and other critical theorists who write
about how the stories of urban residents represent signs of resistance.
Drawing on critical geography and multiculturalism, Haymes believes that
urban residents should share their spatial stories of struggle in order to
create a *pedagogy of place* that examines meanings of urban, culture, Whiteness, and the world.

According to Haymes, "Because inner-city Blacks live on the margins
of White supremacist domination and privilege, they have no other alternative than to struggle for the transformation of their places on the margin into spaces of cultural resistance" (p. 113). This struggle may take the
form of activism, the "construction of homeplaces" (see Haymes, 1995,

p. 113; see also hooks, 1990), and the redefinition of identity, community, and power against the backdrop of mainstream standards. Phillip
struggled to make sense of community changes in his writing and literacy
performances as he engaged in a "reading [of] the world" (Freire, 1998;
Freire & Macedo, 1987). Even in his discomfort with saying "White people"
—a discomfort that also pointed to how moments of silence can represent
acts of resistance—Phillip acknowledged the presence of White people
("them"), although "nobody talks to us." In this acknowledgment, he did
what Haymes advocates: resisted White domination and privilege by telling narratives of his "place on the margin" (p. 113). This involved both
the telling of counternarratives against negative images of this urban community as "jungle" as well as the documentation of perceived past (e.g.,
"everybody looks out for everybody else") and present (e.g., "nobody talks
to us" and "corner cafés") community conditions. As Phillip implied, his
performance was a result of the highly complicated relationships caused by
gentrification. Such relationships positioned "us" against "them," "White"
against "Black," and "newness" over "oldness."

Phillip's story is an example of how he was *acting* upon, *reflecting* on,
and being *challenged* by social and political conditions in Harlem. These
conditions included a new glitzy Apollo, new condominiums, renovated
apartments, and expensively priced brownstones. They also involved increased police presence in the area. His acknowledgment of these conditions echoed Freire's (1970/1997) belief: "People, as beings 'in a situation,'
find themselves rooted in temporal-spatial conditions which mark them
and which they also mark" (p. 90). On being marked, Freire states, "They
will tend to reflect on their own 'situationality' to the extent that they are
challenged by it to act upon it. Human beings *are* because they *are* in a
situation. And they *will be more* the more they not only critically reflect
upon their existence but critically act upon it" (p. 90, emphasis in the original). For Phillip as well as Khaleeq, Samantha, Kim, Damen, Ms. L, and
some of the other teachers at Harlem High School, the desire to take up
Freire's advocacy to "critically act upon" one's reflections and oppressions
came through in the many interviews we conducted and writings we exchanged. They sought to keep alive the mission of Freire's "cultural workers," or *conscientizacao*, people who work with and directly involve the larger
community in promoting educational achievement through various
curricular and community activities while working against oppressive
structures. The foundation of Freire's mission is to increase one's critical
consciousness by engaging in reflection, discovery, action, and social transformation of oppressive conditions as one travels through the world. This
traveling involved interpreting signs of community change, engaging in

critical conversations, and, among other things, negotiating identities and critiquing power dynamics.

In Phillip's resistance to "White-ification" and his obvious embrace of "Black-ification" was a larger conversation about how he saw Harlem as an educative place of Black cultural events. His Harlem included "the Black people on the streets, the Apollo . . . and the attitude that everybody looks out for everybody else." His Harlem also included what he referred to as signs of struggle and culture, such as local public schools, historic churches that "give Harlem style," and the numerous painted murals on the storefronts of local businesses that detail stories of hope and possibility. For Phillip, such signs inspired his literacy narrative because they "tell important stories that don't get told when a community gets gentrified. . . . Harlem has stories that shouldn't be forgotten."

Phillip was motivated by many signs, from the historic Apollo Theater and the Schomburg Center for Research in Black Culture, to the Hotel Theresa and the Harlem YMCA. These signs, along with digital pictures, journals, videotaped community documentaries, mapping of community spaces, and interactions with residents at local community meetings, served as catalysts by which Phillip, Khaleeq, Damen, and Rebekkah created literacy narratives. In their narratives, they positioned Harlem as a major historical site of social and political activism. Youth and other teachers at Harlem High, whom you will meet in Chapter 6, also shared stories of place, identity, and gentrification that informed our literacy experiences and ways of (re)reading community conditions. Together, these stories painted the community as a site of "history, Black culture, the Harlem Renaissance, struggle, and hard work" or, as I name it, a location of contradictions embedded with rich signs of Black-ification that spanned socioeconomic groupings and supported Black traditions.

After Phillip expressed anger over White-ification and gentrification, I pushed him to consider the educative lessons that can be learned from the local community. He admitted that in community sites and encounters, one can learn how to be "responsible," how to "take pride" in Black culture, and how to "talk back" to injustices. This way of being, of learning, is a type of education that "you don't get in schools . . . it happens on the streets of Harlem." In this discussion, Phillip listed prominent figures such as Langston Hughes, Malcolm X, and Adam Clayton Powell Jr. as people who engaged Harlem as an educative place for Black people: "I can't imagine the education people got from listening to Malcolm X giving speeches and going to political events, and just from living in Harlem then . . . a deep experience in the 'hood." Phillip's reflections on the past in comparison with the current Harlem were further embedded in his belief that Black education, cultural activities, and political life happened in the streets and, thus, contributed to the idea of Black-ification. He expressed how such community education resisted White-ification in Harlem: "We don't need them taking over our community;" "We just gotta work against White-ification by looking at struggles Blacks already gone through." He also believed this education was not exclusive to school space: "We gotta preserve our 'hood and turn to the streets for real learning to happen."

On various occasions, Khaleeq echoed Phillip's belief that "real learn-ing" about White-and Black-ification was not a part of the work that he and his peers did in school. During one of his many visits to my university office, Khaleeq told me that he gets "bored sometimes" in school, "or maybe I'm just frustrated cause I gotta write on demand when teachers tell me. No time to take things in." When I asked him to elaborate, he insisted, "There's gotta be a way to learn there [school] and, well, talk about how that stuff ties to the stuff we be seeing happening in the community." I must admit that such confessions often baffled me, given that I observed how Ms. L interacted with her students and taught insightful lessons that are essential to their literacy skills, practices, and ways of thinking in and about the world. However, I realized, at Phillip and Khaleeq's urging, that Ms. L is only one teacher with more than 25 students per class for less than 50 minutes a session. So, I asked Khaleeq and Phillip to find the connec-tions for themselves, to think about the ways in which school-sponsored learning connected to community-based learning. I wanted them to think seriously about what Ms. L encouraged all of her students to do: to make self-to-self-to-text-to-world connections as they sought to uncover ques-tions, dilemmas, and counternarratives on various topics. Slowly, Phillip and Khaleeq accepted my challenge and began to dig deep in order to consider how school and community learning, and the literacies within, intersected, connected, and differed.

TAKING IT TO THE STREET: EGYPT, HARLEM, AND ACTS OF PLACE-MAKING

You remember the stories you told me about that town called Egypt? And the lines in that poem you read to me back in the day? The one that fifth or sixth grader wrote about living in Texas? You remember, right?

Phillip was referring to a poem written by Jasmine, a sixth grader who was a student in my 2004 summer community writing course in Egypt,

Texas, a rural, primarily African American town on the outskirts of Houston, Texas. The original settlement, named Mercer's Crossing, dates back to 1829 when Eli Mercer "established a plantation and ferry on the Colorado River at the San Felipe–Texana crossing" (The Handbook of Texas online). It quickly became known as Egypt, in reference to the Bible, after a severe drought forced the town to supply corn to the surrounding settlements. Today, the town houses a neighborhood store, a small post office, two local churches, a town nightclub, a small slave museum, old plantation quarters, and many flat and duplex houses where the families of my former students, middle school–age African American and Latino/a adolescents, resided. Farther away from the main road, which visibly divides the working class from the middle class, are fancier houses owned by either longtime White residents or Black natives returning to the area. Despite that White people are not the majority, signs of a changing community are quite visible: The town's first Wal-Mart opened a few years ago, along with some fast-food chains. Although the influx is slower than in Harlem, White-ification and the (re)appropriation of space are gradually occurring in Egypt.

During my work with students in Egypt, we examined "community," paying attention to geographical boundaries (e.g., imaginary lines; spatial markers) that distinguished poor and working-class areas from upper-middle-class areas. The following lines are excerpted from a longer poem written by Jasmine:

> The picture of my community is old
> Old makes me think of the history of this Black community
> With its old stores, slave houses, and old family memories
> With its peaceful streets
> And its green trees growing everywhere
> With its new changes every day
> Between us and them
> And everywhere in old Egypt.

Jasmine penned the above words after a class walking tour of the local community. Of eight girls, she was the first one to be amazed by the presence of historical artifacts: dilapidated servants' shacks, "the big house," and the slave museum. In her process of making sense of a town of "history," "old stores," and "peaceful streets," a town that is experiencing "new changes every day," Jasmine was grappling with contradictions within the community. The following lines from a longer version of the poem indicate this point:

> The old things are next to new things
> We like the new things
> We forget the old things
> This is my picture of Egypt.

When I shared my experiences in Egypt with Phillip and Khaleeq, they identified various text-to-self connections that contributed to their use of critical literacy skills. According to Phillip, "Man, different spaces, but many of the same things going on. I like Jasmine writing about changes between people. She says something like *us* and *them*. That relates to Harlem." For Phillip, "us" refers to Black people across socioeconomic groupings (Blackness), and "them" refers to White people who are benefiting from "gentrification and our [Black people's] struggles" (White-ification). Highly problematic in these socioeconomic groupings is the absence of people who are neither Black nor White, such as Latinos, who comprise a large segment of Harlem's population. Even more challenging is Phillip's reading of Egypt because it is a town with a growing population of Latino/a residents who do not comprise such fixed racial categories of Black or White. Therefore, discussions of White-ification and Black-ification cannot overlook the presence of Latino/a, Puerto Rican, African, and Asian people in New York City's Harlem community. Clearly, Jasmine's Egypt was neither Phillip's Harlem nor Khaleeq's Upper West Side. Her town was rural and their communities were urban. Yet, during one of his community walk-through sessions, Phillip could not help but invoke Jasmine's Egypt into his space: "See, the signs are all around us and they make me think about the history of this community. There's a lot of old stuff, but that's good. And there's a lot of new stuff, and that can be . . . [he paused, and I said 'intriguing'] yeah, intriguing, and dangerous."

Phillip, Khaleeq, and Jasmine were trying to make sense of *us* and *them* at the same time that they were documenting community stories. These acts and activities related to Maurrasse's (2006) attempt to capture the changes in Harlem by listening to the community, "from churches to small businesses to activist organizations to block associations and beyond [that] have stressed organization as a means to improved social change" (p. 41). While Jasmine was more interested in "the history of this Black community/With its old stores, slave houses, and old family memories," Phillip was more concerned about the costs of White-ification in relation to the possible displacement of longtime Black residents: "They don't take into account the people who already live here and their community organization. People move in at a price. Sometimes that price is too much for the working-class man and woman to pay. So what you gonna do? Listen, then act."

While quoting Jasmine's poem, Phillip used his digital camera to cap-ture various images throughout Harlem: the Apollo ("You see, they've redone the Apollo like big time"), the Police Athletic League center ("That's the PAL where kids go to get off the street and play ball"), and the Studio Museum of Harlem ("I don't see any White people going in there, and that's a good museum"). In his mention of the Studio Museum, Phillip, inter-estingly, seemed to be inviting White people into one of Harlem's cultural institutions after previously rejecting their presence in such spaces because of gentrification and race. This is an important turn of events in Phillip's thinking about Whiteness and access, one that eventually led to his inter-actions with White residents in Harlem (see Chapter 5). He said, "I won-der what Jasmine would think of this. I bet how she thinks of her Egypt as us against them don't come close to what I see in Harlem on the regu-lar. But she's out there, like me, making sense of what's going on. That's what we do . . . go in the 'hood and make sense."

Phillip recognized the value in Jasmine—in her rural town and with a sixth-grade sensibility—taking education to the streets to perform nar-ratives of community. Although Jasmine's Egypt was different from Phillip's Harlem, Phillip connected them in his literacy narrative: Both locations have a large African American population and a rich history of struggle, and both are being confronted, although in different ways, with the possibility of White-ification. Egypt has historic slave quarters, new retail businesses, gentrification, and incoming White residents; Harlem is considered a hotbed of rights movements and is rapidly becoming a site for new retail businesses, gentrification, and incoming White and middle-class Black residents. Therefore, the literacy narratives that Jas-mine and Phillip are performing serve as powerful inquiries into spatial change and fabricated efforts toward democratizing already democratized communities.

In other words, Phillip's Harlem and Jasmine's Egypt are spaces that have rich histories and can serve as sites of rich literate possibilities. Both Phillip and Jasmine actively turned to writing in order to document sto-ries of community: "our home, neighbors, parks, and even our schools" (Phillip); "the picture of my community is old" (Jasmine). As educators, we should identify and encourage the performance of literacy in the work that youth do as they "take it to the streets" and as we discover ways to build on their experiences inside classrooms. For example, the following principles, which I believe can be brought into our classrooms, were at the center of Phillip and Jasmine's individual investigations:

- Engaging in writing and reading activities to make a difference. Phillip and Jasmine were writing and reading about the community with a sense of purpose as they addressed a pre-identified theme: community change. This is an example of literacy activism.

- Adopting multiple perspectives in order to understand a topic or an issue in various ways and through different lenses. This is an example of critical literacy.
- Questioning other people's perspectives in order to enhance their own perspectives and to have their positions/perspectives challenged in return. This is another example of critical literacy.
- Sharing what they learn with others and encouraging others to share what they learn with us. In this way, they try on different voices and identities as a way to understand agency. This is an example of reciprocal learning.
- Creating experiences around words, images, languages, and in the presence of differences and diversities. This is an example of multimodal literacy.
- Critically thinking about what happens to communities that are gentrified, changed, or "improved" through talking, questioning, writing, and mapping. This is an example of both critical and multimodal literacy.
- Debating how communities change for various reasons and based on many different circumstances—gentrification, demographic trends, and even economic/ financial and housing crises. This way of making critical text-to-self-to-world connections by being aware of sociopolitical realities is an example of critical literacy.

Whether we were examining gentrification in Harlem or historical artifacts in Egypt, Phillip and Jasmine were making their *own* meanings from the realities of their lives and the literacies around them. The skills they displayed—critical literacy, reciprocal learning, multimodal literacy, and establishing specific connections—connect to present and long-term educational goals that foster high academic achievement for students as they prepare for participation in a larger world. Thus, the educational prospects of their community involvements can enhance their facility with words, engagements with complicated ideas, and approaches to problem-posing and problem-solving activities. These things, among others, are at the heart of my own pedagogical practices and democratic engagements with youth and adults.

CHANGING THE (URBAN) NARRATIVE OF HARLEM

Phillip and Jasmine's stories about the politics of location are not readily accounted for in larger political debates about gentrification and community change. The ways in which they saw their communities—as places of hope and struggle, history and culture—often conflicted with images sprawled across the news and in popular culture of community abandonment, neglect, and danger. Phillip, for example, saw parallels between *his* urban Harlem and Jasmine's rural Egypt: "She talks about the old stuff and I can see some of Harlem in what she's saying. When the new come, then there's White-ification. That's for Egypt and for Harlem." For Phillip, emphasizing the value of "old stuff" contradicted larger narratives that portray communities of color, particularly urban, as dangerous and in need of gentrification.

This is not a new phenomenon. Urban communities like Harlem have rich histories that are forever being rewritten and re-presented by the presence of newness, differences, and changing demographics. Harlem has been many things for many people: It was once a settlement for indigenous inhabitants, Dutch settlers, the White bourgeoisie, and poor and working-class Black people, many from Southern states. However, the fact of cyclical change does not diminish the uniqueness of Phillip's struggle, given the history of his family in, and the heritage of the place known as, Harlem. As early as 1925, for instance, Harlem was widely considered "the capital of the Black world, where Black artists, intellectuals, and entrepreneurs thrived, Black police officers walked the beat, and Black dreams need not be deferred" (Kelley, 2003, p. 10). Over hundreds of years of change, the decades of the Harlem Renaissance uniquely defined the literate tradition of Black Americans. This old Harlem, as perceived by Phillip and many of his friends, is not represented in public discussions about community, culture, and struggle.

When I push them to think through their perspectives about the absence of discussions on community and culture in their schools, writ large, both Phillip and Khaleeq hesitantly admit that Ms. L "teaches us a little about these things, but, see, that's one teacher in an entire school." Instead of the presentation of alternative viewpoints, they believe images of decline, talk of strife, and perceptions of urban cities and communities as "jungle" are pervasive. A look at Marsh's (1934) artwork, *East Tenth Street Jungle*, which is set in Lower Manhattan; the movie *The Blackboard Jungle* (1955), based on violence in a large urban high school; or the documentary *Detroit's Agony* (1990), about the collapse of the Motor City, confirms their belief. Hence, youth stories of place that connect the histories of renaissance movements to rich cultural and literacy practices within communities can serve as responses to larger political debates and negative popular culture depictions of urban areas and urban education.

In many classrooms across America, students are taught to take on an identity that contradicts their familial identities, customs, and ways of being in the world (see Luttrell & Parker, 2001; Moje, 2002). Youth stories of place, belonging, struggle, culture, and identity are often devalued in schools. For many youth, the only place where they feel they can openly question, resist, and challenge authorial voices is in the community. Phillip proved this point when he talked about the educative value of a place like Harlem: "It's in the 'hood where I learn the important lessons that I need to learn, where I can disagree with what I see, and tell my story about it without feeling like I'm in the wrong."

Phillip told and performed *his* community stories as a counternarrative of Harlem as a site of history, hard work, and Black culture in resistance to what he called the "White-ification of the 'hood." He viewed Harlem as a community under invasion through gentrification. Much like Jasmine did in her poem about rural Egypt, Phillip wondered about the relationships between "us and them." As educators, we know that "them" includes teachers and administrators. Therefore, I believe Phillip's wonderings can open a larger discussion about community, race, and differences in school spaces. Phillip was not only writing a story about community, but performing it by reading about, questioning, critiquing, and racializing the artistic, cultural, and spatial artifacts (art, dance, music, traditions, Black cultural spaces) of and debates within Harlem. This type of critical engagement has the potential to influence how educational stakeholders see relationships between power and politics in schools and the surrounding communities. It also has the potential to create direct connections between youth and teachers, and ultimately, between historically disenfranchised peoples and the presence of Whiteness, White privilege, and White-ification in urban communities. I believe that these stories of change, community, belonging, and youth involvement have a place in our classrooms, our curricular work, and, as Fecho (2004) describes, in our immersion "in looking closely at the transactions we make across cultures" (p. 157). How can we start this conversation? In my work with Phillip, Khaleeq, and other youth, we took a direct approach: The youth turned their mics and cameras on "them" in an attempt to understand the motivating factors behind gentrification.

LISTENING TO OTHER VOICES: RECIPROCAL LEARNING, CRITICAL LITERACY

For both Phillip and Khaleeq, the narrative of "us" versus "them" was so engrained in their thinking about gentrification that they needed to hear other perspectives. To further create their individual community literacy narratives, they willingly agreed to have conversations with White Harlem residents. Their willingness was not an easy feat. Initially, they scoffed at me for even making the suggestion, arguing that "we already see them here all over Harlem anyway" (Phillip), and "they gone talk to us?" (Khaleeq). I challenged them to consider the value of multiple meanings and conflicting perspectives for their arguments on gentrification: "How can you talk against gentrification without talking with and listening to people whom you categorize as *them*? And how much mileage do you actually think you'll get from saying *White-ification, White-ification, White-ification*? Now really, is that fair?" They considered my questions and then inquired into *my* position on gentrification, which, up until this point, I really had not shared. In finally being forced to claim a stance, I admitted that I was inspired by their positions on gentrification, White-ification, and community. I read Harlem as a major site of Black life and struggle in the United States. And I resisted the changes occurring in the community, but could not really blame "them" for moving into an area that "they" considered affordable.

The blame partially results from the inability of people with different racial, cultural, and economic backgrounds to talk about community histories, demographics, and change. In fact, all communities change, whether for good or bad, which, for me, is a subjective yet political judgment. My hope was for community and cultural preservation and not for displacement, which is a devastating reality for too many people of color throughout the Diaspora. Hopefully, preservation could be accomplished if groups of people learned how to work together in light of racial, economic, cultural, and linguistic differences. I recognize that this is a huge request, given the ways our society talks around differences. My brief confession was enough for Phillip and Khaleeq. They were interested in my emerging position, insisting that maybe *I* had something to learn from White residents as well. They agreed to do the interviews.

Over the span of 7 months—from January to July 2007—Phillip, Khaleeq, and Damen, along with researchers Rebekkah, Marcelle, and me, interviewed approximately 10 White people about their stories of place, power, and community. We posted advertisements on local Web sites, school and community bulletin boards, in a local post office, and in grocery stores. We also distributed flyers at local tenants' association meetings and rallies held to protest gentrification in the community. During the summer of 2008, I conducted brief follow-up sessions with available interviewees. Although Khaleeq, Phillip, Rebekkah, and I collaboratively developed an interview protocol, we did not stick to the script. Often, and depending on the nature of the interview, we digressed from the questions in order to engage in a conversation with the interviewee. The questions focused on identity, reasons for moving to Harlem, feelings about gentrification, and levels of participation in community events. They included the following: How long have you lived in Harlem? Would you have moved to Harlem 5 to 10 years ago? What do your family members, friends, and associates think of Harlem (e.g., perceptions, beliefs, stereotypes) and of you living in Harlem? Have you met any opposition to living in Harlem (e.g., from coworkers, friends, family, neighbors in your building or in the community)?

Many of the interviews reinforced what the youth claimed were public perceptions of the community, but also showed that White residents resisted blanket stereotypes. One interviewee, Kent, a White male from the Northeastern region of the United States, insisted, "People who aren't from the city have this kind of clichéd notion of what Harlem is. . . . I feel like I kind of avoided that." This perception for many people, according to Kent, describes Harlem as "primarily a Black neighborhood with high crime rates and not a place that you want to live if you can avoid it. I think that's the perception 10 years ago. I think there have been factors that are changing that. . . . I think that's kind of the reputation that the area has, especially for people living outside of New York City." When Khaleeq followed up by asking what factors contributed to changing that public perception of Harlem, Kent shared: "I think there's been some emphasis [on] promoting the artistic and cultural contributions of Harlem residents to Black culture and American culture in general. I think efforts to kind of celebrate Black culture in terms of visiting the Schomburg and raising awareness of Black poets like Langston Hughes . . . and also celebrating Strivers' Row [town houses once home to famous Black artists, activists, and politicians] and soul food restaurants that have been staples of the community for a really long time are now being celebrated." Kent thinks that these cultural institutions in Harlem deserve attention and the focus on them is gradually changing people's perceptions of the community.

Yet, as a White person living in Harlem, Kent admitted that he did not see himself as part of the community. He did not participate in cultural or community-sponsored activities, did not have particularly long conversations with neighbors, and could not imagine raising a family there. His confessions confirmed Phillip and Khaleeq's idea about how some people—in this case, a White male graduate student attending the prestigious Columbia University—did not immediately see the value of establishing connections in this community. In Kent's words, "I sleep there [in Harlem] and that's pretty much all I do there. This [the university] is my community. I spend very long days here." His reaction to the idea of participating in the community of Harlem had to do in part with the reality of his busy school schedule and also with not having grown up in a large urban area: "I'm from [the Northeast] and from a rural area and I don't want to raise a family in the city." However, if he ever chose to raise a family and live in Harlem, his "existence in the community and contributions would be different. I'd be more aware of what schools are offering. I think I'd be more alert to activities . . . to family activities. My lack of contributions to the community is dependent on my role here." In other words, Kent saw his current role in the community more as a graduate student studying at a local university and less as a resident confronting gentrification in Harlem.

Phillip found Kent's perspectives interesting on the one hand, and troubling on the other. After the interview ended and Kent left, Phillip commented, "I get that he's a student and all, but he lives in Harlem and does nothing for the community." Kent's perspective on contributing to the community is not that much different from the perspectives held by those who live in college towns across the United States. However, the unique political situation of Harlem requires one's attentiveness to community change and civic forms of engagement. Instead of focusing on these elements, Kent's position reiterated the youth's perceptions of privilege and the influx of newness in Harlem.

The importance of family to community investment intersected with points raised by Bonnie, a White female who has been living in Harlem with her daughter and husband since 2005. In her interview, she talked about how Harlem has its own "feel" and said it is apparent that not a lot of White people live in the area. Her argument is striking, given that Harlem has experienced an increase of White residents in the last 5 to 8 years (see Maurrasse, 2006; Freeman, 2006). According to Bonnie, "you're very aware that you're one of very few White people when you're down, walking around 125th Street. There are probably more . . . [White] people coming to and from the subway" where Columbia University borders with Harlem. Her interesting awareness of the presence, or absence, of racial differences did not stop her from spending time in Harlem. She would often get on the subway at a popular Harlem stop as well as walk from her apartment to fashion stores (e.g., Old Navy; H&M) on 125th Street.

In addition to talking about racial differences, Bonnie expressed confusion over what she perceived as cultural differences (e.g., the long lines of people inside the local post office). She commented: "You go to the Harlem post office on 125th Street and there's like always the longest line ever. Takes forever. But there's a self-serve thing that no one is ever at. So I can just walk in, do self-serve, and I don't know if it's that no one has a debit card because you have to have some sort of debit card/credit card to use the self-serve machine. I'm the only person ever using that machine. . . . Seems like a cultural difference." What Bonnie's confessions ignore, or fail to appropriately acknowledge, is that most of the post offices in and across New York City are overcrowded with long lines because people tend not to use available machines to have actual conversations with a worker. Conversations with other White people residing in SoHo, Greenwich Village, and Brooklyn suggest that the dynamics within New York City's post offices are not based on "cultural differences."

From her latter comment and many others, it appeared that Bonnie was regularly confronted with race and class issues in Harlem, particularly in comparison with the times she lived in the Bedford Stuyvesant area of Brooklyn, a majority African and African American community. Regarding her experiences there, she shared: "I never felt part of the community. Partly I think it's just different expectations you have for your amenities or what you do with your free time. So the neighborhood I lived in in Bed Stuy, there was just nothing that was open past a certain hour . . . maybe because of crime." Both Bonnie and Kent individually connected people's perceptions of Harlem to African American communities that are similar to Harlem (e.g., Bed Stuy; neighborhoods in central Philadelphia).

They both also admitted to feeling like outsiders. Kent often reiterated how he was not "from the city." Bonnie referenced being an outsider when she commented, "I don't really mind being different, but it makes life feel more stressful when you feel very different or when things are not as easy because you don't have access to things as easily as you want to." During one of our post-discussion sessions days after the interview (when our interviewees were not present), Khaleeq and Phillip posed a response to Bonnie's confession that she is an outsider who does not have immediate access to resources and amenities she believes should be available in the community. "How's that different from what we go through everyday" (Khaleeq)? Phillip added, "The stress she talking about ain't nothing compared to what Black people struggling here in Harlem and other places been going through our whole lives. We always have the burden of wondering why we don't have access. And not just Black people but all us minorities. See, you thought I was tripping when I mentioned White privilege in my video, but it's alive." After a brief pause, he continued, "Talk about being different, not having things easy, and . . . she said something about access. . . . walk in my shoes just for a day, then you'd know."

Phillip and Khaleeq and the other project members highlighted themes that emerged from the interviews: being an outsider, having access, and associating differences (e.g., long lines; not using self-serve machines) with cultural practices. From here, we noted that of the 10 people we interviewed, most described gentrification in socioeconomic terms. Bonnie explained gentrification by saying: "I think it's about socioeconomics, by definition. I don't think it's about race. I think race and socioeconomics are so closely linked in our society. It's perceived as being a racial thing, but it's really not. I mean, it's really about money." On this point, she continued: "Who's bringing it into the community, who's investing, why are they investing? But I see it as a gradual thing [gentrification] that happens. It's not just something that happens overnight." Khaleeq simply raised his eyebrows at this remark. Phillip, however, said, "Oh, okay, okay. Really now. I see."

George, a White male who is originally from the Southwestern region of the United States, echoed Bonnie's sentiments. A former Peace Corps worker who completed graduate school and currently teaches youth at a New York school, George explained that gentrification is not primarily about race, but about socioeconomic status. He said, "There's gentrification of middle-class wealth here—African Americans, too—and it's more of a class thing where people are moving into places that haven't been made up nice or kept up nice. It's a way to make a living, I'm sure, for some people." Associating gentrification with capitalism, George continued: "It's a way to make profit, I guess make value out of something . . . that's how our economy works. So that seems to be the motor behind, at least in my mind, the motor behind gentrification, that people are trying to make money." George did acknowledge that with gentrification comes the possibility of displacement for some of the poor and working-class people who might not be able afford its cost. He reiterated arguments made by the youth and their teachers at Harlem High School when he said: "The thing that happens then is that folks who are there [in gentrifying urban communities] living before the remodeling happens end up getting pushed out. . . . I heard stories about folks already feeling the pain of gentrification in Harlem."

For George, as for Bonnie, Kent, and some of the other White interviewees, gentrification should be addressed from a socioeconomic perspective. For Khaleeq, Phillip, Kim, Samantha, and the youth from the Schomburg program, gentrification is as heavily defined by race—"White-and Black-ification"—as by socioeconomic status, or wealth. When some youth from the Schomburg program wrote on their surveys that their mothers and fathers are "struggling to pay the rent," they were not just sharing a class reality, but also a racial reality. One youth wrote, "We are minorities, and this our home. Now all of the White people want to come take it away." Many youth were aware of the dynamics between class and race, but they did not easily describe the impact of gentrification on their familial networks by positioning one factor as more significant over the other. They talked about both—class and race—and the challenges that come with living in the midst of urban gentrification. This is an important point because it identifies racial and class-based realities of gentrification that many people ignore in justifying spatial changes as either an economic or a race issue. In my opinion, it is too simplistic to define gentrification as a class concern because it makes invisible displaced, racialized faces and bodies, a point I discuss later.

Linda and Beth, two White females who graduated from Columbia University and lived in Harlem, jointly talked about gentrification from class and race perspectives. Wanting to be a part of the community, but sensing their positions as outsiders and "others," they tried not to assume roles of power or exercise feelings of ownership in Harlem. Instead, they acknowledged that gentrification is a reality that has the potential to displace countless residents of color. Both Linda and Beth wanted to be more active in the community and wanted to participate in local cultural activities there. "I'd want to be involved, but I don't want to impose," explained Beth, as Linda nodded her head in agreement. They recognized the limitations of their Whiteness in a primarily African, African American, Latino/a, and Puerto Rican community; they were afraid that they were not welcome there because of their White skin. Like Linda and Beth, George acknowledged how his Whiteness contributed to the attitudes and perceptions of his neighbors, especially when they realized that he lived on *their* block: "I live in a very Dominican building [but] I'm fluent in Spanish," which, as he sees it, is very helpful as hc navigates through local language differences and attempts to de-position his assumed authority because of his Whiteness. The White residents we interviewed were aware of how others in the community (i.e., non-White residents) may see them and may, at times, feel threatened by their presence. Nevertheless, George and the other White interviewees believed that gentrification would eventually change the community for the better or the worse. All of the interviewees insisted that, overall, they felt comfortable enough in Harlem. They also expressed appreciation for the history of the community and its artistic, literary, and cultural legacies. Still, their expressions seemed to be directed at a past "renaissance" Harlem and not a current "protest gentrification" and "protect Black cultural and educative forms" Harlem.

Participating in the experience of interviewing White people about their perceptions of community and gentrification allowed me to witness how Phillip and Khaleeq confronted and attempted to understand differences head on: "These some . . . deep thoughts they talked about. They don't even noticed their privilege, though. Just because you stressed over not having access don't mean you entitled to it. You an outsider" (Phillip)! During the various interview sessions, Phillip and Khaleeq were not afraid to ask critical follow-up questions, ask for clarity on points that were being articulated, and listen attentively to other people's opinions even if they disagreed with them. As Khaleeq inquired of one of the interviewees: "Do you like being in Harlem or just tolerate it 'cause it's convenient?" Although we were not having specific conversations about reading and writing practices, we were, without a doubt, engaging in significant meaning-making experiences that helped us consider different ways of seeing gentrification and reconstructing our worldviews. Through a critical literacy framework, we were better able to examine gentrification both within and across race and class positions. Thus, we were listening to other voices in order to re-read the world, rethink our emerging stories about community change, and re-present our writings about gentrification in a local context. In my opinion, our experience of listening to other voices parallels experiences of engaging in "talk" in the classroom, especially in terms of how students and teachers debate the implied meanings, writing styles, and complex ways of interpreting texts (e.g., canonical; contemporary; written; visual; spatial). For Khaleeq, "I'm ah think 'bout all this so I could maybe . . . revise how I see gentrification."

SINGING IN MULTIPLE KEYS

In opening this chapter, I talked briefly about Phillip's growing activism, even when he did not realize it was there. I have often reflected on his comment:

> Whose story is going to be told? I see this on the regular—how this Black community is changing from how it was back in the day, how Black folks being pushed to the edge, and from the edge to being completely pushed out of Harlem? Who can afford the cost of gentrification?

As I listened to Phillip's voice, I also recalled the lyrical lines from Jasmine's poem singing in my ears:

> The picture of my community is old
> Old makes me think of the history of this Black community
> With its old stores, slave houses, and old family memories.

In a resounding voice joins the chorus of residents who are new to Harlem—residents who are young, professional, and White. To be honest, gentrification is not a tune that is easy to dance to. But it is the soundtrack that is already playing in Harlem. Old stores are closing and new stores are opening. For the last 10 years and counting, the demographic makeup of the community has been slowly altering along race and class lines. It is the same old song in many other communities across America. How do we answer Phillip's refrain: "Whose story is going to be told?"

To tell stories about the community—history, culture, change, artistic wealth—is to account for the ways in which stories are shared and contested, remembered and represented. For Kent, the White Harlem resident from the Northeast, his story of Harlem is a new one, yet to be fully formed, still emerging. He entered Harlem not to be a longtime resident in the community but because he wanted to be near the university where he is studying. He is hesitant about raising a family in Harlem and he does not participate in the life of the community. Yet there is still a story for him to tell about his "outsider," rural-bred perspective on Harlem. Kent, Bonnie, George, Linda, Beth, and the other White residents interviewed presented perspectives that challenged those of Phillip and Khaleeq. They pushed Phillip and Khaleeq, as well as Rebekkah and me, to rethink the idea of White-ification. It is no longer an abstract concept to which we can simply turn as we state the obvious—that there is an increasing presence of Whiteness (e.g., people; mainstream values; practices; privilege) in the area. White-ification now has faces and voices, and these faces and voices neither look the same nor sing the exact same tune. In fact, these faces that we tend to associate with White-ification are *not* all White.

In relation to literacy, I believe the perspectives held by youth and adults should be accounted for in narratives of place and belonging in our communities and schools. Phillip's connection to the text of Jasmine's poem and her rural community of Egypt, Texas, helped him expand his understanding of gentrification from something that is "only happening here in Harlem" to something that is occurring "in various parts of the world, like urban, rural, and other places" (Phillip). Jasmine and Phillip's individual encounters in their respective communities encouraged me to reconsider the stories of youth that I have listened to and collected over the last few years. In turn, I am able to have different types of conversations with my teacher education students, with Ms. L and other teachers in public schools, with the youth with whom I work and encounter on a regular basis, and with my own former high school teachers and administrators who live and work in and between the borderlines of the urban and the rural. Exchanging literacy stories, engaging in acts of listening and questioning, and reflectively reconsidering positions on important topics are the types of learning that should occur in all classrooms across America and throughout the Diaspora. Literacy learning should be based on old, new, and yet-to-be-written stories, multiple perspectives, differences and diversities, and ongoing, open exchanges. We should not ignore topics of importance in the lives of our students, their families, and maybe even to us: gentrification, community change, cultural practices, race and White-ification, privilege, and, as Delpit (1995) describes, "codes of power," which represent specific rules (ways of talking, acting, interacting, and dressing) for participating in various contexts (e.g., mainstream and familial).

What happens, then, when teachers have 25 or more students in a classroom? How does the type of learning that I am advocating move from ideas on a page and experiences with one or two youth to encounters experienced by a classroom of youth and their teachers? To answer that question, to which I return in Chapter 7, I recall my experiences as a teacher-researcher (2007) at Perennial High School in East Harlem. Invited by the principal to teach an English class 5 days a week to more than 25 seniors (at the same time that I was teaching full-time at a local university), I contemplated ways to listen to each of my students' unique stories, which were, at the time, unfamiliar to me. I had to learn about their daily struggles outside of school, academic success compared to community success, and their sense of ownership and belonging in the community versus in school. From that significant classroom teaching experience, I learned the importance of asking students to *really* engage in writing activities that put their thoughts center stage. I witnessed one student, Damya, taking digital pictures of Harlem, reading Kozol's (2005) *The Shame of the Nation: The Restoration of Apartheid Schooling in America,* and writing poetry on the topics of community, race, gender, and power in response to class readings. Through these literacy experiences, Damya was able to craft an argument on changing community conditions, present it to the class, and submit a collection of her original writings on increasing community involvement as a course assignment. Damya motivated other students to think about community change and their roles in it. She, along with Phillip, Khaleeq, Jasmine, and other youth with whom I have worked, were singing in multiple keys and being responsive to the question posed by Phillip: "Whose story is going to be told?"

As a way to sing in multiple keys while contemplating Phillip's question, I offer the following ideas and strategies:

- As educators, we can invite students to explore local and global community-based issues by having them adopt both insider and outsider positions. These positions can be based on their affiliation as a member of a specific local community and as a nonmember of an identified national and/or global community. This could support our students' practice with creating counternarratives and wearing multiple identities in various contexts.
- We can teach students how to participate in peer feedback groups in order to exchange perspectives, question positions, and reformulate their own arguments on course topics. Involvement in such

groups can help students reconsider their articulated stances on topics and issues and eventually to revise their written arguments.

• We can have students write their own reflective journal responses or poems on a defined community issue before studying published authors' writings on community. Then, they can juxtapose their writings with the authors' texts to create found poetry, oral or digital responses, and critical research-based presentations on this learning experience.

Clearly, there are multiple other ways for educators to support students in learning to sing in multiple keys around texts, classroom exchanges, and course assignments so that they can enhance their critical literacy skills.

Gentrification in Harlem

By Rebekkah Hogan, Project Participant

When I think of gentrification, I wonder if—like any process of change and growth—it is necessarily an exercise in removal and displacement of one group in favor of another, or a practice of growth and productive expansion. Are either of these things what we call "development?"

The conversation around gentrification in the New York City neighborhoods where I live and work centers on feelings of paternalism and colonization. Often, these feelings result from the presence of local real estate developers, wealthy people, and a large, prestigious research university. These groups pay lip service to the idea that they will include the community in their expansion plans by creating jobs and opportunities for local residents and locally owned businesses. However, such unproven declarations add fuel to the fire of distrust, displacement, and resentment that are prevalent throughout Harlem. It appears to many people that, once again, wealthy people have set their sights on an area that 20 years ago was essentially ignored, riddled with crime and violence, and left to urban and social decay with no productive assistance from the government or police force. Yet the Harlem community continued to grow and foster its sense of culture and self.

Buildings were eventually built on top of lots that had been abandoned for 20 years. Luxury condos selling for millions of dollars were erected next to "affordable" apartments whose rent had increased 50–80% throughout the decade. Many people who had spent their entire lives in Harlem, the cradle of the Black Renaissance in America, can no longer afford to live, shop, and eat here. Columbia University uses the concept of "eminent domain" as a legal argument for its right to purchase and rebuild a section of Harlem called Manhattanville. This legal argument, when applied to gentrification, or development, does not take into account the long history of community and struggle in Harlem. More than just pricing out longtime residents and raising the threat of eminent domain, gentrification has changed other elements of this cultural landscape. Historic soul food restaurants like Copeland's have closed, citing higher rent and fewer customers. Independent clothing stores have fallen to the likes of Old Navy and American Apparel. The aspects that make Harlem unique are being sacrificed in order to make the community more like Lower Manhattan, where you are never more than 5 blocks from a Starbucks. There are now two Starbucks on 125th Street. I cannot help but wonder: What will these changes do to the modern and historic view of Harlem? Will Lennox Avenue continue to be called Malcolm X Boulevard? Does that matter? Is there a way for "development," "progress," and "gentrification" to balance the past and future, while being inclusive of everyone regardless of class, race, or history?

I occupy an interesting location in the matrix of gentrification. By matrix, I mean that grid of intersection where race, social class, ethnicity, language, cultural value, and ownership exist. While I am a young Black woman who has lived in Harlem, in the Inwood section of Upper Manhattan, and now in Brooklyn, I am also very educated, comfortably in a middle-class job, and working for a large university that is one of the main perpetrators of the kinds of gentrifying offenses the Harlem community is so rightfully afraid of. My skin color provides access to these rapidly disappearing neighborhoods. When I go into a Dominican bakery or a Senegalese grocery store, no one questions my belonging. People talk about how the rent for their apartment has increased, how there are no more soul food restaurants in Harlem anymore, and how "they" are making it so we cannot live here anymore. While I agree with those sentiments, I often feel guilty because I know who "they" are, I can better afford "their" rents, and I like arugula, organic sorbet, high-speed wireless Internet, and groceries that can be ordered online and delivered to my house. I accept these aspects of gentrification, but resent that until recently those things were not available in Harlem.

The tensions in this situation are not new ones; there have always been issues between race/ethnicity/class and values. Those issues will continue until we decide to honestly address them, and place a higher value on the true meaning of cultural and economic diversity. It's hard not to focus on the negative aspects of gentrification, but I try to look at the potential that exists. When we interviewed White Harlem residents, we started by asking participants to give their definition of gentrification—with a lot of interesting responses. I'd like to offer mine: Gentrification is an opportunity for persons with substantial monetary means to collaborate with the residents of a neighborhood on economic and cultural revitalization efforts that benefit all parties involved.

CHAPTER 5

Crossing 125th Street

Youth Literacies in 21st-Century Contexts

"We in the 21st century, but Black people still struggling to prove our-selves. We still gotta fight for our rights," shared Phillip during one of our discussion sessions on why young people and adults should build coali-tions in order to preserve the historical legacy of a community like Harlem. Such sentiments, paired with Phillip and Khaleeq's engagements in the community, attendance at tenants' association meetings, interviews with local residents, and processes of rethinking the value of schooling, con-tributed to their increasingly sophisticated use of 21st-century literacy to critique changing community spaces. By "21st-century literacies," I am talking about the multimodal, multisensory, print, visual, linguistic, and cultural practices that youth and adults employ and are confronted with on a daily basis. Such practices speak to how ongoing changes, including globalization, immigration, advanced technology, and economic duress,

should be accounted for in educational research in ways that are attentive to problem solving, meaning-making, analysis, and collaboration
(Cushman, 1996; Dyson, 2005; Hill & Vasudevan, 2008). Phillip and
Khaleeq are all too aware of some of these changes in relation to gentrification and racial shifts in Harlem.

For example, after we interviewed Bonnie, a White resident, about
gentrification in Harlem (and after the interviewee left), I asked Phillip to
share what he had jotted down during the meeting. He had been scrib-
bling something while the interviewee talked about not wanting to raise
kids in Harlem. Phillip told me, "I wrote lots of things, but can tell you
what I was thinking 'cause I was mad at first. She can live here in Harlem
to go to TC [Teachers College] but not have kids and raise 'em here? What's
that about? Before, I would have been mad to hear her say that, I wouldn't
even listen to her. But now's different 'cause with this project, we're listening." He continued, "I'm really listening, figuring out where different
people coming from. By just writing down keywords or something from
what she say, I'm taking time to think. To question why I . . . disagree. To
even like consider my beliefs 'cause I'm mad, but I'm putting that aside.
Putting that on hold to think about a different point of view I don't have."
To this, I said to Phillip, as Khaleeq attentively listened, "That's one way
to use writing" to reflect on and react to other people's thoughts in noncon-
frontational ways. Phillip continued, "Yeah, that is. Who would've thought
writing ideas down before blurting 'em out would control my emotions,
put me in check? It . . . helps me listen to what people say and to their
positions so I could think about how I'm feeling about the topic."

Whenever I reflect on this example, I am reminded of Schultz's
(2003) description of "the power of the conception of listening to teach
to transform . . . ideas about teaching and teacher education" (p. 168). She
discusses the power and meanings of listening in order to teach across
differences. This way of teaching is critically attentive "to the voices that
are loud and those that are silent, the perspectives that define the classroom group and those that are missing" (p. 171). I use her framework for
listening to youth in Harlem and to the social, community, and cultural
fabrics of their lives. Teaching was definitely happening in the out-of-school
space of my university office, and it was shared and reciprocal. Phillip's
decision to listen to the interviewee, although he was "mad to hear her
say that" she would not have "kids and raise 'em here," spoke to his growing willingness to be a part of conversations of conflict, discomfort, and
disagreement. Doing so gave him, as well as those with whom he engaged,
an opportunity to experience alternative meanings and means of teaching and of being taught. Hearing the interviewee's perspectives reinforced
for Phillip critical literacy skills in listening that encouraged him to be both

emotional (e.g., reactionary; inquisitive) and interpretative (e.g., reflective; questioning). Specifically, Phillip was putting into practice his ability
to listen closely and carefully by demonstrating an understanding of the
value of writing down ideas, considering follow-up questions, and being
open to opinions that differ from his own.

Khaleeq was also demonstrating increasing confidence with listening
to other people's stories as he made sense of his own by sharing it with
others. After attending a tenants' association meeting at the Adam Clayton
Powell Jr. State Building (March 2006), I told Khaleeq that I was glad he
raised his hand an hour into the meeting to speak about his views on
gentrification. When given permission to speak, Khaleeq, Phillip, and I
went to the front of the room to talk about our project and interest in
understanding community change. Phillip praised Khaleeq's action by
saying, "Yeah, I was surprised, too. That was brave, man." When I asked
Khaleeq how it felt, he shared, "Well, people got stories. Everybody wanna
tell stories." He was referring to how tenants from various rent-stabilized
buildings in Harlem talked about their experiences with gentrification and
the threat of displacement. "Thing about it," according to Khaleeq, "is how
you tell your story with purpose. It's not just the story you tell. It's how
stories point to larger problems." When Phillip asked him what he thought
about the maps of Harlem they created and presented at the meeting,
Khaleeq responded, "Our maps are stories. Signs of writing, literacy. That's
it, literacy! How we making sense of our world by writing . . . mapping the
community, getting up in a room with strangers, listening, presenting stories." I asked Khaleeq if he considered the maps to be visual stories that
represented visual forms of literacy. He said, "Right. That's about literacy.
At least for me, figuring out how to create maps, listen to stories. Stand
up and talk what I see. I never thought about literacy that way, but that's
it. I got something to add."

Phillip and Khaleeq's mapping of Harlem, an activity that started in
the lounge at Harlem High School and extended into discussions that we
had in my university office and in the community, served as a multimodal
literacy practice. As they sought expanded ways to communicate ideas on
community change through print, visual, and oral forms, they created
images based on textual readings of and oral discussions on gentrification.
They also began to reconsider the value of their community video walk-
through sessions on their literacy narratives. Through the use of signs,
symbols, images, writing, and language, their mapping of Harlem represented multimodal literacy, contributed to their various modes of learning, and spoke to Khaleeq's belief that "I got something to say."

In terms of the tenants' association meeting, I asked Khaleeq if he
identified with the personal and political space of the meeting as well as

with the experience of sharing his own stories. Khaleeq responded, "It's about identifying with the space and people, seeing how you belong. We all belong." To this, Phillip responded, "We got stories that are, you know, they say something about gentrification. See, people be thinking, 'oh, yeah, gentrify Harlem 'cause that poor urban place need some changing. We gotta take the danger and scariness out of there. Make it safe.' But they don't know our story, our life. People need to back it up and get them negative stories about Black people in urban communities outta here." Khaleeq ended the discussion by adding, "That's right. They need to . . . take time and come to the meetings [tenants' association], get our stories. Maybe they'll see we don't need all that repairing they think Harlem needs."

Asking to present the maps of Harlem and to address an audience of nearly 50 Harlem tenants proved that Khaleeq was invested in taking an active role in the community, even if he lived on the Upper West Side and not in Harlem. Khaleeq questioned widely popular views of urban communities in disrepair, decline, and in need of gentrification, suggesting that White residents should "come to the meetings . . . see we don't need all that repairing they think Harlem needs." Khaleeq, Phillip, and I talked regularly about how negative images of urban communities are too often sprawled across the covers of national magazines, on billboards, and in news reports. Pictures of abandoned buildings, poverty, and homelessness portray a large problem with how public understandings of urban have moved from signifying "features of social organization—including a sense of community, positive neighborhood identification, and explicit norms and sanctions against aberrant behavior" (Wilson, 1987, p. 3) to qualities of "ferment, paradox, conflict, and dilemma" (Clark, 1965, p. 11). Public and historical views of urban communities tend to focus, however unfairly, on factors of decline (e.g., crime, unemployment, abandoned space, and times of financial depression) and not on stories of struggle, protest, love, and community. This point comes through clearly in Phillip's belief that "they don't know our stories, our life."

According to Beauregard (1993), focusing on what people think are the negative aspects of the urban overlooks "the material contradictions and the cultural ambivalences that make large cities the sites for decay, disinvestment, and degeneracy" (p. 305). People's diverse experiences in cities help narrate larger stories about meanings, representations, and portrayals of urban landscapes that are often overlooked. This way of seeing the urban does not encourage multiple stories on community to flourish. It also does not fully consider the struggles, identities, and lived experiences of people who reside within, and may be displaced from, the gentrifying community. Instead, it ignores "the material contradictions"—shared, contested, and competing forces—of urban communities by focusing on decline over community survival, segregation over communal forms of collaboration, and images of neglect over shared stories of struggle. Not to focus on these contradictions is to embrace "normalization," which, according to Foucault (1984), imposes homogeneity by encouraging people "to determine levels, to fix specialties, and to render the differences useful by fitting them one to another" (p. 197). Foucault's resistance toward normalization and Beauregard's attention to contradictions echo the work of youth in this project to document multiple stories, or truths, across boundaries (e.g., urban landscapes/stories of struggle and success; gentrified communities/ stories of newness and belonging). In what ways can we re-imagine urban communities from negative and abandoned to positive, artistic, and even contradictory? What do local stories tell about the history and resurgence of art in communities facing gentrification and "renewal?"

This chapter explores how youth use art forms to transform negative depictions as well as public perceptions (e.g., mass media; popular culture) of an urban community. As they uncover the artistic value of Harlem, the youth gradually influence adult learning and activism in the community, which has significant educational implications for teaching and research. Education, traditionally, operates from set positions of power, whereby adults "teach" young people inside schools. Participants in this project understand the shifting roles of students and teachers within educational contexts, since education is a reciprocal, shared experience in which youth can provide important lessons for adults (i.e., teachers and community members). In this way, the historical struggles and cultural resources of people of color demonstrate the significance of preserving a community at the crossroads while critiquing tensions that exist in efforts toward urban revitalization and gentrification.

Continuing their investigations of literacy, race, and the Whiteification of place, Khaleeq and Phillip documented art forms (i.e., through mapping, photography, and video interviews) by being attentive to signs of decline and responsive to the value of art. We explore in this chapter how Phillip and Khaleeq confronted the politics of space to influence adult learning in the wider community. They crossed, however hesitantly, the borders of 125th Street to enter into the space of a local university setting that "does not look like home" (Khaleeq) and that "feels even more foreign than my high school English classes do" (Phillip). Khaleeq and Phillip talked with White graduate students, many of whom wanted to teach in urban schools, about community, art, and struggle in Harlem. In thinking about "Harlem as art," Khaleeq and Phillip expanded their definition of art from poetry, music, paintings, and artifacts within museums, to songs of human struggles, tools that stimulate community conversations, and visible signs of everyday life—housing projects, abandoned storefronts, "rubble," and the busy 125th Street thoroughfare that connects Harlem's west side to its east side. Dewey's (1959) artistic aesthetic, or "art as experience"—in which individual objects of art are directly connected to the lives, experiences, and realities of local culture—is a basic principle in this definition. The youth stories of Harlem speak to Khaleeq's belief that "stories point to larger problems . . . that's about literacy."

HARLEM, ART, AND LITERACY

Many times, we do not critically observe the communities through which we travel as we go to school, to work, shopping, or even home. What can we learn from the everyday of urban landscapes? From architectural designs to cultural activities to the role of local communities in civil rights movements, urban places and spaces are rich in history. We can study how communities function as sites of conflict, or, according to Mary Louise Pratt (1991), as "contact zones," as well as how they serve as spaces of safety, what bell hooks (1990) describes as "homeplaces." I believe we can engage in this learning by listening to what people, especially youth, have to say about their neighborhoods.

On a Sunday afternoon in Harlem, I observed Phillip and Khaleeq's observations of the community. I was compelled to document their conversations on the stereotypes they believed people have about urban communities. Many complex ideas about Harlem as art were revealed, ideas that I believe connect to 21st-century literacy learning. I had not considered many of these ideas until I started working with Phillip and Khaleeq and intimately listening to their feelings about community and change. Here is an excerpt:

> *Khaleeq:* Harlem as art.
> *Phillip:* Harlem is art, ya' heard!
> *Khaleeq:* People shouldn't be talking 'bout places like Harlem like it's some bad, dangerous area or something. Harlem's not to be criticized but appreciated.
> *Phillip:* People talk 'bout Harlem, our Black community with its crowded streets and our Black schools with its crowded seats. They don't know 'bout the rhythm that's our madness. It's the art in how we walk, baby, and the art in how we talk, man. Harlem is art. This thing they call gentrification can't take that from Harlem. It might separate people like Black people from White people because of who can stay here, but Harlem's always gonna be art to me.
> *Khaleeq:* Harlem is art. . . . Harlem's literacy even if we ain't like the other side of town, like how rich White people live on the

east side. Harlem's art and literacy, well, at least for the Black
kids I know living here.

Phillip: Man, see what's gonna happen is we'll have a New York
City with Black students/Black communities like Harlem that'll
soon be gentrified and White students/White communities like
the Upper East Side that's a different world.

Khaleeq: It's a different world, but Harlem's still art.

Concerned with disparities between "Black students/Black communities like Harlem that'll soon be gentrified and White students/White
communities like the Upper East Side," Phillip, Khaleeq, and I initiated a
conversation on how art in Harlem can serve as yet another literacy response to gentrification. With our shared rhyme books, or journals, which
served as our paper space to pose questions about community change, we
routinely exchanged ideas on the art within Harlem, including architectural designs, murals painted on the sides of buildings, and the poetic
sounds of words we heard spoken by people on the streets. From our rhyme
books, community observations, and participation in community meetings, Phillip and Khaleeq continuously practiced ways to engage in data
member checking sessions (Lincoln & Guba, 2000) at the same time that
they were becoming comfortable using language to search for deeper
meanings of gentrification. Doing so encouraged them to critically consider their conflicting responses to community change (e.g., "separate
people"; "what's gonna happen"; "even if we ain't like the other side of
town"; "it's a different world).

As discussed in previous chapters, Phillip and Khaleeq both had a
strong fondness for Harlem's famous 125th Street. They focused on 125th
Street as a site where "art is in constant process" (Phillip). In a clip from
his video documentary of the community, Khaleeq made the comment,
"Harlem is already art. It has been for decades, although the community
is now being gentrified to create a sense of art [Phillip interrupted: "A fake
sense of art"]. If this new art and new Harlem gon' to improve our community, why's it displacing so many Black residents who've lived here for
years?" Phillip could not help but respond, "it's time that young people
stand up and talk about the value of Harlem. Look, where else can you
find so many symbols of Blackness in one community?"

Throughout this book, I have described some of the symbols of Blackness that Phillip alluded to, such as the Apollo Theater, the Studio Museum
of Harlem, the Adam Clayton Powell Jr. State Building, the Schomburg
Center for Research in Black Culture, the Harriet Tubman Gardens, the
Frederick Douglass Houses, and local high schools and enrichment centers. He also referred to inscribed passages from speeches by Malcolm X

that appeared on the sides of buildings just as much as they appeared on T-shirts worn by young and adult residents of Harlem. Phillip also saw the value of stories "as art" embedded in local and national histories of people's struggles for rights (e.g., education; housing; voting; economics; political).

By turning to art forms to make sense of community changes, Phillip, Khaleeq, and other urban youth were able to create honest, descriptive stories to challenge negative images of urban space (Beauregard, 1993) and inform adult learning and activism. Khaleeq's sentiments, "people got their stories," was not just a call for youth to tell their stories, but for youth and adults to exchange their stories "with a purpose." Khaleeq's emerging ways of looking at the power of stories and their meanings can lead to intergenerational collaborations in which people exchange narratives, whether shared or competing ones, about identity, belonging, and struggle. Such exchanges can serve to protect, preserve, and privilege the histories of understudied communities.

Khaleeq's belief that "people shouldn't be talking 'bout places like Harlem like it's some bad, dangerous area or something" connected with Phillip's argument that "Harlem is art, ya' heard." They "stand up and talk about the value of Harlem" (Phillip) by recognizing struggles, sociopolitical tensions, and the transformation of people in changing spaces. They read the local newspapers, attended tenants' association meetings, and took pictures of historical community landmarks. At the same time, they struggled to understand why schools do not readily account for the literacies within local communities. Then, they questioned why people, including former President Bill Clinton and New York City Councilman Bill Perkins, would want to live or open offices in Harlem. For Phillip: "Clinton moving to Harlem looks good, but then our rent goes up . . . and Perkins, he another story." On this latter point, Khaleeq shook his head in agreement before inquiring, "Don't Perkins got an office off 125th?" Phillip continued, "He had space like around 121st [Street] when he was running for election. Now ask if I seen him around since then. See, that's the thing. Where's the real commitment? People come in, but do they stay?" As Phillip and Khaleeq discussed the transformation of Harlem space, I took it upon myself to listen to their voices, stories, experiences, and points of disagreement in much the same ways that I wanted them to listen to me: with an open heart, a critical mind, and a questioning soul that was always in pursuit of more stories. It is this pursuit that convinced me, in the words of Khaleeq, that "Harlem is art. . . . Harlem's literacy."

Phillip stated, "It's the art in how we walk . . . the art in how we talk." This art that makes up Harlem is not simply about the artifacts of art (e.g., drawings; books), but the people of Harlem themselves. He refers to the knowledge and power that made Harlem a mecca of Black life for people of color at the brink of the 1920s Harlem Renaissance. During this time, meanings of literacy (e.g., writing about pain, reading literature by people of color, interpreting history, and engaging in apprenticeships) and experiences of human struggles (e.g., racism; discrimination) took an artistic turn. "People," according to Phillip, "from what I know, were making music of their lives, out in the community with action, not just sitting waiting for something they don't like to up and happen." For Khaleeq, people were not "like machines waiting on a button to be pushed so they could get up." Instead, they were teaching one another about living in the world in ways that beckoned action. On this latter point, I can still hear Phillip say, "See, schools try to create us into machines. Gentrification is a machine. With schools and gentrification I can't sing my own art."

Feelings of confusion mixed with the desire to really understand forced me to contemplate Phillip's statement of defeat: "I can't sing my own art." As an educator and researcher, I was dismayed by the argument that schools produce student "machines," given my observations of Phillip and Khaleeq when working with Ms. L at Harlem High. Initially, they both appeared to be going through the motions involved with the routine nature of traditional school-sponsored learning. When they eventually recognized Ms. L's passion for teaching and working with students, they gravitated toward critical literacy opportunities. Yet this was just one of many classes and teachers they had encountered during their educational journey, and for them, the "bad" far outweighed the "good." Additionally, I recalled their ongoing insistence that I read the words "can't sing" silently and then aloud over and over again so that I understood the larger points being made. In doing so, I realized that all along Phillip wanted to sing his own song, make his own art, and dance to the meanings that emerged from those multiple experiences.

Extensive follow-up conversations with Phillip and Khaleeq taught me new ways to see art as "action you don't get permission to create" (Phillip) and as "what we got inside us that wanna get out" (Khaleeq). Seeing art as action signified their processes of making sense of the changing world by exploring meanings of freedom and expression in Harlem. It also helped them question the purposes of schooling that, for Phillip and Khaleeq and their peers, "don't be teaching about public spaces" (Phillip) and "what's happening where people live, go to school, stuff like that" (Khaleeq). As Phillip and Khaleeq examined "Harlem as art" and "how schools try to create us into machines," they were beginning to see how other people metaphorically described spaces of interaction: "global-local," "location," "third space," and "the city" (Keith & Pile, 1993, p. 1). Examining spatial descriptions, reflecting on their schooling experiences, and arguing that "Harlem is art" contributed to how they approached gentrification through a literacy framework.

When they decided to cross 125th Street, Phillip and Khaleeq were aware of how one's cultural practices and identities—especially for people of color in poor and working-class urban and rural communities—are often negatively portrayed by mass media. They agreed with Soja's (1990) insistence that space is created to conceal consequences—that is, space often functions to hide human reality, differences, and diversities that exist throughout the world—because "relations of power and discipline are inscribed into the apparently innocent spatiality of social life" (p. 6). In Phillip and Khaleeq's acceptance of Soja's belief, they pondered ways to encourage adult members of the community to use art (e.g., billboard campaigns, local museums, historical buildings, and avenues and boulevards) to improve and protect the area. These ways included displaying works by local artists at community festivals and in the windows of local businesses, as well as requesting that neighborhood museums and theaters devote the first or last Friday of each month to celebrating Harlem's literacy heritage and its contemporary street artists. They wanted adults, including teachers, business owners, shoppers, and longtime residents, to have positive community identities. They wanted them to willingly cross borders by understanding that the historical construction of borders— cultural, physical, and psychological—can both prohibit and permit "particular identities, individual capacities, and social forms" (Giroux, 1992, pp. 29–30). Phillip and Khaleeq did not want to be prohibited from living and/or participating in the community, even if it is gentrified. Additionally, they did not want the cultural practices and identities of the residents of color in Harlem to be ignored, erased, and forgotten. One way that Phillip and Khaleeq exerted influence over their urban communities was by using photography and video interviews to capture Harlem's changing conditions.

DOCUMENTING "HARLEM IS ART"/"HARLEM AS ART"

See, the hard part of this project on Harlem and art is facing them new people who ain't from Harlem and think this community is all about new things popping up: the Disney Store [now closed], Magic Johnson Theater, Old Navy, Aerosoles [shoe store], and Mac [cosmetic store]. By the way, I wonder how many people now coming into Harlem know that right around the corner from Aerosoles and Mac is the Hotel Theresa. They don't know. They

overlook these things that we see on a regular basis, important
things that part of our history like the Theresa. (Phillip)

Located at the intersection of West 125th Street and Adam Clayton
Powell Jr. Boulevard, the Hotel Theresa opened in 1913. After the hotel
was desegregated in the 1940s, numerous African Americans stayed there,
including Louis Armstrong and Lena Horne. The hotel is now an office
space and an official New York City landmark. It is popularly known as
the location where Malcolm X held meetings for the Organization of Afro-
American Unity (OAAU), where Fidel Castro of Cuba stayed during his
first visit to the city and the United Nations (Castro also met with Malcolm
X at the Theresa), and where boxer Joe Louis celebrated his various victo-
ries. Upon discovery of the history of the Theresa, both Phillip and Khaleeq
found this site to be a historical marker that represented Black power and
activism.
    After Phillip explained to Khaleeq and me the value of historic sites
throughout the community that people "overlook," Phillip and Khaleeq
exchanged perspectives on Harlem as art:

Khaleeq: Yeah, like the way the old Apollo was before the glitzy
    lights and expensive tickets. You think we [Black people] can
    afford to go there now?
Phillip: You mean before all the White people started feeling safe
    enough to take over Harlem and community spots? The new
    Apollo is their new "art space" in what they think's an exotic
    Black neighborhood. That's funny!
Khaleeq: But what other people think is . . . art in Harlem isn't the
    real of . . . the everyday.
Phillip: Not the conditions we have to live in. Why do I have to live
    in an apartment building with a cheap fire escape when right
    around the corner is a new building with real balconies for all
    the new apartments? Why do I have to deal with trash and
    signs of crime and drugs when they don't have to? And we all
    right here.
Khaleeq: Yeah, and across the street from my projects are condos
    with balconies. Right across the street! It's so different across
    there. These are the things people don't want to see. They
    believe what's going on here in the community is like a second
    renaissance . . . another Harlem Renaissance.
Phillip: A second what . . . Harlem Renaissance? Don't get me
    wrong, there's a lot of newness in Harlem, some for the good,
    some for the bad, some I just don't understand yet. But how

> can the new replace the old: condos versus projects; Whites
> versus Blacks; balconies versus fire escapes; silence versus
> community gatherings; not knowing neighbors versus having
> people's backs. And this is a renaissance?
>
> *Khaleeq:* Clean surroundings versus trash and crime, drugs, funky
> smells.
>
> *Phillip:* It's an either-or situation we're living in, so to say Harlem
> is going through a second renaissance ain't right. Don't get me
> wrong: There's art underneath all this rubble. You just gotta
> look really hard for it.

Khaleeq and Phillip's exchange echoed Haymes's (1995) discussion
of how a "pedagogy of place" should focus on issues of race and struggle
in urban communities. This pedagogy involves the physical area, material
conditions, and changing landscape of Harlem, or the "old versus new."
For Khaleeq and Phillip, the relationship of "old" versus "new" included
visual images of and spatial changes occurring throughout Harlem. The
Theresa Hotel, the Schomburg Center, community cultural events, and
the crowds of people on the streets talking with street vendors represented
the "old." Conversations among community residents, business owners,
and activists about who and what belongs in Harlem—such as, Whites
versus Blacks and other minority groups, condos versus housing projects,
and balconies versus fire escapes—pointed to signs of the "new." When I
asked them to talk about art in Harlem, or as Phillip called it, "Harlem as
art," their concern became one of belonging to a community undergoing
rapid changes associated with gentrification, shifting demographics, and
forgotten histories.

Khaleeq, Phillip, and I documented stories of change through photography, mapping, and video documentaries, beginning with the areas
surrounding their home spaces. Khaleeq's documentation began with a
reflexive look at art in his community. He grappled with how to document
art in "the Frederick Douglass Projects when all around me are people who
don't seem to care, who throw paper [trash] on the ground, who sell drugs,
who just hang out." He added, "I get tired of seeing this. I know the art's
there, since Harlem is a history landmark of African culture and struggle
. . . and that history trickles into the Upper West Side." Here, I believe that
Khaleeq is expressing a desire for community normalization—he wants
his neighborhood to "be okay, clean, safe, you know, like how it is across
the street." However, his position shifts away from normalization to con-
tradiction when he expresses angst over the visible changes that the neighborhood is experiencing—"the too expensive [stores] redone for White
people," and "the signs of history that's vanishing." Nevertheless, Khaleeq

eventually pointed out to me the name of his housing complex, Frederick Douglass, as he directed Phillip to get a video shot of the signs that bear this ex-slave's name. Although Khaleeq was unable to tell Phillip and I on the spot the significance of the name of his housing development (see Chapter 2), he did remark: "When I think of Harlem as art, I gotta look around where I live, to get a better handle of history here."

A few days later, after he had researched Frederick Douglass, Khaleeq said, "Douglass was a slave and then an abolitionist. That's important for Black people to know. That's art through, um, struggle." After a long pause, Khaleeq composed himself, silently struggled with the words he wanted to use to convey his true feelings, and continued: "That's art and history. That's what we don't learn in school. I never studied [these connections] in my history class, geography class, English class, or nothing. I never had a standardized test ask me what I think about that, either." In fact, teachers at Harlem High School do include Douglass as well as other important figures in their curriculum. Khaleeq's comments, however, point to disconnections between *teaching* Douglass and *establishing relationships* between Douglass (e.g., life; struggle) and local history in the curricular lessons being taught in the space of classrooms. Khaleeq then went into his backpack in search of his rhyme book. "I bet he looking for his rhyme book," Phillip said, to which Khaleeq responded, "I'm looking. Something I wrote relates to what we talking 'bout. Valerie, you got my notebook, I think." I did have his rhyme book, and Khaleeq told me to "just look in it later for the passage talking 'bout the things students see in their community that's signs of history, but we don't study in school." Khaleeq wanted to say more, as indicated by his body language, and both Phillip and I waited until Khaleeq found the words that he wanted to use: "We talk about how things so separate: poor from rich communities, Blacks from Whites, gentrification and White pride [Phillip corrected, "White privilege"]. Why don't teachers ask us about this? These things scary for me and people my age, but no one's asking our opinions."

As we stood there with Khaleeq's powerful words going into our ears and moving through our hearts, noises from the crowded M100 bus on one side and hard hat construction workers on the other side brought us back to the changing space of New York City. Despite the noise, I thought what Khaleeq had said: "Harlem as art," "art in Harlem," and also "signs of history," "struggle," "why don't teachers ask us." When I did locate Khaleeq's rhyme book, I quickly turned to the passage that he was referring to:

> I talk to Val and Phil . . . all the time. We talk about things going on
> that matter. I see the community going thru lots of changes I don't
> understand. It makes me scared. . . . I don't have a place to think

about these things but when we together. I try talking to teachers, they seem interested, but "gotta move on with the business of the day." I'd like just to have one day in a class that we talk about real signs of history in front of us. Maybe write about what the signs mean, how they make us feel. I can support that writing by drawing on evidence in the community: gentrification's a sign that new [things] coming. How I know? Look at how many new, high-price apartments going up we [poor and working-class Black residents in Harlem] can't buy or rent. We should force schools to talk about this and history, teach us to tell stories about that.

As Khaleeq recognized signs of history in the community and acknowledged that *some* schools do not engage students in critical discussions of such signs—"gotta move on with the business of the day"—he also told a story of belonging through art forms. With a digital camera, he took pictures of the Frederick Douglass projects, the row of abandoned storefronts adjacent to the projects, and the condominiums with balconies across the street—"why the apartments where White people live have balconies and right across from them you have Black people like my family with apartments that have raggedy fire escapes?" (Khaleeq). He then took Phillip and me on another video walk-through of the area. As he described his negative feelings toward gentrification, he pointed out how the creation of newness (e.g., new condominiums, new residents, and new businesses that will enter the community) often occurs without regard to the local schools, small businesses, and housing projects that quickly fall into disrepair. Khaleeq's visual texts (e.g., photographs; video interviews) represented what linguistic modes of communication could not fully capture: "aesthetically communicative power" (Vasudevan, 2006, p. 214) of a youth using art forms to create stories of community. His stories were about spatial, or geographical, struggle, and they contributed to his emerging definitions of art, community, and power.

Much like Khaleeq, Phillip had a story about art in his immediate surroundings, particularly the art of the new (e.g., renovated apartments; balconies; influx of White people) versus the art of the old (e.g., old apartments; fire escapes; longtime Black residents). Phillip accepted Khaleeq's acknowledgment of "signs of history" just as much as he related to Khaleeq's feelings about local sites left in disrepair: "There are projects, abandoned lots, in the center of this new art, and nobody seems to think this crazy? If nobody stands up to this to show people how Harlem is art, has been for years, what's going to be left? Will they take away the Adam Clayton Powell Building cause they need that block of space for more high rises?" Phillip continued by talking about the Apollo Theater as a local space where new talents performed on "Amateur Night" and where one could get an inexpensive ticket to see famous acts "do their thing on stage." This was no longer a reality for Phillip, who expressed shock at seeing a long line of White people going into the Apollo on a Wednesday night in May 2006. He commented:

> We [Phillip and Valerie] were walking from the Powell Building, just left a meeting where activists were complaining about living conditions, increased rent, unfair conditions by management in their housing complexes. Next thing I know, we approach the Apollo, and there they are . . . claiming our community art spot as their own. Probably not even realizing that the artwork on the concrete and fenced walls next to the Apollo was created by a local working Black artist. I'm glad I had the digital [camera].

With the camera, Phillip took pictures of "White people in front of the redone Apollo." In our shared rhyme book and in subsequent interview sessions, he compared the pictures to those he took of Black people going into the Studio Museum of Harlem and waiting for the bus in front of the Powell building, and of construction sites for new condominiums near where he lived—just eight blocks south of 125th Street. In his comparison, he highlighted the race of the "White people in front of the redone Apollo" as an indication of a changing, soon-to-be gentrified community: "They were never here when I was growing up. They were too afraid to come to Harlem, and at night! Never would've happened." Phillip admitted that the presence of "lines of White people" in Harlem made him uncomfortable because "they change the face of this community and take away the real meaning of art in a place like the Apollo. Blacks always been going to the Apollo, the museum, whether they live in Harlem or just visiting." He continued: "Most Blacks know Harlem or live in a similar space. We share that struggle. But Whites know Harlem as an artsy place because of gentrification. It's not the same kind of knowing." Contrary to his initial understanding of Black-ification and White-ification, Phillip's sentiments were now grounded in critical thinking and pointed to a more developed articulation of these terms. That is, Black-ification is not just about middle- to upper-class Black people moving back into and changing Harlem. It is about Black people, across individual experiences and class statuses, recognizing their long history of civil and political struggle in the United States in comparison to White (mainstream) values. This is an important distinction to make because it demonstrates Phillip's increasing understanding of connections among race, place, and identity for Black people. That is, acts of place-making (e.g., creating safe spaces and fostering positive social encounters) for Black people, historically, are directly connected to a shared struggle for the creation and preservation of safe spaces, which Phillip and Khaleeq are beginning to acknowledge.

During one of his video walk-through sessions near the intersection of Frederick Douglass Boulevard and 117th Street, Phillip pointed out the renovated apartment building on one corner, the new drugstore on another, and the "crazy priced" new dry cleaners. He spoke of an abandoned Laundromat in the same breath that he talked about a vacant lot that is now barricaded, the latter where many community members met for social events:

> This is what I see on the regular. I didn't pay much attention to it before, but now I do. And do I see any art in all this rubble? New condo over here, old apartment building over there! New dry cleaners there, closed Laundromat here! Right here in Harlem. Yeah, I have to, if I want to remember history. I believe the old is more of art than the temporary new. But nobody, except you and Khaleeq, asked me. Nobody else really wants me to tell my story about what I think I want in the area.

I told Phillip that I believed he was already engaging in critical literacy as he theorized ideas around struggle, art, community change, and gentrification. I also encouraged him to find ways to think through these same ideas in the context of his high school. During an independent reading and writing session in Ms. L's English class, I walked over to Phillip and asked him, with his teacher's permission, to begin describing with words and visuals what he talked about in his community walk-through video: what he would want and what he was willing to fight for as the debate around gentrification in Harlem increased. Over three separate independent reading and writing sessions, we collaborated (with input from other students and Ms. L) to create a visual representation of what he wanted. Figure 5.1 is an illustration of the result of that particular school-based collaboration.

Phillip's visual depiction, in his own words, "is about not getting rid of the old because new things coming. Like I said in my video, the old is important, it's more art than the temporary new. I'm struggling to embrace the old art and not get caught in the new." Phillip's struggle speaks beyond education in the classroom to include local literacies. Clearly, "to embrace the old art" is rarely considered in public debates over the corporatization of schools and the gentrification of urban communities. Yet I firmly believe that "the old art" should be embraced and critiqued alongside the new as Harlem and other communities across the United States undergo

Figure 5.1. The Struggles of Youth Participants

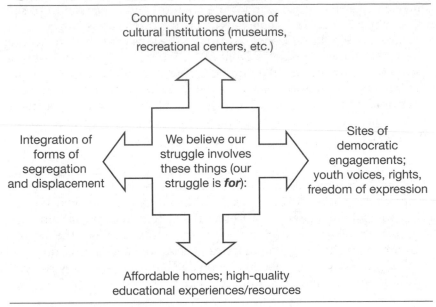

Community preservation of cultural institutions (museums, recreational centers, etc.)

Integration of forms of segregation and displacement

We believe our struggle involves these things (our struggle is *for*):

Sites of democratic engagements; youth voices, rights, freedom of expression

Affordable homes; high-quality educational experiences/resources

major spatial, racial, and economic changes that have dire consequences for the youth and adult residents who cannot afford to stay. Thus, the idea of crossing—whether that means crossing the physical borders of 125th Street or crossing the emotional and psychological barriers associated with change—greatly impacts one's level of involvement and activism in the community. Phillip and Khaleeq know this reality all too well.

To speak of this struggle more widely, Phillip, Khaleeq, and I met Vivian, Barbara, Thelma, John, and a host of other adults at a community action meeting held at the Adam Clayton Powell Jr. State Building. The meeting focused on "saving the community" from gentrification, increased rent, and the displacement of Black residents as well as preserving "the old." In this case, for Phillip, Khaleeq, and many longtime Black residents in the area "the old" signified a spatial history of struggle and survival. In this moment, documented representations of art and community captured by youth influenced adult learning. By engaging in conversations with and explaining their perspectives on gentrification to adults (i.e., residents; teachers; me) who were invested in protecting the community, Phillip and Khaleeq encouraged them to question current community practices (e.g., the value of gatherings and meetings and taking care of/protecting the community) and assumptions (e.g., young people have no voice, and they

do not care about the community). At the same time, the adults encouraged Phillip and Khaleeq to study the community's long history of struggle
(e.g., segregation; fights for civil rights) and political leadership (e.g., Malcolm
X; Adam Clayton Powell Jr.). In this context, learning became reciprocal,
active, and transformative for both the youth and the adults. Youth activism was met with adult learning. With this point in mind, Khaleeq, Phillip,
and I created a diagram during a session in my university office that describes what we are working "against." We presented it to other adults.

The diagram serves as a response to Phillip's diagram on, "We believe
our struggle involves these things (our struggles are *FOR*)." At the same
time, it speaks to what Phillip and Khaleeq, and some of their friends,
including Damen, were struggling to prevent, such as gentrification, displacement, and White-ification (see Figure 5.2). In creating the diagram,
Phillip and Khaleeq recalled brief conversations they had with Vivian and
other adult members of the community, adults who either lived or worked
within the immediate neighborhood or whom they met at local tenants'
association meetings. Those conversations helped the young men understand how their words and actions influence adult activism: "When we
presented the maps and pictures and things at the meeting, they [adults]
had lots of questions for us. They asked things like, what can we as adults
do? How can we help you keep up the work y'all doing? What can our

Figure 5.2. The Struggles Against Gentrification of Youth Participants

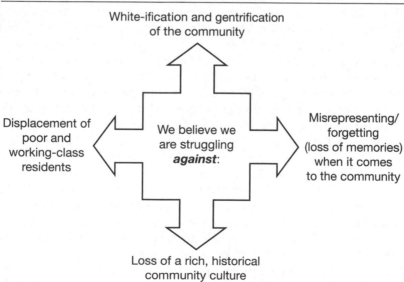

stories offer?" (Phillip). Khaleeq then recalled, "They were listening to us and seem like they believed we serious about this. We showed the maps, talked about the pictures . . . told them about some community stories. They were learning. We were teaching."

Phillip and Khaleeq spent the next few weeks examining their digital pictures of Harlem. They also began to imagine, as Vivian asked them to do, the untold stories of adults in both the community and school in relation to Harlem's past. Their imaginings led them to consider how the past—"what was here before"—served as a precursor to the *real* Harlem Renaissance (which began in the 1920s, and not the so-called renaissance currently taking place leading to gentrification and spatial change) and the many civil rights protests that occurred throughout the United States and the Diaspora. Their study of Harlem's long history was captured in their many photographs, video interviews, and conversations. These artifacts attested to their growing interest in collaborating with adults to document stories and protect Harlem from gentrification and commercialization.

How did the youth view "Harlem as art" in relation to the influx of newness in the community? On the one hand, they were curious to see the new chain drugstores; on the other, they were dismayed to no longer participate in certain community rituals that occurred in the empty spaces stores now occuppied. Their dismay led them to view newness as nega- tive, as an attempt to disguise and/or ignore the art of Harlem's past. Ac- cording to Phillip, "Lots of stores in this area have opened, bringing different people. This changes the whole feeling of Harlem, including what we be talking about as the arts." Khaleeq agreed, insisting that Harlem has al- ways been a place where art forms dominated, even on "less than popular [neighborhood] streets, even the ones on the edge of Harlem like mine." Both Phillip and Khaleeq believed that before the new stores, there were a lot of conversations, museums, parades, festivals, and block performances, a point corroborated by longtime adult residents in the community. How- ever, "We don't have them as much because lots of people left since they can't afford to stay" (Phillip). Even with this reality, Phillip and Khaleeq still insisted that Harlem is art and "gentrification can't take it away" (Khaleeq). Khaleeq and Phillip's pictures of the Cotton Club, the Studio Museum of Harlem, the Harlem YMCA, the Audubon Ballroom, Abyssinian Baptist Church, Duke Ellington Statue, and Marcus Garvey Park reiterated this point. Their pictures captured a legacy of artistic and political action in Harlem and throughout the African Diaspora. Their images portrayed art as a vehicle that opened the doors to African, African American, and Latino expression of the Harlem Renaissance to contemporary times.

The pictures spoke volumes to their emerging definition of "art as experience" (Dewey, 1959) and as visible signs of everyday life. For Phillip and Khaleeq, the pictures were connected to what they called the 1920s "youth and adult arts movement" of the Harlem Renaissance. In their photo collages, they referenced the likes of African American literary scholars Langston Hughes, Zora Neale Hurston, and James Weldon Johnson. Their collages and journals recognized the value of young artists apprenticing with adult members of the community, which helped make Harlem a major site of Black cultural expression. In the 1920s, the significance of art in Harlem paralleled the community's historical struggle with representation, racism, and socioeconomic strife. Now that today's Harlem is undergoing gentrification, I wonder, "Where are the adults, the Black and White and Latino/a and Puerto Rican residents and political leaders, the people who are supposed to protect the community? The social activists, the politicians, the teachers, the artists? The people we are told to follow? Where's everybody, the other Vivians? And where are the apprenticeship models from the Harlem Renaissance?" (Khaleeq, Phillip, & Valerie, inquiry questions).

SEARCHING FOR LITERACY APPRENTICESHIP MODELS

Khaleeq: I look at Harlem and think art is more than writing, poetry, drawing, dancing, and singing.

Phillip: Art is also struggle. That's Harlem.

Valerie: Seems as if we believe the same things about "Harlem as art."

Phillip: But not too many adults would say that. I don't think too many adults believe people like me and Khaleeq have anything important to say about art and Harlem. It goes back to something I said before . . . some people think they have the right to talk and others don't. Some think that Harlem is just a lot of poor Black people living in projects who don't care about the community.

Khaleeq: We care, that's why we doing this project. We know we have to care. It would be good if adults accept this. You know, adults can learn a lot from us. . . . Vivian did.

Valerie: Like what?

Khaleeq: Like the changes happening in Harlem affect hardworking, struggling people who've been living here for a long time. Young people like Phillip and me know that, we see that, and we documenting changes with our cameras. Telling stories that need to be told.

Phillip: You [adults] just can't sit around and complain all day long about the changes without listening to what other people got

to say. We are a part of those other people. Adults need to
know that young kids in Harlem can do something about the
changes . . . by staying focus on life and getting their voice out
there. More adults should recognize that young kids want a
better future and know the changes that need to be made are:
less violence, more education, better leaders.

Khaleeq: Clean and safe communities! These all have to do with
Harlem as art.

Valerie: So, Harlem is art in the sense that it has all of the traditional art forms—museums, entertainment venues, lovely
architecture, a strong literary history, festivals, the history of
the Harlem Renaissance and the artists who came with that
period. But if I am hearing you right, Phil and Khaleeq,
"Harlem as art" encompasses human struggles with place and
race, what you call "rubble," Phillip. Is this right?

Phillip: That's right. And the rubble is the sounds of the 'hood, the
people, the struggle, our whole history. That's the rubble;
that's the art . . . the experiences.

Valerie: I think adults can learn a lot from this work.

Khaleeq: We know. We know. You think they know?

Phillip and Khaleeq were aware of the distances between adult and
youth efforts to document changes in Harlem, whether through art forms
or presentations at local meetings. They were excited by the brief but critical
engagements that occurred once they presented their maps, digital pictures,
and aspects of their literacy narratives at a tenants' association meeting.
Nevertheless, they were a bit discouraged that, after their presentation, it
appeared as if the "adults continued their usual talk without mapping out
solid strategies to handle what's happening in Harlem" (Phillip). "Solid strategies," for the youth, included adults writing and collecting community narratives; creating brochures, newsletters, and leaflets that provide action
points (strategies and plans) to protest gentrification; and proposing alternatives to gentrification and rental increases that they would send to local
governmental offices, mass media, and activist organizations charged with
preserving the community. These things did not immediately happen.
Khaleeq and Phillip struggled to understand that distances and differences
in problem-solving approaches often result from conflicting perspectives,
ways of knowing, and struggles that can prevent intergroup relations. There
is tension around who should, or can, represent the *truths* of a changing
Harlem and who has the right to speak. This tension exists between generations, but it also crosses age groups to include race and class.

Phillip's assertion, "White people in front of the redone Apollo" and Khaleeq's belief, "What other people think is . . . art in Harlem isn't the real of . . . the everyday," illustrated their awareness and discomfort with signs of "otherness." How can educators and community stakeholders respond? For one thing, adults can begin to examine how "Harlem as art" is a call for people of various ages and races to coexist across imaginary, physical, and cultural boundaries. During Khaleeq and Phillip's invited class presentation in one of my former colleagues' English education courses, a White female teacher education candidate raised a significant question: "Is there room for cooperation across groups and across communities, public schools, and universities as gentrification becomes a reality?" This book, and specifically this chapter, begins to imagine answers to questions about how art in Harlem can serve as a vehicle that connects different groups of people to one another, about negotiating power in Harlem by discussing how gentrifying spaces impact the lives and cultural practices of countless youth and adults, and about the influence that gentrification has on schooling, achievement, and success.

For Phillip and Khaleeq, where they lived and/or attended school had a direct impact on how they interpreted struggle and identified with change. It also influenced how they viewed art as experience and how they considered the value of the Harlem Renaissance in the lives of today's youths and adults. Khaleeq and Phillip wanted to have conversations with adults in the larger community who would serve as their mentors as they sought additional ways to document art forms, call attention to ongoing activist efforts, and exchange stories of struggle and survival in the community. They wanted what they started to believe adults wanted: a safe community, clean streets, political activities, transformative action, and a call against community "normalization" (Foucault, 1984) or the homogenization of communities. They believed, from the example of the Harlem Renaissance, that these things can happen through the arts and through apprenticeship models for literacy learning. Within their belief that "Harlem is art"/"Harlem as art" in this postmodern, postindustrial neighborhood undergoing gentrification existed a call for reciprocal learning between young people and adults. In the words of Khaleeq, "adults can learn a lot from us."

This work taught me that, as an adult committed to preserving Harlem's history, I must take responsibility for the stories of community and struggle that I share. I, as well as other adults, can better value civic participation, create counternarratives to negative portrayals of urban communities, and collaboratively inquire into historical signs that make communities artful. We can also increase levels of activism and establish apprenticeship models with other adults and youth. Doing so can enhance public understandings of how and where learning happens, can draw positive attention to the lived realities of young people in urban communities, and can offer models for how youth cross the borders and boundaries that separate communities and people from one another. Khaleeq and Phillip participated in a process that involved "crossing 125th Street" to understand how Harlem as art is present in the spaces, conversations, and engagements that they have with others, such as longtime Black residents, new White residents, and White university students. This process occurred within as well as beyond the local community.

CROSSING 125TH STREET

What do boundary crossings consist of and mean? Phillip and Khaleeq experienced one "crossing" in their physical movement from a familiar community to a university setting. On many occasions, I invited them to talk with my or my colleagues' teacher education pre- and in-service candidates who were completing their master's degree in English education. They also presented to a graduate class of teacher education candidates in art education. During the 2006 summer session, I worked with graduate students who were full-time teachers in school districts in New York; Washington, D.C.; Connecticut; New Jersey; and Michigan. On average, they had approximately 5 to 7 years of teaching experience across elementary, middle, and high school. The class was comprised mainly of White female students, with one African American female and one White male. Their interests included using model texts in literature classes, engaging students in active reading and writing, teaching literary criticism to youth, and having classroom conversations with students on themes of race, class, and gender. In one of our class sessions, I briefly described the work that I was doing around gentrification and youth writing, and I showed a video clip of Phillip's first community walk-through session.

In this particular video clip, referred to earlier in this chapter, Phillip focused on signs of renovation and gentrification that were occurring in the area. With gentrification, Phillip argued, come "crazy priced" stores that some of the residents cannot afford. Standing in front of a senior citizens' caretaking facility, Phillip described his feelings of "being stuck in the middle" of all the newness. Then, he questioned, "What you gon' do?" When I showed this clip to my teacher education students, they raised various questions: "What are people doing about these changes?" "Is Phillip working with any local organizations to address these concerns?" "Is he being pushed to think about these issues as current events in his history,

English, and art classes at school?" One graduate student even commented, "Similar things are happening in the area where I teach in Washington, D.C." I informed students that Phillip was going to join us in a discussion of gentrification.

Fifteen minutes later, Phillip walked through our university classroom door, smiled widely at everyone, and started asking my graduate students about their interests: "So, what do y'all do, like study?" After initial introductions and after telling Phillip that the students in the room were all teachers working on a master's degree, he looked at me with a bit of hesitation. At that moment, I believe he became aware that he was not only crossing the borders of 125th Street, but also the boundaries between students and teachers, youth and adults, race and class. I videotaped the remainder of the class session in order to capture on film what words alone could not: Phillip's act of crossing over—entering into a space that was unfamiliar to him and did not look like his familial community—to talk with teachers about a topic of importance to him.

> The project is basically we going around Harlem 'cause there's a lot of new buildings being built up in Harlem that, buildings weren't there, torn down, and they build new buildings at a high price for certain people that can't afford it. So . . . my building that I used to live in, I moved across the street to the building I live in now, and that building looks better than the building I'm living in now. Then there's a new building on the right, on the left, and up the block. So I'm in the middle. So it's just about time before they get to my building. So with this project, I'm trying to educate young people that this is going on in our community and it might hit your community next. So I'm trying to teach people what it is, you know, like try to stop it. Not even try to stop it, but like make the rent affordable.

Students attentively listened to Phillip talk about people working together to "make the rent affordable" in the face of the inevitable: gentrification. He said he believed people should have the right to stay in their apartments and to talk about what is happening: "So I'm going around taking pictures, showing people new buildings and old buildings. New buildings next to old buildings." On this last point, Phillip looked around the room and, correctly assuming that none of the teachers lived in Harlem, asked, "What makes you think they not gonna get to the old buildings next?" As he talked and the teachers listened, his confidence increased. He talked about the journal writing he was doing, the pictures he was taking, and the young people and older people who were sharing their stories.

Phillip's eventual ease in talking with this "strange group of White teachers," as he initially referred to them during our follow-up discussion, contributed to his act of crossing. Documenting and understanding gentrification involved more than just talking about and taking pictures of the community. It involved, according to Phillip, taking the message, or story, about Harlem to different people including "teachers, and not feeling like I'm just a student and they [are] teachers." Phillip eagerly engaged in conversations with teachers and felt a sense of ease being asked the following questions:

> I was okay being asked by the one White guy, "Can you talk about the role of writing in your project?" Or the White woman saying, "What kinds of conversations you have with your peers?" See, we gotta be able to talk. And the other White teacher asked me, "Do you see yourself as an advocate?" Or what about the Black teacher when she asked about "Other groups or organizations talking about community rights that we're involved in?" See, I gotta listen and talk with people, even teachers.

As he gradually adjusted to the physical and emotional acts of crossing the 125th Street border that separated Harlem into sections (e.g., Central Harlem, Manhattanville, and Morningside Heights) to talk with teachers at a local university—"See, I don't be coming up here to Columbia 'cause I don't feel comfortable"—he became aware of another act of crossing. This crossing involved exchanging perspectives and having conversations with people who were not from his community; however, they were invested as educators in the topic of inquiry, which was gentrification, or community change. Phillip engaged with "others" who were from different racial, socioeconomic, and age groups, but who were all invested in the literacy lives of youth.

Phillip's engagement with people, especially White people, whom he once described as "outsiders coming in" and whom Jasmine (see Chapter 4) referred to as "them/they," led him to join Khaleeq and Rebekkah in a discussion of gentrification in one of Dr. Pat Z's graduate courses at Teachers College. This particular course focused on literature and pedagogy in English education, and students had just read Ernesto Quinonez's (2000) novel *Bodega Dreams*.

The novel is set in New York City's Spanish Harlem. One of the central characters, a man with big dreams and enough money to realize those dreams, is William Irizzary, whom everyone knows as Willie Bodega. Willie is a former member of the 1960s Young Lords liberation and human rights movement who has traded in that identity to become both a drug lord and a "slum" landlord in the area. He purchases derelict, abandoned apartment buildings, renovates them, and rents them at below market value to his patrons, who have either been loyal to him or from whom he is seeking loyalty. As he gives youth in the neighborhood grants to pay for college, runs detox centers, underwrites the start-up cost for community fruit stands, and sells drugs, Willie says that he wants more for Spanish Harlem. He envisions the community (e.g., the apartments; businesses; cultural and professional activities), which is unknown territory to people who live below East 96th Street in Manhattan, as a neighborhood completely owned by Spanish residents. Clearly, Willie is invested in creating a version of Lyndon B. Johnson's "Great Society" in Spanish Harlem, and as he works to achieve this goal, readers are introduced to other characters in the novel. Chino is the narrator; Blanca is Chino's Spanish, Pentecostal wife, who is described as "a White Spanish" (p. 153); Vera lived in Spanish Harlem, but married a rich man and moved to Miami; Nazario is Willie's front man; and Sapo is Willie's henchman and Chino's best friend from childhood.

Although there are many topics on which one may focus in Quinonez's novel—finding a place in the world, shifting identities, race, language, struggle, crime, and cultural conflicts, among others—I gravitated toward Willie Bodega's desire to create a *new* Spanish Harlem. Though he relies on criminal ventures to finance his personal and community deeds, Willie is passionate about turning the community into a Spanish remake of W. E. B. DuBois's (1903) "talented tenth." This would involve young Latinos getting a quality college education, returning to the community, and assuming roles of leadership and power.

Both Phillip and Khaleeq were fascinated with the summary of the novel (minus its criminal activities), and made connections between it and their own interest in gentrification. During their visit to Dr. Pat Z's class, they talked less about the novel and more about "our interest in the community, making it into something for the people here" (Phillip). In his discussion of the community, Phillip shared the following with the class: "[We] interview people and you don't have to live in Harlem 'cause the changes happening everywhere. . . . A lot of homelessness taking place around my block and a lot of drug dealing, like what y'all read about." Here, Phillip was establishing a connection between what he witnessed in his own community and what he knew of Quinonez's vision.

A student asked Khaleeq, Phillip, and Rebekkah about the overall purpose of the gentrification project. Phillip stated: "I'm surrounded by it. Rent increases, old and new buildings. So, I have to do something. I don't have to be a grown-up or very, very, very smart to do that. I just put what I'm learning together with what's going on around me." Khaleeq talked about the pictures he had taken of the community and what they represented in terms of change. He pointed out Riverside Church, Frederick Douglass Boulevard, and various brownstones. He then shared a story about trying to get into a building to take pictures, but being denied access because "I wasn't a member. I gotta be a member to get into a public building?"

Much like Willie Bodega, Phillip and Khaleeq were astute observers of their community and were outspoken about the need "to do something" (Phillip). While Willie engages in criminal activities to create his version of a "Great Society," Khaleeq and Phillip visually documented artifacts from old Harlem alongside the emergence of a new Harlem. They attended community meetings and presented literacy artifacts—maps, digital pictures, and journal entries—that expressed their opinions on gentrification. They talked with teacher education candidates about the need to focus on linguistic and cultural practices within their students' changing community spaces. They responded to questions about the role of writing in their project by describing their initial hesitation when it came to engaging in voluntary writing that "I wasn't getting judged on for grades (Khaleeq)," but that encouraged freedom of expression and the discovery of multiple ideas. Writing, in the context of the gentrification project, became a regular part of our work together. Phillip and Khaleeq were responsible for making critical observations of signs that Harlem was spatially and racially changing. From their visual observations, they relied on the act of writing as a way to recall memories, question positions, exchange perspectives, and critique, in print, their immediate world in relation to their sense of belonging in the larger world. Together, these observations materialized into their production of literacy responses to gentrification. Phillip and Khaleeq did these things as they hesitantly crossed boundaries (e.g., physical; psychological; geographical; racial; metaphorical; imaginary) in order to participate in conversations with others who did not live in or near Harlem.

As Khaleeq explained, "I had to put myself out there. . . . I didn't see the changes in the community until after I did the project. Now around my block, I live on the Upper West Side [he chuckled into the audio recorder when he confessed this] where there's a lot of Whites and Blacks and diversity . . . it's not too long before they might tear down the projects." On this latter point, Khaleeq continued: "Maybe these companies, they're not aware of what they doing. That's reason why we have to talk with different types of people, see what they think and let them see what we thinking."

There are barriers—physical and psychological, racial and geographical— that people often believe work to prevent conversations across 125th Street.

The presentation in Dr. Pat Z's class ended when one of the teacher education candidates commented on the bravery in the act of crossing. She said that Phillip and Khaleeq "are stepping out there" and hoped that her future high school students would follow their example by recognizing the value of their community: "What's really being lost is neighborhoods . . . and then what's replacing them are these cold, concrete kinds of buildings that are being reconfigured, that are isolating people. And you don't have that street life 'cause Harlem has an incredible street life. . . . That must be really awesome for you guys because lots of people don't have that growing up and that's part of being in a neighborhood. I admire what you are doing to keep your neighborhood."

YOUTH LITERACIES IN 21ST-CENTURY CONTEXTS

One might ask what this chapter on "Crossing 125th Street" has to do with youth literacies in 21st-century contexts. To answer this question, I would turn to recent reports from the National Council of Teachers of English (NCTE), the Conference on College Composition and Communication (CCCC), and the American Educational Research Association (AERA) that attempt to re-imagine and expand the definition of literacy and what *literacies*, particularly in the world in which we live, include. Literacies encompass not only the ability to read and write, but also to make sense of our lives and to critique multiple positions and perspectives. Literacies involve questioning our roles in the world, assuming multiple identities to consider various perspectives and experience empathy, and interpreting complex meanings of texts that may or may not include our voices, stories, lived experiences, and truths. As Dyson (2005) writes, "If you listen, you can craft in writing what you've heard others say and thereby give voice to your own responsive truth" (p. 154). Phillip and Khaleeq were listening to community members and graduate students, and they were being listened to as they publicly thought about the impact of gentrification in Harlem. As they were listening and being listened to, they crafted, recrafted, and redesigned their positions on gentrification. Doing so allowed them to "give voice to" their truths and to cross 125th Street to speak them.

This process of crossing is a difficult one for some students to experience, especially in the absence of organized opportunities. For many of the students at Harlem High School, for example, the act of crossing was often limited to the areas surrounding the school or, if they lived outside of Harlem, to the areas surrounding where they lived and through which they traveled on their way to school. In my opinion, some schools across New York (maybe because of time, maybe because of resources) do not offer enough opportunities for students to talk with adult members of the community, at local universities, and even at school about gentrification in Harlem, Brooklyn, the Bronx, Queens, and even in Southern states where many of their extended family members live. When I asked Phillip and Khaleeq to talk with my and my colleagues' teacher education students about gentrification, they both hesitated before asking, "You mean, talk with White students? Do they know anything about Harlem?" (Phillip). As Khaleeq put it, "I don't think they'd understand me. I'm not as educated as they are."

After acknowledging Phillip and Khaleeq's genuine concerns, I asked them to write about their honest reactions to the idea of talking with White students and their assumption that they themselves were not as articulate or educated. We talked about how Black males are often misrepresented in mass media's glamorization of urban identities and communities. We then talked about stories of academic achievement and schooling that tend to assume that Black males are not as smart as their White counterparts. Khaleeq read to us the beginning of his response: "I think they see me as dangerous, I'm not, maybe this how I feel on the inside from how they look at me." Phillip reacted, "Yeah, they see us that way. I wear my clothes the way I want to because that's me, but when I open my mouth to talk, they so shocked like 'oh, he can talk.' Yeah, I can play the role."

Their confessions prepared them for the physical act of crossing 125th Street. After we talked about stereotypes and the assumptions they had about White people and what they assumed White people thought of them—"Whites seen as smart and rich . . . Blacks seen as academic failures and as poor" (Philip)—they agreed to talk with teacher education students at the university where I worked. After talking with more than five classes of students at Columbia University, we revisited their initial impressions of "talk[ing] with White students" about gentrification. Discussing their initial impressions with their already emerging understandings and observations of "Harlem is art"/"Harlem as art" discussed in the beginning of this chapter proved why acts of crossing boundaries relate to 21st-century literacies. Over the course of that year, Phillip and Khaleeq became more confident and expressive in their opinions on gentrification in Harlem. They more willingly answered questions that were posed to them by teacher educators, and they publicly contemplated responses to questions that they had not previously considered. Without my asking, they turned to writing to jot down ideas that stemmed from their classroom engagements, and they revisited those questions in their rhyme books and in follow-up interview sessions. Doing these things contributed to how they were imagining literacy in 21st-century contexts—as communicative acts and practices that can happen across differences; as visual signs and symbols that can be captured, described, and debated; and as opportunities to listen and to be heard. For Phillip and Khaleeq, doing these things allowed identities to be constructed, questions shared, voices heard, and learning to happen.

These ideas did not stop with Khaleeq and Phillip's classroom presentations at a local university. In fact, they extended into the interview sessions and conversations in which we engaged with teachers at Harlem High School. The work we did outside of school worked its way back in. As with the university class presentations, interviews with high school teachers (see Chapter 6) revealed the importance of discussing community conditions, demographics, and identities, as these things impact the lives, languages, and literacies of youth and adults. In the next chapter, I explore ways to extend the conversations by including teacher portraits and perspectives. When we learn about our students' lives and let them in on aspects of ours, then reciprocal learning across boundaries and differences is more likely to occur. Such learning, grounded in reciprocity and mutual respect between students and teachers, can take many forms. I invite you to consider the following:

- The challenges students encounter as they are asked to cross boundaries—physical, social, psychological, and academic—that may be unfamiliar and uncomfortable. How can we work with students in critical ways that model for them meanings of and reasons to engage in boundary crossings?
- The responsibilities students have to their families and communities that we, educators, are often not aware of, and hence, the assumptions that we sometimes make of their academic performance and disposition. In what specific ways can we really get to know our students as we listen to their voices, stories, and community lives?
- The potential of students to make their own meaning from world events, course readings, and written (academic) assignments instead of being directed by adults to accept a particular answer or stance. How can students and teachers learn from one another as meanings are explored, positions are considered, and perspectives are shared in multiple forms and across multiple contexts?

Predators and Victims

By Valerie M. Orridge, President of the
Delano Village Tenants' Association in Harlem

Gentrification is a process by which developers buy property in mainly low-income areas for the purpose of displacing the indigenous residents and replacing them with a higher social and financial population. The objective, in my opinion, is strictly monetary. In the case of Harlem, this community has been viewed as the last frontier in New York City. It is very significant to note that Harlem is not a frontier, but rather a well-established community with a strong history of cultural practices and traditions. In fact, contemporary Harlem consists of mostly African Americans who have resided in the community for many years.

At the onset of the process of gentrification, there were numerous unclaimed vacant lots and abandoned buildings in the area. Developers by the scores descended on the respective community boards with pleas for purchase and proposals for development. The involved community boards eventually and unfortunately granted necessary approval to developers, and the building of luxury condominiums, cooperative apartments, and high-income rentals began.

Thereafter, a new breed of developers conceived of purchasing large *rent-stabilized* complexes and smaller apartment dwellings. The new concept ignited a movement, which quickly spread to other New York City communities and boroughs, including Queens, the Bronx, and Washington Heights. Properties were usually sold for far more than what they were worth. The buyers, therefore, were financially driven to refinance these properties for more than the original purchase price. Portions of the shares were parceled out to private investors, which can lead to the creation of a hedge fund. According to *The New Oxford American Dictionary* (2001), a hedge fund is defined as "a limited partnership of investors that uses high risks methods, such as investing with borrowed money, in hopes of realizing large capital gains" (p. 788). The success of this was contingent upon evicting the current tenant population, renovating the vacant apartments, and renting at fair market price. The eviction plan, to a large extent, was abortive, as tenants' advocates and organizations aggressively resisted such tactics by hiring attorneys, going to court, and utilizing the Division of Housing and Community Renewal (D.H.C.R.) housing and code laws. New tenants moved in and then quickly moved out because they refused to pay high, fair market, and deregulated rents for inferior services. Thus, many apartments were left vacant and unrented. This, in conjunction with the global financial crisis that took off in 2008, as evident by the current crash of Wall Street and the sinking economies worldwide, has left many owners in dire straits, unable to pay interest on loans and placing them on the brink of foreclosure.

Gentrification, in my honest opinion, is evil. It is evil for real estate developers to conceive of a plan to evict people from their homes in order to use the property for investment reasons and as a tool for becoming millionaires. Gentrification evokes the worst in human beings. It motivates the gentrifier to utilize the most brutal of methods to achieve financial goals. Threats, intimidation, denial of services, lease renewal refusals, primary residency challenges, and frivolous court suits are only a few of the methods exercised to evict the victims.

Gentrification evokes the worst in people, particularly its victims. There are those who acquiesce and those who become militant. For those who acquiesce, pack up, and leave, there is a psychological trauma of having been so timid as to give in to the powerful. For them, there is the ever-present feeling of powerlessness and defeat. For the militant, the strong, and the fighting, gentrification evokes the most vicious acts of revenge. By any means necessary, nothing is too brutal for the predator. Gentrification is an ugly, waging battle that I do not intend to lose.

CHAPTER 6

Teacher Talk

*On Gentrification, Urban Youth,
and Teaching as Survival*

"But why we even doing this work when nobody cares anyway?"
(Phillip)

Although they argued in favor of preserving Harlem's cultural, historical, and aesthetic value, both Khaleeq and Phillip were aware of gentrification's inevitability. They were often dismayed by the rapidly increasing presence of gentrification, which seemed to spite their efforts to document Harlem's old and new history, discuss meanings of community, and exchange ideas with others—youth and adults—about maintaining an affordable Harlem for current residents. Often, our conversations on Harlem took a pessimistic turn. During one of our rap sessions, Phillip described his love for Harlem in the same breath that he declared, "They just gone take it over." Khaleeq eventually added, "We not talking 'bout this in other places, so does it matter?"

It matters for Phillip and Khaleeq, and it also matters for their teachers. The youth frequently expressed frustration at not publicly addressing the impact of gentrification when in school. From Ms. L's reflective piece at the end of Chapter 3, it is clear that many teachers are trying to be more attentive to spatial, political, and cultural realities in communities that surround their schools, communities where their students live. Ms. L, for example, frequently asked students to visit and write observations about cultural institutions in Harlem in order to expand the ways in which they thought about connections among art, literature, and written composition. She also invited them to investigate local neighborhoods that serve as the settings for the literary works they studied in school, such as the neighborhoods presented in the autobiography of activist and former Black Panther member Assata Shakur. Such invitations establish meaningful connections between school-sponsored learning and community involvement, and demonstrate how teachers are attempting to attend to the rich histories and literacies within local communities.

This chapter provides portraits and perspectives of three teachers from Harlem High School interspersed with critiques from Phillip, Khaleeq, and Ms. L. The teachers are Ms. Cunningham, Mr. Walker, and Ms. Brown. Their perspectives illustrate their awareness of gentrification in Harlem and the importance of addressing community concerns and literacy stories in school spaces. The stories reflect their willingness to negotiate identities and responsibilities in the presence of a changing Harlem. They openly talked about gentrification and identity, and how they sought to create collaborative, democratic learning environments with youth by describing and reconsidering connections among race, place, and community change.

TEACHER PORTRAITS AND PERSPECTIVES

The teacher interviews, much like the community walk-through sessions, were videotaped. They occurred in the teachers' lounge and ranged from 40 to 60 minutes, depending on interviewees' availability and engagement with the questions. All of the interviewees agreed to have the sessions open to anyone who wanted to participate and pose questions. Phillip, Khaleeq, Ms. L, another teacher and another student, and I were present for most of the interviews. Once the interviews concluded, I prepared post-interview thoughts and questions and gave them to Ms. Cunningham, Mr. Walker, and Ms. Brown. Instead of conducting follow-up taped interviews, we talked one-on-one and at random about their interviews, my follow-up questions, and any concerns they expressed. These follow-up exchanges occurred between classes, during their lunch breaks, or during planning periods.

Ms. Cunningham and a Sense of Place

Ms. Cunningham was a 27-year-old White teacher completing her second year at Harlem High School. She taught English language arts across grade levels 9 through 12. When describing how she identified herself, Ms. Cunningham said, "You could say I'm White, but usually I identify with the nationalities of my heritage more—American or Italian or German." She then explained that she was now a part of the middle class, which was "a very, very recent thing," because until this point in her adult life, she was "very much lower, lower middle class." At the beginning of our videotaped interview, I asked her to explain her understanding of middle class. She explained that to identify as a member of the middle class is to be in a position to "have enough for everything that you need and then maybe a little bit extra for something else. . . . You can afford all the basic necessities of life such as rent is not a problem for you to pay, when your credit card bills come each month, you can pay them, making student loan payments or the electric bill . . . buying food." Phillip commented that he respected Ms. Cunningham's admittance of her middle-class status in a school that attracted students from poor and working-class backgrounds with a few students who "might be lower-middle-class, if that" (Phillip).

Ms. Cunningham was able to claim a status of middle class, in part, because she did not live in close proximity to the school where she worked. By living in Queens with her family, she avoided the increasing costs associated with renting an apartment in "the City." In many ways, this was a comfort because she was able to save enough money for her eventual move to Upper Manhattan—"Harlem, Washington Heights, or Inwood." In other ways, the distance between home and work was quite frustrating for her because she lived "all the way, like all the way out in a part of Queens [that] takes 1 hour and 15 minutes to get to work, and that's one way." When Khaleeq asked her to describe the neighborhood in Queens where she lived, Ms. Cunningham talked in detail about how her family has lived there for a long time and how she called it home because it was the only home she really knew. She described the area as suburban and "very, very residential and the only businesses in the area are like local businesses that cater to the people." In contrast to Harlem, she explained that the racial and ethnic makeup of her neighborhood is comprised of mostly White and Asian people with some Greeks, Italians, Koreans, and Chinese. There are also "a lot of immigrant families [in] the area" and an increasing demand for more housing options. Associating the housing demand with the higher costs of renting apartments close to mass transit (e.g., bus stops; subway terminals), Ms. Cunningham said she believed gentrification was already affecting this part of Queens. She explained, "They've been tearing down a lot of houses to build up newer properties. Not particularly high rises like here in Harlem, but apartments that hold multiple families and the rent just keeps going up and up and up."

When asked to define *gentrification*, Ms. Cunningham was quick to say that she defined it "as the [pause] renovating and cleaning up of apartments, or building new developments that allow people to charge higher rents in neighborhoods where rent wasn't as expensive before." After a moment of silence, she continued, "Then after the rents go up and the people move in, you get this idea of other stores coming in and particularly big, chain, corporate stores that push out the local businesses and the local chains." Gentrification, according to Ms. Cunningham, is not race-based, but "class-based because it's really about money." On this point, she said, "I think race and culture are affected by gentrification, but the whole movement starts because of class. Basically, I have money to live in this neighborhood or I don't have money to live in this neighborhood. That's the first defining factor." As she glanced at everyone present during her interview session, she became a bit animated as she further explained her point: "Then after that comes 'Do I want to live in this neighborhood because these types of people live here or these types of people don't live here?' But you can't decide unless you got the cash." When I inquired into relationships between class realities and financial power, Ms. Cunningham said, "Right! Because financial power ultimately leads to how much power you have in other spheres." To this latter point, Khaleeq whispered, "But in America, power's also about race, how you look. People don't like thinking Blacks got money." Phillip added, "Yeah, that scares a lot of White people."

Many of Ms. Cunningham's ideas about gentrification were ones that Phillip, Khaleeq, and I discussed in our in- and out-of-school rap sessions. Although Phillip and Khaleeq realized that gentrification includes class issues, it was hard for them to hear White people—including Ms. Cunningham; Kent, Bonnie, and George (see Chapter 4); and teacher education students (see Chapter 5)—place culture and race in the background. As Khaleeq stated, "It's afterthoughts to them." I believe Phillip and Khaleeq's resistance to hear some White people explain gentrification as a class issue had to do, in part, with their own sense of belonging in a community that is primarily African and African American. Even in light of this visible racial makeup in Central Harlem, it cannot be ignored that Harlem is not and has never been exclusively African and African American. East Harlem, referred to by many as "El Barrio," is located in Manhattan's north-central section and sits adjacent to Central Harlem. It is a predominantly Latino/a and Puerto Rican neighborhood. According to statistics released in 1993, the population of East Harlem for the year 1990 was approximately 51.9% Latino (which included 40.9% Puerto Rican), 38.9% African American, and 7.1% White, the latter of whom resided in the neighborhood's south-ernmost section (see *Annual Report on Social Indicators,* 1993; see also Jackson, 1995).

East Harlem, at the beginning of the 20th century, was home mainly to Italian and Jewish families. Fiorello LaGuardia, an important Italian American politician in the 1930s and 1940s who founded several art schools in New York, was from East Harlem. German and Irish families resided in parts of the community. However, World War II changed the demographics, and as a result of new people moving into the area (e.g., African Americans; Latinos/as), many local residents relocated to the Bronx, Queens, and Brooklyn. This movement had more to do with changing demographics, racially and ethnically, and less to do with the economic costs of gentrification, given that most of the local businesses continued to be owned by former (non-Black, non-Latino/a) residents.

Clearly, Harlem has an immensely rich history for many people, especially disenfranchised people of color in the United States. In addition to the economic, civic, and political struggles of African, African American, Latino/a, and other people of color in Harlem, this community has served as a "safe space" (Fine, Weis, & Powell, 1997; Weis & Fine, 2000). Gentrification is causing this safe space to be changed and rewritten, a reality of which Phillip, Khaleeq, their peers, and their teachers are all too aware. Along with offending their sense of belonging, Phillip and Khaleeq's resistance to hearing White people talk about gentrification as a class issue had to do with their experiences as African American males who lived and/or attended school in a community that was experiencing visible spatial, economic, and racial changes. For Khaleeq, "living here, almost in Harlem, but really Upper West Side" has taught him how safe spaces can also become "contact zones" (Pratt, 1991). When Ms. Cunningham described her feelings of "White guilt," which she associated with White privilege and histories of oppression, Khaleeq said, "African Americans, and like males, I'm looked at like a criminal. I'm not going to sit there with guilt, think about what the cops gonna do to me today. I have to keep living life, work for change . . . you should, too." Here, Khaleeq was asking Ms. Cunningham to critique the reasons (historical, racial, and power) for her guilt as she learns to cross borders to do "her work for change." This work, as revealed from her interview, is embedded in her teaching practices, pedagogies, and approaches. Just as Khaleeq crosses physical, emotional and psychological boundaries (e.g., talking with teacher education candidates and interviewing White residents), Ms. Cunningham has a responsibility to do the same as she recognizes her privilege and engages in teaching for social justice.

Ms. Cunningham did place culture and race in the background to class when describing gentrification: "It's definitely about economics, about class, at least that's what I believe." However, when asked about the community in which she worked and the impact of gentrification there, she talked, first and foremost, about Harlem's communal vibe: "There's more of a sense of people knowing each other, which you really don't get in Queens." This echoed ideas expressed by a White teacher education candidate who insisted, "Harlem has an incredible street life" (see Chapter 5). Ms. Cunningham then talked about having students in her classes who "know each other not just from school, but from seeing each other in the neighborhood. That never happened to me in high school. Never! I was never neighbors with my friends." At this, Phillip and Khaleeq glanced at one another as if to say, "Really?" Ms. Cunningham explained how she liked Harlem and has "always had a lot of respect for Harlem because it's been this great community that's given birth to so much culture in the United States and that's just incredible to me." Phillip agreed and remarked, "Interesting how everybody thinks it's a great place, but been scared to live here with the minorities before. Now comes gentrification, right?"

Ms. Cunningham's respect for Harlem and awareness of its cultural significance made her question the presence of new White residents in the community. She admitted, "That's a really big problem that I'm currently having because, like I said, I really want to move to Manhattan, but I can't afford to live anywhere below 125th Street." In considering moving to Harlem, Ms. Cunningham explained, "Living here would be amazing. Then the other part is like, do I belong here and if I'm coming here, am I starting this trend of kind of killing all the things that make Harlem Harlem? It's just like this awful debate that goes on in my head. . . ." She believed that a move to Harlem would make getting to and from Harlem High School more convenient and time efficient. She could teach and live in or around the community with her students. However, she struggled with the idea, knowing that a move to Harlem would further contribute to the community's White-ification (see Chapter 4), given that the area is a "rich Black community with a rich culture." Although culture and race were in the background to class in her thinking about gentrification, they were at the forefront of her thoughts about moving to Harlem, which could potentially, in her words, be seen as "killing all the things that make Harlem Harlem."

As I listened to Ms. Cunningham's ideas and engaged in follow-up discussions with her, I began to wonder: What do people who have never actually lived in Harlem see as "great" about this community? Is it a vision of a Hughes-, Robeson-, Ellington-, and Hurston-inspired Harlem, where art was created and celebrated in the streets, coffeeshops, entertainment venues, and in apprenticeship relationships? Is it the 1960s Harlem of riots and demonstrations for the rights of people of color? The Harlem of Malcolm X and Adam Clayton Powell Jr.? The Harlem and its significant Renaissance era that we are taught and that we teach in high school? Will it be the same Harlem after gentrification? Will it retain some of its historical, literary, and Black cultural artifacts in its movement into 21st-century newness? As I think about these questions when I am alone, hunched over field notes and videotapes, or when I pose them to Phillip, Khaleeq, Ms. L, or whoever is willing to listen, I wonder: Do people who live in this community consider it to be "great" in the same ways nonresidents do, nonresidents who have access to the financial freedom of spatial movement? What about nonresidents who have chosen, up to this current moment of gentrification, not to live in Harlem? For Damen, the abbreviated answer to this latter question was, "No, not really. 'Cause we live here. We know Harlem in certain ways others don't. We know what goes on every day. We know who's here and we could tell you who doesn't live here and looks out of place." Damen continued, "Everybody don't know the routine. People come in and tour around then they just leave. Many of us can't leave if we wanted to."

When I asked Ms. Cunningham about this issue, she referenced the novel *A Tree Grows in Brooklyn* by Betty Smith (1943). She mentioned that the novel reminded her of how people and places change: "[It] is about Williamsburg at the turn of the century and how it was all Irish and Jewish then. And then Williamsburg changed over the years, [its] ethnic and racial makeup and now it's going back. . . . It's like White people are moving back to Williamsburg, but it's not the same White people." She admitted that *A Tree Grows in Brooklyn* helped her consider how various stories of and within communities are eventually altered and become different stories. If we do not learn those stories and about the people who lived in those communities, then we are not fostering a continuum of stories and histories to teach, learn from, and share. Hence, there is a connection between literacy and explorations of community change. Clearly, Ms. Cunningham was committed to learning more about Harlem—its history, culture, literacy events, and residents—before deciding to move in, author her own stories, and contribute, however unwillingly, to gentrification. I just wonder, as do Phillip and Khaleeq, how she will make sense of her feelings of guilt if she moves to Harlem and continues teaching for change, equity, and social justice.

Ms. Cunningham, concerned with finding ways to situate herself as a White woman in debates on urban gentrification, struggled to critique issues of race, place, and gender in local narratives of belonging and identity. On the latter point, she said, "I'm White and I want to be a revolutionary. If I want to be for racial equality, I'm not allowed to be proud of being White" because "they have a history of oppressing people." Although she identified as a part of this White group, she often said "they" in referring to those who are doing the oppressing, not "we." Rather than blaming herself for advancing Harlem's gentrification, Ms. Cunningham was encouraged by the students and teachers in the lounge to recognize her Whiteness and the roles—both positive and negative—it could play in the gentrification process. For example, Ms. L said, "You can't change your Whiteness, right? So what are you willing to do with your privilege?" Phillip added, "As a teacher, you challenge your students to open their minds, to learn new stuff. That goes for you, too. If you don't do it, how can you teach it?" Ms. Cunningham accepted these challenges and asserted her dedication to learn more about the history and pressures of urban gentrification in Harlem in her ongoing work with the students she teaches and the colleagues with whom she works at the school.

Mr. Walker and Living in Harlem

Mr. Walker, a White male teacher at Harlem High School, was approximately 26 years old at the time of the interview. He taught a combination of sophomore-, junior-, and senior-level English language arts classes, and was known, at least among some of the teachers, as an easygoing guy. When I told him about the project and invited him to be interviewed, he did not hesitate to take me up on the offer. Having written a thesis on gentrification in Lower Manhattan, he was familiar with the topic, passionate about hearing other people's perspectives, and invested in knowing what other people were doing to address community change. As opposed to starting the interview by describing aspects of his identity (e.g., race; class status; familial community), Mr. Walker jumped right into the interview by telling us where he lived and what his position was on gentrification.

He lived on West 144th Street between Amsterdam and Broadway and described the area as "largely a Dominican neighborhood with some African Americans and in the last 2 years, a large influx of Caucasians." I recognized the area that he was referencing. I had once lived less than 8 blocks and a cross street away from him, and yet our paths never crossed.

As for gentrification, Mr. Walker explained that it is harmful for the long-time residents of a community, and admitted his awareness of how some urban communities like Harlem are becoming increasingly White. For a long time, he was the only White person in this particular Harlem neighborhood. Now, according to Mr. Walker, "it's changed dramatically and what I see is not so much people like me, professionals, but artists moving in, people who might describe themselves as hip, and that to me is where you know that the gentrification process is really sort of gone full force because . . . they don't necessarily exist in the community to be a part of the community." Khaleeq whispered, "And the professionals do?" Mr. Walker then talked about how "these people" tend to come into communities like Harlem as a way to attract others to the area and to "carve out their little niche and make it their own, which in turn makes it more desirable for others. Then rents go up, property values go up, and so on." As he talked about the types of people moving in, I could not help but to wonder: How is one defined as "hip"? And what makes the movement of "hip" people into the community more threatening than the movement of other people (i.e., "professionals"), given that rent prices will continue to increase and demographics will continue to shift?

When asked about the specific effects of gentrification on the long-time residents of the community, Mr. Walker, unaware of this, reiterated sentiments that had previously been expressed to me by Phillip, Khaleeq, and other youth at Harlem High School. He commented, "Well, usually, it just pushes them out." To support his point, he talked about how "a largely rental building" has recently turned into a cooperative building, which meant that renters either have to "buy the place in which they live that will be renovated or leave. And a lot of times they end up leaving and moving to other communities, which, I think, largely are lower-income communities in more concentrated areas." Phillip agreed with Mr. Walker on this point and said that it will not be a surprise when the costs of gentrification force residents to seek other places to live that "are nothing like what they call home now." For this reason and many others, Mr. Walker did not fully support gentrification in Harlem, despite his awareness of racial dynamics in the area and the way others perceived him as an outsider, or as one of "them" White people.

His reasons for not supporting gentrification extended beyond a debate over whether the community did or did not need to be changed. In other words, Mr. Walker insisted that gentrification "does a disservice to the people who have inhabited the area for a long time and have really made it their home" but are forced to relocate without sufficient public assistance.

Turning his attention to the students who were present during his interview, he said that gentrification is a complicated issue that does not solve all the spatial issues of a community and, in fact, that it has more to do with capitalism than anything else. Khaleeq asked Mr. Walker to elaborate by talking about the good and/or bad sides of gentrification. At this request, Mr. Walker explained, "There's a lot of negative aspects of gentrification. As far as positive, I guess it works positively for some people if you go ahead and invest in some properties in the neighborhood and within a year or 2, you make a lot of money. That's great for them, but at what costs?" The youth seemed to agree with Mr. Walker's assessment of the effects of gentrification for those who have the money to invest in it. They encouraged his honest confession: "A lot of the times, the people that make that money off investments don't have any concern for those that it hurts." The youth also agreed with Mr. Walker's comments about the value of Harlem as an artistic site (see Chapter 5), a point that he believed people who are calling for and supporting gentrification may have forgotten.

Ms. L asked him a pointed question about race and place: "How do people react to you in your neighborhood?" To this, Mr. Walker admitted that the reaction of residents was mixed. "At first," he said, "it was pretty cold. When I first moved in, people wouldn't say anything to me. Now, I've been there . . . I think they kind of see me, in my building, they see me as more of a long-term person, maybe." When he walked the streets of Harlem, Mr. Walker indicated that some people struck up a conversation with him about gentrification in the area. Others would yell at him, "calling me White as if that isn't obvious. . . . But for the most part, I find the community I'm living in pretty accepting or totally ambivalent to my being there." I found Mr. Walker's conclusion a bit odd because of his in-depth reflection on the verbal reactions he received from people on the street who stared at him while making references to gentrification and his being White. Nevertheless, this led to our discussion on definitions of gentrification, which Mr. Walker considered a class issue: "I think most of the issues in this country get hidden by culture wars. But you can't deny that it [gentrification] is also, there is some element of race and culture that goes into it." For him, too "many neighborhoods in New York City are pretty homogeneous, so it's [gentrification] cultural, but I think it's more of a class issue." Like Ms. Cunningham, Mr. Walker believed that people should focus on the class elements behind gentrification: "I think the struggle against gentrification would be, well, if it was looked at as a class issue, it would be easier to kind of fight gentrification because, I don't know." It becomes easier to fight because White people, particularly those in positions of power, are more likely to conceptualize gentrification in this way (e.g., class privilege and socioeconomic issue), making invisible the Black and Brown bodies that may be displaced from the community. Although he did acknowledge that he was hesitant to relegate race and culture to the background, his comments articulated his position on gentrifi-cation and the economic forces behind it. In this case, race and culture were not primary factors, a point that caught the attention of Phillip, who said, "It's no longer surprising for me to hear White people say race don't have much to do with it. But how do we explain all the Black people right here being displaced? Yeah, money and class, but you can't tell me race ain't got nothing to do with it."

Mr. Walker's ideas were provocative, especially because Phillip and Khaleeq later admitted to me that they had no idea that this teacher in their school was "so open" (Khaleeq) and "yeah, straight up about gentrifi-cation" (Phillip). When I pushed them to explain their shock, they said, "You don't know sometimes" (Khaleeq) and "He's a White teacher, a male at this school with us, so you don't get to know what teachers think" (Phillip). Their points led me to a question that Khaleeq had posed to Mr. Walker: "Do you think people move to Harlem because they have no-where else to go?" In response to this question, Mr. Walker asked Khaleeq (in order to avoid making assumptions), "When you say 'people,' who do you mean?" Khaleeq responded, however hesitantly, "Caucasian people." Mr. Walker said, "You can say White if you'd like. That's fine," and Khaleeq remarked, "Okay." This example represented engagements across positions: Khaleeq—a youth and a Black student at Harlem High School—was ask-ing Mr. Walker—an adult and a White teacher at Harlem High School—about the reasons why he believed White people are moving into Harlem. They communicated with language that was accessible, pointed, and non-threatening. Here, Mr. Walker and Khaleeq were not talking over and around race, but directly at and with race (see Ladson-Billings, 2009; Ladson-Billings & Tate, 2006; Weis & Fine, 2000). The way in which Mr. Walker encouraged Khaleeq to "say White" so as to make race visible and present in their discussions of gentrification paralleled Phillip and Khaleeq's belief that "you gotta name it. . . . If it's racism, say racism, not 'somebody said something inappropriate to me.' If it's gentrification, say gentrification, not 'the community is looking a little different from before.'" This act of naming things, or saying "it like you mean it, 'cause it's staring us right in the face anyway" (Phillip), served a fundamental role in how I worked with teachers and youth from Harlem High School and pre- and in-service teacher education candidates at the local university. By nam-ing things, which can greatly contribute to our pedagogical practices, the youth, adults, and I powerfully engaged language, talked about race, and participated in rich meaning-making activities. At the same time, we called into question acts, actions, and institutional policies that appeared ineq-uitable (e.g., schools not accounting for students' lived experiences and community obligations; teachers ignoring students whom they believe are underperformers or vernacular speakers).

The open and accessible language between Mr. Walker and Khaleeq also showed itself in Mr. Walker's response to the question "Do you think [White] people move to Harlem because they have nowhere else to go?" Mr. Walker responded, "I think a lot of people, a lot of young professionals, move to Harlem largely because the rents are cheaper than everywhere else." Then, he talked about local publications such as *TimeOut New York* and *Village Voice* printing stories that say, "Harlem's not dangerous anymore." He insisted that rhetoric is used "against the community by changing [the name] to West Harlem, so there's this distinct difference now between East and West Harlem." In regard to this latter point, which raised the eyebrows of many people in the room, Mr. Walker explained, "People think East Harlem is scary and West Harlem's safe, and they [the media] really show pictures of people in the neighborhood. You see artists, you see White people . . . and the media plays, well, plays the gentrification process because people see it. Now they understand West Harlem as being a place that they can go, be safe, and pay cheap rent."

I believe that such stereotypes—East Harlem as unsafe, West Harlem as safe—harm communities and tell stories about the people who live there. These stories are negative, one-sided, and use a language of *divide and conquer*. The willingness of Mr. Walker and the students to use descriptive language to discuss stereotypical messages about communities and their residents pointed to their involvement with active listening in the presence of differences (e.g., racial; age; place; positions; ideological beliefs) and critical learning across assigned positions (e.g., adult/youth; teacher/student). It also reiterated important lessons in regard to talking about the act of naming, a point we discussed when describing the rezoned area around Columbia University that is named Morningside Heights, but is widely known as South Harlem by local residents.

Throughout Harlem, East and West, are signs of urban redevelopment initiatives. On the one hand, such initiatives are marked by the presence of longstanding "housing projects," unemployment, and an ongoing demand for affordable housing options. On the other hand, they are marked by the presence of renovated, expensive brownstones, the expansion of businesses and corporate-owned stores, and the development of high-rise condominiums. These signs and the stories that are told about them are indicative of a changing community that has obvious racial, class, and economic dichotomies. When Mr. Walker talked about media portrayals of East and West Harlem (i.e., safe versus dangerous), both Phillip and Khaleeq agreed that some people "buy into stereotypes and don't try getting the truth themselves" (Khaleeq). This point, in my opinion, speaks to how certain stories are valued over others, how some voices and perspectives get privileged over others, and, in a more practical sense, how the literacy experiences and cultural practices of many students are, often, not honored in classrooms.

Mr. Walker's focus on the class aspects of gentrification did not fully ignore the aspects of race and culture in Harlem. As much as he explicitly established connections between gentrification and class, and gentrification and privilege, he implicitly alluded to connections between gentrification and racial dynamics as well as gentrification and the spatial and cultural significance of Harlem. Together, these connections have implications for the ways in which teachers and researchers can think about and address community change, class issues, and literacy stories with their own students. As Mr. Walker shared, "Everyone has a story or two. It's our responsibility to hear and talk about them."

Ms. Brown, Harlem, and Making It Make Sense

Ms. Brown, another teacher at Harlem High School, was a 23-year-old African American woman who taught special education. When asked to describe herself, Ms. Brown quickly said, "I identify myself as a Black American." She then explained the complexities involved with identifying as African American: "I don't feel like I deserve to put that [African] as part of my identity" because she has not yet traced her roots. She then went on to say that she "was raised lower-middle-class" in the state of Georgia, and "would probably classify as upper-lower-class, maybe middle-lower-class" in New York. In relation to the cost of living, Ms. Brown did not believe she met the middle-class income requirements as outlined by New York State standards.

Before her recent move to the Inwood section of Upper Manhattan, Ms. Brown resided for a brief period of time in Harlem on 117th Street and Frederick Douglass Boulevard, which is in close proximity to where Phillip lived. She described the neighborhood as having "a lot of Senegalese people that live there, Black people, and [pause] when I moved in, however, I moved into a brand new building and so I felt like the minority in my building." Ms. Brown was living in "a gentrified building" and her new neighbors "were really happy to see me and my roommate move in because . . . the tenants were predominantly White." The racial dynamics were quite visible to her. On the one hand, Ms. Brown moved to Harlem with her roommate to be close to her new job and to pay a more affordable monthly rent—affordable in comparison to other New York City communities. She was quite familiar with Harlem's local history and its significance in the lives of countless African, African American, and Latino/a people. She loved seeing other people in the community who "looked alike," which she explained as people who racially resembled her and her roommate. Finally, Ms. Brown was living in Harlem, a community that she respected, had learned a lot about during her own schooling, and that served as a site where civic, literary, and political action flourished.

On the other hand, the building in which she lived was different architecturally from the others in the area and did not house the diverse human realities (racially, culturally, and linguistically) which could be found on the surrounding streets. She shared: "Our building had just recently been finished . . . and is like an eyesore. You walk on that block and you come up from 110th Street and boom! You hit these big, gaudy, monstrosities that don't fit in the neighborhood." Her comment paved the way for Phillip to say, "I know which ones. You right." Ms. Brown's description of the new apartments allowed her to reflect on two by-products of gentrification: spatial change and displacement. She remarked: "You know that there was someone who lived in this space before this building went up and it makes you feel really bad because I'm thinking . . . in general, it makes you feel like you displaced somebody when you know it's a brand new building in the middle of everything in this part of Harlem." However, her reflection resulted in one of her confessions: "It kind of gives you this feeling, kind of like guilt, but I felt like at least I'm Black moving in. At least I'm not somebody coming in and changing the demographics."

Ms. Brown's comments spoke directly to the conflicting relationships between issues of race (e.g., White- and Black-ification) and social class status and mobility in discussions of urban gentrification. In our critique of Harlem's spatial and racial changes associated with White-ification, Phillip, Khaleeq, and I often ignored, or took for granted, the presence of Black-ification, given that the community has a large population of African, African American, and Latino residents. This point raises the question: Can certain people be exempt from contributing—willingly or unwillingly—to the gentrification of urban communities of color because they share the same racial identities as longtime local residents? Taylor's (2002) research addresses economic issues between White people and people of color, on the one hand, and between Harlem's "Black gentry" (p. 86; i.e., middle-class; homeowners) and their poor and working class neighbors of color (i.e., "lower" class; apartment renters) on the other hand. While Ms. Brown did not consider herself to be a member of the gentry—"[I] classify as upper lower class, maybe middle lower class" (Ms. Brown)—in some ways she was participating in what Taylor describes as "economic changes in gentrifying communities" (p. 87), or what Phillip and Khaleeq referred to as gentrification's human faces of various races, whether White or Black or other minorities, who have "heavy money bags." In this way, the visibility of Black-ification took on an expanded meaning. Up to this point, we have understood Black-ification as the presence of Black bodies, cultural forms and practices, and political influences that shaped Harlem into a major site of Black life and culture. Now, the idea of Black-ification also includes the reality that Black middle- to upper-class people are moving back to Harlem and reclaiming the space from media perceptions of "decay" and "decline" to a site of Black power and prestige, as members of Taylor's (2002) new "Black gentry."

Throughout her interview, Ms. Brown made references to Harlem as a community that, in the words of Taylor (2002), represented "'our place,' claiming that the move to Harlem strengthens . . . connections to the Black community" (p. 87). Yet, while she identified with the long-time residents in both an economic and a racial sense, she made the choice to move into a new, expensive apartment building, "an eyesore," to use her words, with other tenants who "were predominantly White." She revealed feelings of guilt over being a possible participant in Harlem's gentrification. Khaleeq acknowledged the tensions surrounding Ms. Brown's position: "Yeah, you Black and you can afford to live in a new building. I dunno what else to say."

Although Ms. Brown expressed some guilt over moving into a new building that displaced local residents and replaced older architectural structures in Harlem, her feelings were different from those expressed by Ms. Cunningham. Ms. Brown did not believe her presence in Harlem negatively affected the community's demographics. Ms. Cunningham, however, feared that her presence as a White resident could potentially contribute to "a trend of kind of killing all the things that make Harlem Harlem." Ms. Cunningham was aware of the ways in which she could be read, whether accurately or not, as a White woman in Harlem: an *other*, an outsider, and a supporter of gentrification. Ms. Brown, however, realized that she could be seen less as an outsider because of her race, and more as an inside *sellout* for living in a newly constructed building where the monthly cost of renting the two-bedroom apartment she shared with her roommate, excluding the cost of electricity, was almost $1,700. Their levels of guilt were different, but were visible in their individual interview sessions. Their openness with talking about these complicated issues in the presence of students contributed to Khaleeq and Phillip's realization that teachers also make hard decisions in relation to community change: "It's not easy. Moving into a gentrifying place means somebody's forced out who can't pay that high rent . . . these hard times, even for teachers. Gentrification ain't making things easy" (Phillip).

Ms. Brown and Ms. Cunningham's individual perspectives led me to recall descriptions of Harlem written by photographer Gordon Parks. In the Foreword to a book by Marberry and Cunningham (2003), Parks wrote of the authors' individual fascinations with the community. Of Marberry, he stated, "What he discovered was a Harlem in the midst of change, a flux of economic and cultural resurgence into an ocean of poverty and decay" (p. vii). Parks continued, "After a seemingly bottomless decline, an economic revival has come to Harlem, though the most deprived and destitute watch from outside the tent" (pp. vii–viii). Ms. Brown, who had lived amid the "economic revival," witnessed the changes and tensions occurring in Harlem. Ms. Cunningham, who had contemplated moving to Harlem or one of the neighboring Upper Manhattan communities, questioned her identity and the perceptions that others might have of her if she became a resident in the community. As teachers in the community, both Ms. Brown and Ms. Cunningham were aware that many of their students were put in positions to "watch from outside the tent."

When asked to define gentrification, Ms. Brown responded that it is the displacement of "the lower class with the middle class or the upper class." For her, gentrification in this community "is viewed as a racial thing because Harlem is historically, within this century, a community with people of color." In addition to gentrification's racial aspect, Ms. Brown "look[ed] at gentrification monetarily: If you have the money, you can force the shift, you can buy the building and build it up. Charge more. Displace the residents. That's what you could do." Her definition of gentrification took into consideration class concerns: "displacing those who don't have the money until they can't afford to live in Manhattan anymore." However, she refused to place race and culture in the background: "People of color in the United States, and we can look at a lot of places, are always being displaced at other people's expense. Gentrification has a lot to do with race, too. We can't ignore that." Khaleeq shook his head in agreement as he smiled at Ms. Brown. Phillip stated, "You one of the first teachers to admit that. Why do people have a hard time talking about race? How can we talk about class, but not race, and we talking about gentrification and displacement? Come on now."

Teachers, especially, cannot ignore the changes that are profoundly affecting the lives of students. The changing landscape of Harlem greatly impacts their sense of self and their dispositions toward engaging as active citizens in the local community and in school. While the opening of new businesses can be seen as an indicator of community improvement, they can also be read as signs that affordable community space, once occupied by poor and working-class residents, is being invaded, or taken over, by resources brought about because of gentrification. According to Ms. Brown, when longtime residents of any community are threatened with displacement, then gentrification becomes an intrusion: "I don't like what it's doing to the residents of Harlem. Yes, it's great that you now have Old Navy here, but I can't condone leaving people unable to benefit from what is happening in their community." Ms. Brown explained that it is convenient for residents who have not had access to particular resources when businesses move into communities because it demonstrates an interest in the area. However, it is problematic when businesses "don't give back to the community, don't put their money here, and the residents suffer." Phillip quickly stated, "We might think it's convenient at first 'til them high prices hit us and we forced out the community. Then it's not convenient. We gotta think about that."

At this point in the interview, Ms. Brown became emotional as she asked, "They say the rent has to increase, but where do you draw the line? Where do you say, 'let's stop it here'?" She talked about the gentrification process involving wealth coming into the community to "make these buildings look wonderful because they are . . ." before concluding, "These people [longtime residents] probably thought they were going to get it and then they don't. They get an eviction notice." With this point, Ms. Brown had fully captured the attention of the people sitting in on her interview. She then established a connection between talking about gentrification in the community and discussing it with high school students: "I've had students who have told me, 'Oh, the building down the street, people are moving out . . . but I'm still going to hang out in front of my block. They're not going to get my building.' It's that sense that it is far away until it hits you."

Believing that teachers should draw on the realities within local communities in their work with youth, Ms. Brown talked about how some students believe "it's some external force that will affect Khaleeq's building, but it won't affect my building. I think thinking in this way, people do become complacent. They say, 'Oh, well, that's down the street.'" Here, Ms. Brown was stressing points that she has often shared with students—that changes are not just happening down the street, but throughout Harlem; that changes do not simply affect one's neighbors, but everyone in the neighborhood; and that gentrification is not an individual issue, but a community concern, local and global, that needs to be addressed not only in the community, but also in the schools. Gentrification, for Ms. Brown, "is just flawed. I think people want gentrification to mean things are getting better, but you come in, things get fixed up by the middle class, usually with the cause of displacement of the lower class." She continued by saying, "The people have to go. . . . The mom and pop shops that people started years and years ago have to go because they're being eaten up by the big fish." For these reasons, adults and youth, teachers and students, should engage in ongoing conversations about the realities of community change as they individually and collaboratively critique meanings of power, identity, and belonging.

LESSONS FROM TEACHER TALK AND TALKING WITH TEACHERS

The learning (e.g., questioning; inquiring; reflecting; talking; exchanging) occurring between adults and youth in the unofficial literacy spaces—the teachers' lounge, hallways, stairwells, and so on—influenced the ways the youth and adults began to rethink the power of literacy. Instead of talking about what it means to read and write, the people present during the various interviews were, in fact, engaging in these literacy practices by exchanging perspectives across race, age, experiences, and positions of authority. No one frowned upon Ms. Cunningham's feelings of guilt for being White and believing, in her words, that she was "part of the majority that has been doing all these bad things." Actually, her admission of this feeling, resulting in part from how she was taught as a child "to approach race, gender, class, and culture," led to an important teachable moment. Ms. L commented, "I do like that part about when you said, when you're White and you're taught not to be prejudiced, but colorblind." To this, Ms. Cunningham further confessed that she started to become more critical of race and class after "sitting in on [Ms. L's] classes and listening to what she had to say to her students. I realized that seeing people as colorblind and not noticing their race is like leaving off a huge chunk of who they are." She continued, "And if I see her [Ms. L] as Black, that means I have to see myself as White." Ms. Cunningham was becoming increasingly aware of the reality that we do not live in a colorblind society where race, racial differences, and class issues do not exist (see Delpit, 1995; Ladson-Billings, 2009; Tatum, 2003). They do exist, even though Ms. Cunningham's childhood upbringing and early educational experiences taught her to act as if the "ideal" were true—that the *Sesame Street* version of Harlem was, in fact, Harlem.

This exchange of ideas, grounded in honesty and openness, affected the ways Phillip, Khaleeq, and many of their peers learned to think about race by using critical literacy skills. They became comfortable asking follow-up questions, listening to other responses, and critiquing conflicting messages of race, class, and change throughout the community. Often, they questioned the absence of multiple readings on race, class, and place within their school curriculum: "How we supposed to learn about different people when we study the same literature and write the same boring five-paragraph essay from class to class" (Phillip)? Khaleeq offered a response to Phillip's question: "Maybe we gotta make the schools give us what we think we need. . . . Bring community people in so we'll learn about the community." Phillip and Khaleeq began to speak up in class when they disagreed with what they heard or with the lessons that they were being taught. This happened gradually, given their reluctance to question school authorities because "nobody ever said we had a right to" (Khaleeq). It also encouraged Phillip, Khaleeq, and me to reconsider the meanings of White-ification, White privilege, and Black-ification in discussions on gentrification (see Chapter 4). No longer could we simply talk about White- and Black-ification as if they were abstract concepts without meanings, faces, power, and consequences. For example, our initial attempts to recoin the term *White-ification*—which had been loosely used to describe how White people are taking over "Black" music—and to provide it with a solid definition were not enough.

Ms. Cunningham's struggle with confronting Whiteness and White privilege helped us better conceptualize White-ification as the increasing presence of Whiteness (e.g., privilege; practices; values) and *guilt* in areas that are predominantly of color (see Chapter 4). After listening to Ms. Cunningham, Mr. Walker, Ms. Brown, and other teachers, Phillip, Khaleeq, their peers, and I extended this definition to include political, social, and economic challenges placed upon minority-occupied communities that are largely the result of gentrification. These challenges included class and race divisions, misunderstandings across different cultures and cultural practices, and misrepresentations of community space (e.g., as being in decay, dangerous, or in decline). Phillip remarked, "I get what [Ms. Cunningham] saying about feeling out of place. That's hard, that's a reality we need to hear. We get to hear her truth and how [Ms. L] helped her see another way and then learn to speak about place and White privilege."

We all heard truth in a comment that Mr. Walker made near the end of his interview: "In a way, gentrification of a neighborhood bleeds the neighborhood of its resources, especially if people are moving out because they can't afford it." He stated that, in many ways, it was difficult for him "to justify why I was there [in Harlem]." He said he "did kind of feel bad" because he always thought that "gentrification was horrible, and then I moved into a neighborhood that was being gentrified." Everyone agreed that there are unique resources in all communities that rely on the people who have lived there for many years, from the locally owned bookstores, neighborhood schools, and enrichment programs to cultural institutions and social activities. When gentrification threatens these invaluable resources—the very resources that we teach students to view as valuable—

one has to question what it means to *belong* in a neighborhood, what types of responsibilities come with "owning" a part of a neighborhood, and what is implied by feeling "bad" or "guilty" when moving into a historically Black and/or minority area. These were teachable moments for educators and students; they provided opportunities to consider the experiences of a White teacher who lived and worked in the community and who is confronted with feelings of "double-consciousness" (see DuBois, 1903). As Khaleeq stated, "I'm learning what I never knew before. I'm thinking about all this . . . and it's hard to say what's right and what's not."

Critical learning, in which teachers were asked to perform stories of place in front of their colleagues and students, or be self-reflexive by sharing their narratives (and apprehensions) about the influence of place on their identities was indeed happening in the space of this interview project. How could it be moved inside the space or time constraints of a traditional classroom? According to Ms. L, "We need to figure out what we can do in the classroom to get students more into the topics. We're sitting here having these great discussions and we should do this in classes." Ms. Brown was also thinking about such classroom engagements, which she described when talking about her interactions with students on the topic of gentrification in Harlem. She insisted that students and adults should study the history of communities: "I want people to know about the history and cultural practices within Harlem, their home and community." This struck a chord with Phillip and Khaleeq. During a later out-of-school meeting, Phillip referred to Ms. Brown's sentiments by asking, "Why we don't learn about these things when in school?" Khaleeq responded, "Maybe we should change school up a little, learn these helpful stories along with other things we have to learn." Clearly, Ms. Brown's interview, in addition to the ones we conducted with Mr. Walker, Ms. Cunningham, and the others, helped Phillip and Khaleeq as well as me re-imagine the purposes and functions of schooling in relation to local communities. Such experiences also helped them consider how literacy happens and is present in the spaces that cut across school and community divisions.

CREATING COLLABORATIVE, DEMOCRATIC LEARNING ENVIRONMENTS

Literacies—reading, writing, communicating orally, performing, questioning agency and identities—were at the forefront of the interview discussions. Although we did not explicitly ask questions related to literacy, we—the adults and youth present during each interview—participated in exchanges that involved sharing literacy stories. Ms. Cunningham's literacy story on identity and issues of race, gender, class, and culture was informed by childhood lessons that had taught her to be colorblind. These lessons, in turn, were informed by her lack of exposure to having school peers as neighbors. Part of Mr. Walker's literacy story on community involved his decision to live in Harlem and to critique the signs of change that presented themselves on a daily basis. These signs involved the artistic aspects, racial dynamics, and engagements with colleagues and students at Harlem High School and within the local community. For Ms. Brown, literacy was at the center of her conversations with students, her insistence to "talk about what's going on in Harlem," and her interest in studying "the history and cultural practices" there. We were not just talking about gentrification in Harlem. We were also re-imagining possibilities with and potentials of literacy across contexts, across race and class, and across individual experiences.

This type of education was collaborative and democratic in nature. We used language—open and honest language that was available to everyone who was present—to discuss gentrification. Often, this available language led to additional conversations in the hallways, stairwells, and outside of school on how gentrification is a larger issue in the United States and throughout the Diaspora. We scaffolded from available language as we increasingly moved complex ideas and terminologies into a discourse that was understandable to students. In doing these things from a place of comfort and respect, our vocabulary increased as we contemplated the extended meanings of White-ification, Black-ification, community, and identity. By talking about an issue that was relevant to the familial lives of many students at the school, teachers and students also demonstrated how literacy is a social practice (Heath, 1983; Street, 1993, 2005) and "a civil right" (Greene, 2008) that fosters democratic engagements (Kinloch, 2005a).

Although I understand that gentrification is not a central factor in the communities, urban and/or rural, where some teachers work, I do believe that all teachers can examine with their students community concerns that may directly or indirectly affect them. The primary focus of such examinations may not necessarily be gentrification, community preservation, creating or sustaining local resources, civic activities, or even violence and police brutality. Instead, the focus may be on events within local communities such as civic engagement, youth-to-adult activism, land preservation, pollution and clean air, and the emergence of poetry and spoken-word venues. In examining such topics, critical lessons might emerge. Such lessons may include using language to engage in socially conscious change, discussing the significance of activism and community service initiatives, reading and re-reading texts through a critical literacy framework, and using writing to express ideas and consider oppositional stances, or counternarratives.

Ms. Cunningham, Mr. Walker, and Ms. Brown, among the other teachers interviewed, were aware of the community in which they worked and where their students lived. They offer models for teachers in many communities to have conversations with and entertain questions from students about connections among place, race, and identity. Their honesty when talking about gentrification pointed to their engagement with local events and their understanding of the need to critique community issues in schools if we truly value collaborative, democratic learning environments for teachers and students. As a way to demonstrate how we, educators, value such critical engagements with our students, I invite you to consider the following points and questions:

- Ask students to take the lead on posing in-class writing prompts related to course readings and/or current events on community, identity, and race. For example, one of my students at Perennial High School asked us—students and me—to write a brief response to the question: How does Jonathon Kozol define *apartheid* and do you think the term relates to what we know about urban neighborhoods in the United States?
- Have a panel discussion with people who represent and will speak from different perspectives. The panel, held during class time or a school assembly, can consist of a teacher from the school talking about teaching for change and the principal or a school administrator discussing challenges with meeting the literacy demands of the 21st century. Joining the panel could be a student who describes connections/disconnections between standardized testing (and academic learning) and community-based learning. An assignment for students that could emerge from this experience might be to craft written responses in which they explain, elaborate, or discuss their own perspectives alongside those of the speakers and the authors they are studying in their English classes.
- Sponsor a class debate in which students first produce written responses (e.g., essays, extended journal entries) on a specific topic. Then, they could be taught ways to critically produce counter-narratives to their own positions in order to present the counter-narratives in a debate.

The possibilities are endless for seriously inviting students to take ownership of their learning by listening to multiple perspectives and experiences as they engage in critical literacy opportunities.

Teaching, Change, and Youth

By Mimí M. Richardson, Seventh-Grade Language Arts Teacher

As a pre-service teacher education candidate, I learned of Valerie's work with literacy, youth, and gentrification in Harlem when she was a professor in New York City. I admired her ability to connect with students, instruct by practice, and demonstrate the ways curriculum comes to life in the real world. At the onset of my second year teaching in a suburban middle school in New Jersey, I am acutely aware of the impact community has on my students and further recognize the magnitude location has on the voice and actions of all students. Valerie's work demonstrates the power that students embrace when they encounter authentic educators who share valuable information relevant to their lived experience. Such educators also offer strategies that youth and adults can implement as they work for social and political change in the world.

As a seventh-grade teacher, I recognize that a constant challenge in many classrooms is student engagement. Entering the classroom presents educators with various questions they anticipate students will ask: Why should I learn this? How will I use this information? How does this information affect me? Confronted with the task of addressing these valid concerns subtly in curriculum design and lesson planning, educators are to instruct students in important and meaningful ways. What is more pertinent for students and their literacy inquiries than investigating where they live? Location, in my opinion, is not simply defined by one's geography, but by the context that informs one's existence and multiple lived experiences.

When educators explore with students the social constructs within our society that influence their lives, we introduce them to the institutions they have been acting within (and, often, against) throughout their educational experiences. Sometimes, this introduction reveals feelings of powerlessness, fear, and silence. When we encourage students to confront and really consider these institutional, political, and social forces, they become invested in their education and active in their learning. This engagement allows students to confront academic and personal challenges with a heightened sense of purpose, commitment, and determination. In my classroom teaching, I am committed to helping my students reach their academic goals as they transform perceptions—often, negative ones—of education. This is not easy, but it is important.

While my school district is within a suburban middle-class community that possesses the funds and fundamental resources needed to actively promote student success, we, too, confront many challenges often associated with urban school districts across the nation. Student achievement, though on average satisfactory, can substantially improve. Much of our population includes families who have only recently relocated from low socioeconomic neighborhoods and urban communities. They, like many other families, are dedicated to their children's educational lives. My colleagues, administrators, and I work to increase parental involvement, promote student extracurricular activities, and broaden our enrichment and support programs by encouraging the participation and exposure that yield well-rounded, active citizens. We work really hard to address cultural and social inequities within the educational system. Clearly, this has a huge impact on the lives of all students residing in various communities (e.g., urban; suburban; rural).

This year in my class introductions, I explained to my students that we were embarking on a journey together. After greeting my new class on the first day of school, I asked them to write about an enjoyable trip they have taken by describing the location of the trip, why it was of interest to them, and who joined them on the trip. They were asked to focus on what and/or how their travel companions contributed to their trip and how their companions added to their memories. At the conclusion of this activity, we discussed their recollections and how the location and the companion informed the memories that remained. Since literature is often alluded to as a means of seeing the world without physical travel, I suggested the settings of the seventh-grade texts as the locations on our itinerary for this year. I hope that this invitation will allow them to recognize the significance of place and the influence of those we meet along the way. Moreover, I hold my students accountable, as I invite them to hold me accountable, for contributing to their various learning outcomes, literacy encounters, and classroom memories.

As I think about my beginning-of-the-year introductions and my students' memories of an enjoyable trip they have taken, I think about Valerie's work with youth in New York City. Her work successfully merges education with action in order to inspire students to become conscientious, effective contributors to the world they are part of and will have a role in further creating. The students she encountered grew confident of the authority of their voices, and sought powerful ways to share their ideas. This model highlights new alternatives to literacy research and practice within the field of education, a field that continues to search for additional forms of instruction that transform and inspire and that take seriously the communities in which our students live. From a focus on community gentrification to the journeys our students take with their companions, we owe it to our students and ourselves to investigate the realities within school and familial communities.

CHAPTER 7

A New Literate Tradition

Classrooms as Communities of Engagement

"We paving a new way by seeing how the community is a part of our identities. That sums up everything for me. That's my literacy narrative in one sentence. That's a wrap." (Phillip)

"Being involved in things we interested in gives us life lessons that never go [a]way." (Khaleeq)

I left New York City for Columbus, Ohio, in September 2007 to start a new job in the School of Teaching and Learning at The Ohio State University. I left both hesitantly and eagerly, with conflicting emotions. With me I took important lessons about language, literacy, culture, and place that have found their way into my thinking about the spatial realities of a city like Columbus. From a new vantage point, I am reliving critical moments from my work in Harlem. Indeed,

Columbus is vastly different from New York City, generally, and Harlem, particularly. Yet there are political, sociocultural, educative, and spatial concerns that both places share.

What I have noticed in Harlem and throughout Columbus is something I have recently rediscovered on my travels back home to Charleston, South Carolina. That is, there are countless youth, primarily of color, who feel disassociated from, out of place in, and ignored within school space. This becomes obvious when I observe their physical dispositions inside classrooms, school hallways, and cafeterias. Yet their verbal exchanges and textual productions (e.g., videos; journals; newsletters; Web sites; virtual classrooms; MySpace pages) around literacies within out-of-school spaces are abundant. One student's video documentary of Harlem and presentation on creating a video and imagining it as text to be reconfigured for multiple purposes is just one example of youth media involvement. I have regularly noticed how youth manipulate and re-create the spaces of online social network systems to construct and reconstruct identities. Many of them feel empowered by the new language they are creating, defining, and sharing with their peer audience. I have also noticed their altered dispositions when they participate in literacy events within their familial communities and assume roles of power, authority, and knowing. Their attitudes shift as they document conversations and visible signs of community history and change, and participate in what I refer to as Democratic Engagements. Such engagements represent interactions (e.g., conversations; presentations) they have with others that are built around mutual respect, reciprocity, and knowledge transference. These interactions occur in contexts that, for them, are nonthreatening. Such engagements tell me that youth around the world—beyond the confines of New York City's Harlem; Columbus, Ohio; or Charleston, South Carolina—are building literate traditions. These traditions are defined by words, linguistic diversities, texts, engagements, multiple identities, and acts of performance within and across various sociopolitical contexts.

How can teachers utilize these literate traditions from out-of-school spaces in our work with youth in schools? This question guides this final chapter. Here, I pose possibilities for extending this research on youth literacies and urban gentrification into a pedagogy of possibility, built around literate experiences, new traditions, and public spaces where youth engage in meaning-making processes. My goal is to demonstrate how the literate traditions of youth, which is not exclusive to particular students (e.g., those of color) in specific communities (e.g., urban), are available to educators who want to push the boundaries of "traditional" school literacy. This push is manifested in numerous ways and supports literacy practices in schools. It includes how youth redefine the purposes of writing and written texts and how they explicitly challenge stereotypical images associated with struggle; with the politics of urban, suburban, and rural communities; and with racialized bodies, which for Haymes are Black bodies that are seen as "the urban Other," the disordered and dangerous (p. 4). This push also involves how they re-imagine the world outside of racial and economic restrictions and into a global space of possibility where their identities and cultural practices are honored. Much like Phillip, Khaleeq, and their peers at Harlem High School, youth around the world are active agents of their own literacy narratives and productions outside of schools. Every day, they redefine literacy, critique dominant narratives of ownership, and question the space of communities. With their bodies and minds, poetry and journals, video cameras and online communities, they produce a new literate tradition that, I argue, can support their school-sponsored literacy work.

"TAKE A STAND": BUILDING A LITERATE TRADITION

Where can we look for models of urban education that push for critical involvement from youth, educators, and community members? How can such models influence the work of teachers and the critical literacy skills of students? Geoffrey Canada, social activist and president and CEO of the Harlem Children's Zone in New York City, presents one model by which to build what I call a literate tradition. Coming from an economically poor community in New York City's South Bronx, Canada has experienced first-hand the struggles associated with defying stereotypes placed upon "urban," "minority," and "at-risk" youth. Believing that every child deserves to receive a high-quality educational experience from pre-kindergarten to college graduation, Canada is pushing the meanings and functions of education in new directions. Throughout Harlem, he is working to restore pride and a strong sense of community to an area that is undergoing rapid gentrification. To do this, he, along with the teachers, administrators, and staff at the Harlem Children's Zone (HCZ), is mentoring youth, calling for the public to recommit its energies to the educational possibilities and potentials of America's youth, and revolutionizing the ways we think of education. Instead of educating one child at a time, Canada believes in collaborating with youth, families, their support networks, and the larger community to advance the educational lives of all people.

Located on 125th Street, HCZ opened in 1970 as a truancy prevention organization. Throughout the turbulent 1980s and into the 1990s, when "the crack epidemic tore through Harlem" (http://www.hcz.org), the organization was determined to remain a positive force in the community. Over time, it opened a Beacon Center, a Peacemakers program, and a Countee Cullen Community Center. More recently, it has added the Baby College, the Employment and Technology Center, the Promise Academy, the Harlem Gems, and the Asthma Initiative to its program network.

These programs, all housed under the daily operations of HCZ, function under Canada's fundamental belief that the way to save America is by actively working to save our youth, particularly youth of color in poor, working-class, and underserved communities (see Tough, 2008; Canada, 1998). In 2007, HCZ worked with more than 16,000 children, parents, and other community adults. Its aim is to work with more than 22,000 people by 2011 in ways that positively affect educational reform locally, which will have implications for education nationally. However, given recent economic woes across America, especially concerning the housing market and the status of Wall Street, HCZ is "scrambling to replace what has been a significant amount of [financial] support" (Canada, quoted in Williams, 2008, p. A21).

These messages come through powerfully in Canada's poetry. In "Take a Stand," Canada (1996) makes explicit references to Corey, Maria, and Charlie—youth whose lives depend on our commitment to positive educational, social, and political change. Canada describes how "Corey is afraid to go/To school," and how Maria "prays each night 'fore bed./Because in the window comes some things/That shatter little children-dreams." He writes of Charlie's "deepest, secret wishes" to be covered "with kisses." His poem ends with:

> And tonight, some child will go to bed,
> No food, no place to lay their head.
> No hand to hold, no lap to sit,
> To give slobbery kisses, from slobbery lips.
> So you and I we must succeed
> In this crusade, this holy deed,
> To say to the children in this land:
> Have hope. We're here. We take a stand!
>   (Canada, 1996, "Take a Stand")

Canada's poem is a summons of sorts, a call to every human to "take a stand" if we intend to protect our youth and provide them with rich literate experiences. His poem values the lives and futures of Corey, Maria, and Charlie, as well as Phillip, Khaleeq, Damen, Kim, Samantha, and countless others. I believe Canada's vision is embodied in the daily work of some of the teachers at Harlem High School, as well as teachers I have visited at other schools in New York City; in Columbus, Ohio; in Houston, Texas; and in Detroit, Michigan. These teachers are committed to working with young people in classrooms and communities because they believe it is essential for every human being to have a right "to better understand,/How to learn to love and give,/And live the life you taught to live" (Canada, online).

One specific way I sought to better understand issues that Phillip and Khaleeq were confronting as they defined for themselves ways to "live the life you taught to live" was by listening to *their* perspectives. For instance, I listened to them discuss how the mass media portray Black males as dangerous, which affects how various people see them and construct their raced and gendered identities. One day, I asked them if this portrayal was exclusive to Black males, or if it included Black females and other people of color. Instead of shouting out an answer, as we had all become accustomed to doing, Khaleeq looked at me, I looked at Phillip, and we all just looked—back and forth—at one another. Then, we started talking about media depictions of Black males, the increasing incarceration of youth, and adult activism and youth political rights. Our discussions always returned to where they began: gentrification in urban communities, the rich literacies of young people, and youth lived experiences. Those conversations, much like the ones that occurred in Ms. L's classes, represented efforts at (re)building a literate tradition through definitions of self and resistance to demoralizing depictions of Black bodies.

To build and/or engage in a new literate tradition meant that we could not easily take off our identities as we had so often done before and replace them with the kind of identities we are often expected to wear in academic settings. We were not "inventing the university" (Bartholomae, 1985), but inventing our own identities in the midst of efforts in urban gentrification. Undoubtedly, many of the literacy stories of Harlem that we came to embrace were heavily political and personal. They required us to try on various identities, consider multiple perspectives that often conflicted with our original perspectives, and debate issues of agency and access. I wholeheartedly believe that our literacy stories and shifting identities point to Canada's vision for a substantially improved educational environment for youth, especially in neighborhoods challenged by gentrification and community change.

As I discussed in previous chapters, youth are aware of the narratives of place by local residents just as much as they are aware of the changes occurring within and throughout local urban communities and the ways in which they, themselves, are negatively positioned within a discourse of spatial transformation. On their way to school, they walk past sites where new spaces have been constructed—the kind of spaces Khaleeq calls "expensive things we can't live in" and that Samantha, after the video recorder was turned off, angrily described as places that are "not for any of us who struggling to make the ends meet. We always ignored." They stand in front of new cafés that sell five-dollar lattes. They rush pass the increased presence of police officers and corporate-owned businesses that have slowly replaced street vendors and the mom-and-pop stores. Young people see these changes on their way to school. Given the heightened demands on teachers to meet specific educational standards, mandates, and legislative requirements, the concern students bring to the classroom takes a back seat. Hence, Canada's vision for an emancipatory, inclusive form of education often and unfortunately is clouded in a haze of "standardized" curriculum.

How should educators "take a stand?" If we are to critically build upon Canada's vision, then we—educators, researchers, and youth—are obligated to critique institutional and community structures that dictate the meanings of education (e.g., literacy; achievement; failure; success), the purposes of schooling (e.g., participation in a democratic society; achieving social class mobility), and constructions of identity (e.g., race; class; gender; professional-public-academic; personal-private-community). Ms. L, for example, worked with her students to engage in such critiques. During a unit on June Jordan's (2002) memoir, *Soldier: A Poet's Childhood*, Ms. L invited her juniors first to examine selected poetry and essays by Jordan. They highlighted themes of community, power, and identity before diving into an examination of *Soldier*. Students created poetry by reorganizing words, phrases, and passages from Jordan's writings and by altering the spacing, structure, and order of the texts until a new poem was found. After these activities, students publicly critiqued underlying messages in the poet's writings before turning their attention to lengthy discussions of the memoir.

I remember sitting in the classroom, witnessing how students became enraged that Jordan's father, Granville, treated her like a boy while also physically abusing her. Then, they became overjoyed when they discovered that at least Granville, a man who did not complete grade school before immigrating to the United States from Panama as a teenager, taught Jordan the beauty of language. He inspired her to write, and in her adult life, Jordan published numerous poems, librettos, and essays. She found hope through literary pursuits, activist efforts, and teaching activities.

Ms. L pushed her students to make connections between Jordan's texts and their own identities. She asked students critical questions related to literacy and identity: How did Jordan understand power? Does her understanding of power contradict or parallel your own understanding of power in the world? How did Jordan use language and writing to make meaning in her family's home and outside in the larger world? When you think about this question, what roles would you assign to language, literature, and literacy? Is your identity influenced by the choices someone makes for you, by the choices you make for yourself, or something else? How can we remember and hold tight to the lessons within Jordan's writings as we enter the world, think about who we are, and define our place in the community?

To Ms. L's questions, I added in my own: What functions did literacy really play in Jordan's struggles? Do you think she passively accepted her father's or even her schoolteachers' definitions of literacy, achievement, and success? What was really going on with her literacy narratives—because, from my perspective, I see problematic relationships between abuse and language as well as between literacy in her home and at school? I shared with students aspects of my own research on Jordan (Kinloch, 2004, 2006; Grebowicz & Kinloch, 2004) before telling them that June Jordan is one of the most understudied yet widely published African American writers in the United States. She was writing and teaching to define her identity as well as to reclaim the identities of disenfranchised people in both national and global contexts.

Manuel, a male student in the class, added, "See, she was like working to redefine things. Not only literacy like we describing . . . but you know, education overall. I think this affected how she went into the community." A female from the back of the classroom interrupted, saying, "You mean into the world, right? The whole world, not just the community she lived in. That's deep." Another student added: "We gotta look at her identity. A Black woman, parents immigrants, father had to school himself 'cause regular schooling didn't do it. She was treated like a little boy by her daddy. . . . These would affect how I enter the world." We invited into the classroom Ms. Orridge, Jordan's first cousin and a local activist for housing rights in New York City's Harlem (see Response at the end of Chapter 5). She talked about Jordan's childhood and the tensions between Jordan's passion to be a writer and her father's insistence that she become a doctor or lawyer. Ms. Orridge also talked about how Jordan would want students to make connections among writing, power, and community organizing: "Community was important to June. She used poetry to talk about what she experienced there. That gave her power, because she always said she felt powerless as a student in school." She continued, "By understanding the value of community, June gained back her power and voice." Students asked Ms. Orridge various questions about Jordan's childhood, memoir, poetry and essays, and her relationship with her abusive father.

Ms. Orridge's presentation complemented students' examinations of Jordan's writings. At the same time, it encouraged students to revise their journal entries and responsive essays as they questioned one another's definitions of literature, literacy, and community. Students began to use details of Jordan's life as they more actively considered larger topics: identity construction (e.g., how Jordan's father played a major role in her identity as a writer), education (e.g., she taught youth of color throughout New York City and at various U.S. colleges), and power (e.g., her father's abuse, her mother's silence, and her growing disdain for compulsory education, which helped her envision emancipatory forms of education—Poetry for the People). Poetry for the People (P4P) is a program that Jordan founded in 1991 at the University of California–Berkeley "for political and artistic empowerment for students" and to support the creation of communities of trust (Jordan, p. 16). In many ways, I believe that Jordan's P4P, paired with her teaching and activist efforts, are fundamental precursors to Canada's vision for improved educational institutions and programs.

Being aware of June Jordan and P4P helped students establish critical connections among power, language, place, and writing. Students produced a variety of assignments from this experience. Some students wrote essays on the "changing roles of Black writers." Others drew on themes from Ms. Orridge's presentation to write about "literacy and community," "community power and personal stories," and "using writing to organize for change in school and at home." In these ways, students considered how stories (e.g., Orridge's presentation), literature (e.g., Jordan's writings), and literacies are "communicative and transformative in the sense that they are used to make and represent meanings" (Moje, 2000, p. 670).

In other words, Ms. L's junior-level students examined writings by Jordan as a way to critique the literature of and within their community and, as one student said, "the whole world." At the same time, they were meeting the demands of academic literacy (e.g., reading; writing; designing arguments; exchanging complex viewpoints; synthesizing information; analyzing and critiquing multiple perspectives). Their classroom involvement extended into the ways they began to re-see the power of literature, the meanings of literacy, and the changing roles of their communities, identities, and academic experiences. They were "tak[ing] a stand" (Canada, 1996) by recognizing and, more important, experiencing education as emancipatory, inclusive, and, at its best, democratic.

ENACTING A PEDAGOGY OF POSSIBILITY
IN TEACHING AND LEARNING

What lessons can we take from Ms. L's classroom in Harlem and apply to public forms of education, nationally and globally? How does the building of a new literate tradition relate to teaching, pedagogical practices, and curricular choices in the context of the 21st century? From my examinations of urban gentrification, I have come to believe that community change greatly impacts the literacy lives of youth in- and out-of-school. For example, in rural communities across America, much like in Egypt, Texas, youth are also thinking about the historical significance of their living spaces. Recall Jasmine, the sixth-grade student in Chapter 4, who wrote about how "the picture of my community is old/Old makes me think of the history of this Black community/With its old stores, slave houses, and old family memories." Her poem acknowledges historical symbols and artifacts in Egypt just as much as it narrates the beginning of a story that uses writing for self-expressive and reflective purposes. In Egypt, local residents, community members, and teachers are questioning ownership rights, land development, and redevelopment in a climate that is dealing with shifting economic forces. In light of this reality, Jasmine's community observations indicate how critical reading and writing can influence how one sees, experiences, and generates meaning from changing spaces/ places. Her observations also contribute to expanded, more critical views of racialized bodies that actually endure the realities of spatial changes occurring within familial communities and network systems.

Additionally, many residents in suburban communities are daily confronting ways to protect their families, preserve community resources, and maintain properties and home values as they attempt to make sense of shifting demographics as well as new, unexpected economic situations. The trembling effects of Wall Street and financial institutions everywhere are hampering social class mobility and movement across America. Concerns over land use patterns, unsold homes in once desirable subdivisions, and abandoned strip mall spaces are some of the many factors altering conditions in suburban communities. During one of her interview sessions, Ms. L described Houston, Texas, her hometown, as "a little mini metropolis that has many suburbs on the outskirts of the city. And a lot of people live in Houston suburbs." She went on to explain how suburban communities are made to appear "so different from inner-city communities like they are safer or something, when the truth of the matter is that they [suburbs] have major issues, too. But no one wants to talk about them like we talk about the inner city." When Khaleeq asked Ms. L to elaborate, she responded, "There's a lot of crime, violence, drugs in suburbs. And I know because my parents' suburban house was broken into like two or three times. So to say these things are exclusive to inner-city communities is just not true."

Ms. L's experiences in Houston and New York City have shaped her identity and teaching. In her Harlem High School classes (and now in her high school classes in Houston), she encourages her students to document community trends and create written and oral presentations on current events as they contemplate their positions in the world. This larger world, for Ms. L, extends beyond her students' urban (e.g., Harlem) and suburban (e.g., the outskirts of Houston) communities and into larger spaces where meanings of democracy, ownership, responsibility, and literacy are shifting and being re-imagined. Engaging in such classroom activities encourages students to read the world as text and to write about the world from an expansive literacy perspective, in which they derive and construct meaning from texts. To do this students should learn to be critical readers, writers, and thinkers who have the ability to use literacy for educative, social, and political purposes in and out of school. All the while, students should critique multiple and conflicting perspectives while questioning their identities—and those of others—in a democratic society.

What are some of the challenges for teaching and teachers? And how do those challenges translate into classroom practice? The following exchange occurred between Ms. L and her colleague, Ms. Stone, a teacher at a different high school in Harlem. I asked Ms. L and Ms. Stone to describe to me their thoughts on seeing local communities and the larger world as texts. Among other topics, they talked about student writings, language variances, and teacher struggles. They also shared specific teaching practices from their classrooms. Ms. L said:

> I incorporate identity a lot in the readings that we do. I don't give them as many opportunities, however, to write about place, and that is probably a problem and something that I want to look into doing more as a springboard into the types of conversations and writings [students] do. But most of what I teach is based on some type of cultural issue and how they, as minority people in this country, fit into the United States as a whole. Most of the books we read, they are grounded in some type of historical context about place or society.

Ms. L then described how she wanted students to engage in sophisticated textual readings and writings regardless of the texts they were studying: "It should go without saying that setting's important in what we study. But maybe I should think more about being explicit about setting, teaching about values and traditions that are in the different settings in our books, whether it is fiction or nonfiction." Focusing on setting, or context, Ms. L continued, "Something that's important to accept is that we [students; teachers] don't have to be from a certain community to study it, to learn about it. If we accept that, then we could ask students about the importance of setting. . . . Maybe some will see themselves in the communities in which our readings are set." I quickly added, "Or maybe students can think about how they don't see themselves in the settings or the communities, and that's okay. Now that could be a great essay for a student to write." Ms. L and Ms. Stone agreed, and Ms. L elaborated on my suggestion that students write essays on connections and/or disconnections they have to the settings in course texts. She stated, "And, well, they'll also be able to critique the language used to describe the settings and they can discuss literary devices, symbols, their meanings. . . ."

Ms. Stone picked up the conversation where Ms. L left off, and shared the following ideas with us:

> My curriculum focus right now is kind of completing this three-pronged curriculum on the shared histories [among] African Americans, Chinese Americans, and Mexican Americans. Part of that curriculum is not only understanding how [pause], becoming more aware of how they [students] fit, as a minority, into the structure of the society that they live in. How they think they fit and not me dictating what I think, but also understanding themselves in relation to other minority groups . . . and the ways they see themselves fitting into a larger society. I think inadvertently I hit on place.

For a few seconds, Ms. Stone paused as she contemplated the role of place in her curriculum. She offered the following candid thoughts:

> The first two novels we read, actually, part of them took place in New York, which I think is accessible because . . . like reading Assata Shakur's autobiography and having stepped foot [Ms. Stone and her students] on some of the streets in which she talks about in the book or that she lived on . . . I think that does have an effect on how [the students] approach the book. Being able to make text-to-self connections. And even the other book, *Paper Son* [2000], which is about a Chinese immigrant [by Tung Chin, 2000]. We went to Chinatown, we were walking on the same streets that the main character used to live on. I do think that being there and being in that place, and obviously it's not the same time period, really does have an effect on how they, how much they dig into the book.

Although they worked at different high schools in Harlem, Ms. Stone and Ms. L often collaborated on designing unit plans and course assignments. One of their co-designed units involved going with students to visit communities described in Assata Shakur's autobiography. Ms. L and Ms. Stone

asked students after reading *Assata: An Autobiography* (1987) to complete
a mini-study of the activities, events, people, and businesses on the same
New York City streets discussed in the autobiography. According to their
observations, students found this assignment valuable because it helped
them learn more about the history and sites in their community. Students
were engaging in active observations of the community by researching,
visiting, and critically writing about areas that they lived near or previously had only traveled through in their daily lives.

When Ms. Stone taught texts that were set in a non–New York City
context, she asked students to creatively imagine the spaces described by
the authors. Then, she encouraged students to establish specific connections
and disconnections to the physical spaces of their own communities (e.g.,
school spaces; familial settings), which led to class conversations, debates,
group presentations, and writing assignments. Ms. L and Ms. Stone talked
further with me about the importance of inviting students to examine the
historical, political, and social purposes of settings, or contexts, and described
how they sought new practices to try in their own classrooms. As I listened
to them, various kinds of assignments came to my mind, assignments that
could potentially result from class readings, investigations, and critical discussions on meanings, values, and representations of place:

- Essays that compare and contrast the purposes of settings in various readings and/or in one's own life. These could be turned into
  literacy narratives (see Chapter 4) that focus on context and
  meaning-making processes.
- Multigenre essays that describe and present researchable ideas on
  a topic (e.g., context and community; identity; power dilemmas and
  dynamics; voice) from various literary angles.
- Multimedia, or multimodal, projects that ask students to re-create—
  visually or orally—aspects of the settings from particular novels,
  essays, or other class readings. To do this, students could highlight
  the main idea, select a series of passages, and represent or re-present
  the setting from the texts in ways that stimulate other points of view,
  questions, and conclusions.
- Poetry sessions, or jams, where students turn passages from class
  readings into found poetry or another poetic form, or craft their own
  original poetry and spoken-word pieces. They could have an open
  mic event in their English class or at a school-sponsored function.

This last assignment idea really seemed to interest Ms. L. I further explained
that, with this assignment, students could keep a journal that records their
stream of consciousness and choices in writing poetry or spoken-word

pieces. They could be asked to consider how their writing choices connect to class readings and to meanings of community that derive from performing selected course texts as student-authored writings. When my students and I at Perennial, an East Harlem high school to which I referred earlier, engaged in a similar activity, I discovered increased student interest in course readings. Students openly critiqued perspectives and meanings, and openly questioned the authors' and characters' intentions as they, themselves, interpreted, re-created, and performed texts.

Embedded within all of these assignment ideas, at least for me, are issues of identity, power, ownership, critical reading, and active writing. Utilizing Canada's (1996) suggestion "to take a stand" and applying it to the work that educators do in classrooms would allow us to creatively envision learning as reciprocal, critical, transformative, and powerful. To do this is to invite students to take ownership of their educational experiences, to show them how they are—or could be—active agents in their own learning, and to locate them at the center of our curricula. In classrooms located in urban, rural, suburban, and other settings, teachers can collaborate with students to examine text-based, local, and/or global communities as a way to stimulate critical capacities that, in turn, can support students' educational advancement. Doing so brings us closer to witnessing how youth understand education, experience learning, and make meaning from a variety of encounters, given that they are already doing these things in their out-of-school activities. Thus, teachers can collaborate with youth in building a new literate tradition that is grounded in a pedagogy of possibility.

RETURNING TO HARLEM: IMPLICATIONS FOR RESEARCH AND TEACHER EDUCATION

In an email correspondence from September 2008, Khaleeq responded to my inquiry in which I was "checking in" on him. In part, he said, "My family's doing good and as far as school, one of my professors said she is going to teach as if we were 'going for our Ph.D.'" I also checked in on Phillip, and an entire month went by before he wrote me back. In his response he said, "Well, I am back at the Harlem Center . . . doing something for my community in a positive way. . . . I am busy with school and just working on my stuff. I started a step-up program with my job." The Harlem Center for Education, located in East Harlem, is a group that provides youth in the community with academic assistance in preparation for college.

In our many other email exchanges, I would ask Khaleeq and Phillip about the community, and they would tell me about the new high-rise condominiums that had recently opened and the fancy corner cafés that they have not yet stepped foot in, and they would describe how the "same thing's going on with gentrification. It might look like it [gentrification] slowed down [because of the economy], but believe me, it hasn't" (Phillip). Clearly, there is more work that could and should be done. Additional research is needed that directly connects to the lived experiences of youth and adults in rapidly changing community spaces. Further studies on the narratives that are taught from and written for pedagogical practices in classrooms are also needed. We owe it to our youth to "take a stand" (Canada, 1996) by exploring ways to bridge the divides (e.g., spatial; literacy) between community and classroom concerns.

In this chapter, I have attempted to raise questions of implication and application by exploring the meanings of a new literate tradition that is grounded in a pedagogy of possibility. Such a pedagogy offers youth opportunities to assign alternative meanings to the places where they go to school, engage in conversations with teachers and peers, and interact in literacy and social events with family and friends. Without a doubt, I believe that this pedagogy can be enacted in classrooms and in teacher education programs, especially since they are—one hopes—stimulating sites of engagement for youth and teachers.

I have also made an effort to discuss ways for teachers to be more attentive to the literate traditions that youth develop and participate in during their out-of-school time. As I try to bring this chapter—and this book—to an end, I recognize that there is a lot more to be said about the interviews I conducted with Phillip and Khaleeq, the surveys that were distributed and analyzed, and the observations that were done of youth and teachers in classrooms, school lounges, my university office, and the local community. As I reflect on my work with Phillip, Khaleeq, their peers, Ms. L and local teachers, and others throughout Harlem, I am more than convinced of the significance of studying community history, conditions, changes, and practices within the context of classrooms. In analyzing videotaped, oral, and written data with follow-up discussions, classroom observations, and community interactions, I discovered that there were more than one book's worth of stories.

Revealed within these stories were the ways in which youth, teachers, and Black and White community members (e.g., Kent; Bonnie; George; Vivian; Barbara; Thelma; John) drew on their analytical capacities, critical energies, and creative abilities to narrate stories of community transformation. Whether they believed that gentrification was a class or a racial and cultural issue, youth and adults talked openly about the perceived causes of gentrification and the impact it has on community structures, residents, history, and cultural institutions. The youth who were included in discussions on and investigations into gentrification—as interviewees, as facilitators of other people's interviews, as experts on their own community spaces, and as videographers who directed school and community sessions—were able to enhance their already powerful voices and thoughtful perspectives. They were directly participating in the decision-making processes within their local community. For the youth and their teachers, this slowly contributed to how they came to view school space not just as routine and a place where "students [are] always being controlled" (Khaleeq & Phillip) but as a site of possibility that was partially responsible for fulfilling students' academic needs, interests, and potentials.

What additional possibilities does this work hold for teaching and teacher education? As discussed throughout this chapter, youth are building a new literate tradition with words, languages, identities, and multimodal communicative forms that are largely absent in school spaces. I witnessed how Phillip and Khaleeq maneuvered the video camera (Kinloch, 2009), taking aim at signs of history in the community while also focusing in on the facial gestures and looks of curiosity of the people we interviewed. I also paid close attention to how they made use of digital cameras as if they were prized journals equipped with pens that never ran out of ink. Their digital cameras went everywhere they went and captured some of the most interesting images that narrate various stories on race and place. Such images and the experiences of digitally documenting them could be turned into writing assignments that accompany other literacy activities we ask students to complete.

Here is how I used what I learned with Phillip and Khaleeq in a high school classroom. When I was teaching a senior English class at Perennial High School in 2007, I invited students to design a literacy narrative that explored aspects of their community. We talked about gentrification by reading published essays, articles, poetry, and news commentary on the topic as well as viewing segments from Phillip and Khaleeq's video walkthrough sessions, popular films, and political documentaries. Together, we developed researchable and reflective questions on the topic of community. Our initial set of questions—questions that I believe are beneficial for teacher educators to utilize and revise—included:

- How do you define *community*? What makes your community a community (or not)?
- How do you define your school? What makes your school a community (or not)?
- What do you do inside your local community? What do you do inside your school?
- What are some of the spaces you go? Or, what are some of the places

you would want to go if they were in your local community or a
part of your school community?

- How do you position yourself in your community? What is your
  role and the role of residents, youth, politicians, and your family in
  the local and school communities?
- What would you change/improve/keep the same in your local community or school?

After developing these initial questions, we spent time debating the meanings of community and the purposes of civic participation across various
in- and out-of-school contexts. Students were establishing connections between their community sites and our course readings, which were
authored by popular writers such as Zora Neale Hurston, Langston Hughes,
James Baldwin, Jonathan Kozol, Paulo Freire, Pat Mora, Jessica Care
Moore, Maxine Greene, Amiri Baraka, Geoffrey Canada, Paul Tough, and
others. After considering the above questions, I asked students to do the
following:

- Take a serious look around your community and pay attention to
  any signs/symbols that are present (examples might include billboards, buildings, historic landmarks, stores, people—anything you
  see). List and describe them in as much detail as possible. You could
  do this in your journals or, if you have a video camera or audio
  recorder, you could tape yourself.
- Think about the following question: What makes a community a
  community? Even if you think that you have already answered this
  question, please rethink your original response and extend your
  answer by providing more details and evidence. Remember, there
  could be 15 or more ways to interpret and respond to these questions. In your answer, use our class texts, artifacts in popular culture, and the local community to support or refute your position.
  You should also think of evidence and arguments that could refute
  your position as you consider multiple perspectives.
- What makes some communities different from other communities,
  and why is this the case? List specific factors, causes, and reasons,
  and be as detailed as possible.

Students approached these questions from multiple angles. Some students
wrote that communities are formed around basic principles and shared
values that include religion, culture, language, and ethics. Others indicated
that communities are not necessarily formed around values—although
most are—but that the people in communities may have been forced into

the same space because of economic situations as well as housing availability and affordability. Issues of access, nonaccess, and democracy surfaced in many student responses. Our discussions took plenty of turns, particularly as I realized that we all shared a general understanding of community, but had different explanations for how communities are formed, sustained, and maintained.

Our classroom engagements led to student projects that are often considered "nontraditional" and "out-of-the-box." I wanted students to grapple with and question their initial definitions of community not only within the space of the classroom, but also in their own actual communities. Some students lived in Harlem while others lived in Brooklyn, Upper Manhattan (i.e., Washington Heights and Inwood), and the Bronx. With these things in mind, my students and I decided to do "Community Action Projects." Working in small groups of three to four peers, students developed a community-based question (e.g., "How is Harlem being gentrified?" "What are the meanings, purposes, and signs of community in the area where I live?"). They submitted to me a Plan of Action (PoA). One group's PoA included: 1) taking pictures of their communities; 2) researching the meanings of those pictures in terms of what they meant for adult residents; 3) collecting, reading, and annotating articles written about their communities; and 4) creating their own multimodal video of the community. A final component of their project was their individually authored essays on community that, along with the video, students presented to the class. This multilayered literacy experience encouraged students to think critically about the unit's guiding questions and to collaborate on interpreting those questions based on textual readings and personal community experiences. Additionally, it invited students to study aspects of their community that they may never have considered. This type of ownership was crucial for my students, and I believe that it is valuable for other students in various contexts to experience.

Much like Phillip and Khaleeq's engagements in Central Harlem around the issues of gentrification, my students at Perennial High School were designing texts that represented particular aspects of their own identities, subjectivities, and community lives. In their designs, they experimented with various meanings of community, interrogated popular notions about the underachievement of urban students of color, and reconfigured school space into a site of critical literacy and reciprocal education, in which learning is shared, mutual, and a democratic process between students and teachers. This example demonstrates how a focus on community can prove beneficial for the ways students and adults see and re-see the world.

No longer can we rely on traditional definitions of literacy—the ability to read and write—without considering issues of identity, culture, community practices, funds of knowledge, access, and agency. We must also consider "funds of knowledge," which according to Moll, Amanti, Neff, and Gonzalez (2001) "refer to the historically accumulated and culturally developed bodies of knowledge and skills essential for household or individual functioning and well-being" (p. 133). Much like Phillip and Khaleeq, countless youth are redefining what literacy means. Their redefinitions serve as calls for educators, researchers, and policymakers to account for the new literate traditions inside of classrooms that youth are creating in out-of-school spaces. Doing so means that we are recognizing the communities where youth are engaging in meaning-making processes, crafting literacy narratives, and questioning their identities. From gentrification, land development, and forms of civic participation to community demonstrations and protests, youth are taking a stand, building a new literate tradition, and imagining a pedagogy of possibility. We should, too.

Afterword

When Professor Kinloch initially spoke with me concerning her research in Harlem, my immediate reaction was that she was trying to do too many things in one initiative. I may have said that to her, but it is our good fortune that she did not follow my advice. She has completed a project that I thought was too ambitious, and she has completed it with excellence and eloquence. In one creative and cooperative effort she has 1) addressed the teaching and learning of literacy in a hard to reach population; 2) engaged teaching and learning persons in literacy production and the effective completion of literacy products; 3) provided an informative example of emic historiography produced from multiple perspectives; and 4) achieved the several ends in the context of addressing problems in urban education and urban gentrification.

A year or two before the untimely death of the late historian of education Professor Lawrence Cremin, he and I were discussing the possibility of our collaboration on the writing of the history of education from the perspective of those being educated rather than from the perspective of those of us who educate. Kinloch's involvement of her students in whom she is trying to develop competence in literacy and in the generation, collection, and interpretation of the data is entirely consistent with what Cremin and I had in mind. In the process they and she have made available to the field grass roots perspectives on the processes of gentrification and the use of such lived experience in the pedagogical process itself. Perhaps without awareness, Kinloch has demonstrated an approach to a problem to which David Teiderman and I called attention in mid-twentieth century. Students are regularly confronted with the paradox of negotiating between the mastery of the data of schooling, which tends to be other people's information that students are expected to learn, and the understanding of the data of their own experiences. In Kinloch's work we see the effective bridging of these two worlds of data in the interest of learning to become literate persons, engaging in the production of literacy products, and in the continuing search for more effective approaches to teaching and learning in dynamic urban communities.

Kinloch adds to this very useful discussion of her work a commentary on the work of Geoffrey Canada at the Harlem Children's Zone. She and I are mutual admirers of the remarkable initiatives in the Zone, but Canada's work is not essential to understanding the central messages of *Harlem on Our Minds*. The work at the Harlem Children's Zone does, however, provide a conceptual model on the macro-level of the values that inform what Kinloch is doing. Education is really about life, and the lives that learners live are important purveyors of opportunities to learn. What we now call *comprehensive education* seeks to orchestrate those various and ubiquitous opportunities to learn into an integrated experience for learners. Canada seeks to do that in a sixty-five square blocks area. Kinloch seeks to help students integrate their thinking, reading, and writing around the symbolic sites of those opportunities found in the community where they live.

Edmund W. Gordon

References

Adams, M. H., and Rocheleau, P. (2002). *Harlem lost and found.* New York: Monacelli Press.

Annual report on social indictors. (1993). New York: Department of City Planning.

Baldwin, J. (1948). The Harlem ghetto. In J. Baldwin, *Notes of a native son* (pp. 57–72). Boston: Beacon Press.

Bartholomae, D. (1985). Inventing the university. In M. Rose (Ed.), *When a writer can't write: Studies in writer's block and other composing-process problems* (pp. 134–165). New York: Guilford Press.

Beauregard, R. (1993). *Voices of decline: The postwar fate of US cities.* Oxford: Blackwell.

Canada, G. (1996). *Take a stand.* http://www.hcz.org/what-is-hcz/about-geoffrey-canada [Accessed October 4, 2008].

Canada, G. (1998). *Reaching up for manhood: Transforming the lives of boys in America.* Boston: Beacon Press.

Charlton-Trujillo, e. E. (2007). *Feels like home.* New York: Delacorte Press.

Chin, T. (2000). *Paper son: One man's story.* Philadelphia: Temple University Press.

Clark, K. (1965). *Dark ghetto: Dilemmas of social power.* New York: Harper & Row.

Cushman, E. (1996). The rhetorician as an agent of social change. *College Composition and Communication, 47,* 7–28.

Delpit, L. (1995). *Other people's children: Cultural conflict in the classroom.* New York: The New Press.

Dewey, J. (1959). *Art as experience.* New York: Perigee Trade.

Douglass, F. (1995). *The narrative of Frederick Douglass, an American slave* (unabridged). Mineola, NY: Dover Publications.

DuBois, W. E. B. (1903). *The Negro problem: A series of articles by representative American Negroes of today.* New York: J. Pott & Company.

Dyson, A. H. (2003). *The brothers and sisters learn to write: Popular literacies in childhood and school cultures.* New York: Teachers College Press.

Dyson, A. H. (2005). Crafting "the humble prose of living": Rethinking oral/written relationships in the echoes of spoken word. *English Education, 37*(2), 149–164.

Ellison, R. (reissued, 1972). *Invisible man.* New York: Vintage.

Fecho, B. (2004). *"Is this English?" Race, language, and culture in the classroom.* New York: Teachers College Press.

Fine, M., Weis, L., & Powell, L. (1997). Communities of difference: A critical look at desegregated spaces created for and by youth. *Harvard Educational Review, 67*(2), 247–284.

Fisher, M. T. (2007). *Writing in rhythm: Spoken word poetry in urban classrooms.* New York: Teachers College Press.

Fishman, J., Lunsford, A., McGregor, B., & Otuteye, M. (2005). Performing writing, performing literacy. *College Composition and Communication, 57*(2), 224–252.

Fitzgerald, F. S. (reissued, 1999). *The great Gatsby.* New York: Scribner.

Fleischman, P. (2005). *Breakout.* New York: Simon Pulse.

Foucault, M. (1984). The means of correct training. Trans. R. Howard. In P. Rabinow (Ed.), *The Foucault reader.* New York: Pantheon Books.

Freeman, L. (2006). *There goes the 'hood: Views of gentrification from the ground up.* Philadelphia: Temple University Press.

Freire, P. (1997). *Pedagogy of the oppressed.* New York: Continuum. (Original work published in 1970)

Freire, P. (1998). *Teachers as cultural workers: Letters to those who dare teach.* Boulder, CO: Westview.

Freire, P., & Macedo, D. (1987). *Literacy: Reading the word and the world.* Westport, CT: Bergin & Garvey.

Gere, A. R., Christenbury, L., & Sassi, K. (2005). *Writing on demand: Best practices and strategies for success.* Portsmouth, NH: Heinemann.

Giroux, H. (1992). *Border crossings: Cultural workers and the politics of education.* New York: Routledge.

Greene, S. (2008). *Literacy as a civil right: Reclaiming social justice in literacy teaching and learning.* New York: Peter Lang Publishers.

Haberman, M. (1991). The pedagogy of poverty versus good teaching. *Phi Delta Kappan, 73,* 290–294.

The handbook of Texas online. http://www.Tsha.utexas.edu/handbook/online/articles/view/EE/hne8.html [Accessed June 1, 2004 & April 20, 2007].

Hardman, L. (2006). The rights and wrongs of language variation: Employing everyday language in a classroom setting. Unpublished master's thesis, City College of New York.

Harlem Children's Zone. http://www.hcz.org/ [Accessed December 8, 2007, July 21, 2008, & October 13, 2008].

Haymes, S. (1995). *Race, culture, and the city: A pedagogy for black urban struggle.* Albany: State University of New York Press.

Heath, S. B. (1983). *Ways with words.* Cambridge, UK: Cambridge University Press.

Heath, S. B. (1999). *ArtShow: Youth and community development.* Videocassette. Partners for Livable Communities.

Heath, S. B., & McLaughlin, M. (1993). *Identity and inner city youth.* New York: Teachers College Press.

Heath, S. B., and Smyth, L. (1999). *ArtShow: Youth and community development, a resource guide.* Washington, DC: Partners for Livable Communities.

Hill, M., & Vasudevan, L. (2008). *Media, learning, and sites of possibility.* New York: Peter Lang.

hooks, b. (1990). *Yearning: Race, gender, and cultural politics.* Boston: South End Press.

Hull, G., & Schultz, K. (Eds.). (2002). *School's out: Bridging out-of-school literacies with classroom practice*. New York: Teachers College Press.

Hurston, Z. N. (reissued 2006). *Their eyes were watching God*. New York: HarperPerennial.

Inside schools profile. http://insideschools.org. [Accessed May 26, 2009].

Jackson, K. T. (Ed.). (1995). *The encyclopedia of New York City*. New Haven, CT: Yale University Press.

James R. Squire Office of Policy Research. (2007). 21st-century literacies: A policy research brief. Urbana: NCTE.

Jewell, E. J., and Abate, F. (Eds). (2001). *The new Oxford American dictionary*. Oxford: Oxford University Press.

Jones, L., & Newman, L. (1997). *Our America*. New York: Scribner.

Jordan. J. (2002). *Soldier: A poet's childhood*. New York: BasicCivitas.

Keith, M., & Pile, S. (1993). *Place and the politics of identity*. New York: Routledge.

Kelley, R. D. G. (2003). Disappearing acts: Capturing Harlem in transition. [Introduction.] In A. Attie, *Harlem on the verge* (pp. 9–17). New York: The Quantuck Lane Press.

Kinloch, V. (2005a). Poetry, literacy, and creativity: Fostering effective learning strategies in an urban classroom. *English Education, 37*(2), 96–114.

Kinloch, V. (2005b). Revisiting the promise of *Students' right to their own language: Pedagogical strategies. College Composition and Communication, 57*(1), 83–113.

Kinloch, V. (2005c). The Heidelberg Art Project as a site of literacy activities and urban renewal efforts: Implications for composition studies. *JAC 25*(1), 101–129.

Kinloch, V. (2006). *June Jordan: Her life and letters*. Westport, CT: Praeger Publishers.

Kinloch, V. (2008). Writing in the midst of change. *English Journal 98* (1), 85–89.

Kinloch, V. (2009). Literacy, community, and youth acts of place-making. *English Education, 41*(4), 316–336.

Kinloch, V. (forthcoming, 2010). "To not be a traitor of Black English": Youth perceptions of language rights in an urban context. *Teachers College Record*.

Kinloch, V., & Grebowicz, M. (Eds.). (2004). *Still seeking an attitude: Critical reflections on the work of June Jordan*. Maryland: Lexington Books.

Kirkland, D. (2008). *Something to brag about: A sociolinguistic perspective on urban black males and literacy*. Presented at the American Educational Research Association Annual Meeting. New York, New York.

Kozol, J. (2005). *The shame of the nation: The restoration of apartheid schooling in America*. New York: Crown Publishers.

Ladson-Billings, G. (2009). *The dreamkeepers: Successful teachers of African American children*, 2nd ed. San Francisco: Jossey-Bass.

Ladson-Billings, G., & Tate, W. F. (2006). *Education research in the public interest: Social justice, action, and policy*. New York: Teachers College Press.

Lee, Spike. (2000). *Bamboozled*. New York: New Line Cinema.

Lincoln, Y. S., & Guba, E. (2000). Paradigmatic controversies, contradictions and emerging confluences. In N. K. Denzin & Y. S. Lincoln (Eds.), *Handbook of qualitative research* (2nd ed., pp. 163–188). Thousand Oaks, London, and New Delhi: Sage Publications.

Lunsford, A., & Ruszkiewicz, J. (2006). *Everything's an argument* (4th ed.). New York: Bedford/St. Martin's Press.

Lutrell, W., & Parker, C. (2001). High school students' literacy practices and identities and the figured world of school. *Journal of Research in Reading, 24*(3), 235–247.

Mahiri, J. (1998). *Shooting for excellence: African American and youth culture in new century schools.* Urbana and New York: NCTE and Teachers College Press.

Marberry, C., & Cunningham, M. (2003). *Spirit of Harlem: A portrait of America's most exciting neighborhood.* New York: Doubleday.

Maurrasse, D. (2006). *Listening to Harlem: Gentrification, community, and business.* New York: Routledge.

McCarty, T. L. (Ed.). (2005). *Language, literacy, and power in schooling.* Mahwah, NJ: Lawrence Erlbaum Associates.

McIntosh, P. (1988). White privilege: Unpacking the invisible knapsack. *Peace & Freedom Bimonthly Journal,* 10–12.

Moje, E. B. (2000). "To be part of the story": The literacy practices of gangsta adolescents. *Teachers College Record, 102,* 651–690.

Moje, E. B. (2002). But where are the youth? Integrating youth culture into literacy theory. *Educational Theory, 52,* 97–120.

Moll, L., Amanti, C., Neff, D., & Gonzalez, N. (2001). Funds of knowledge for teaching: Using a qualitative approach to connect homes and classrooms. *Theory Into Practice, 31*(2), 132–141.

New Oxford American Dictionary (E. J. Jewell & F. Abate, Eds.). (2001). New York: Oxford University Press.

Pike-Baky, M., & Fleming, G. (2005). *Prompted to write: Building on-demand writing skills.* San Francisco: Jossey-Bass Publishers.

Pratt, M. L. (1991). Arts of the contact zone. *Profession, 91,* 31–40.

Quinonez, E. (2000). *Bodega dreams: A novel.* New York: Vintage.

Reynolds, N. (2007). *Geographies of writing: Inhabiting places and encountering difference.* Carbondale, IL: Southern Illinois University Press.

Rich, A. (1993). *What is found there: Notebooks on poetry and politics.* New York: W. W. Norton.

Schultz, K. (2003). *Listening: A framework for teaching across differences.* New York: Teachers College Press.

Shakur, A. (1987). *Assata: An autobiography.* Chicago: Lawrence Hill Books.

Smith, B. (1943). *A tree grows in Brooklyn.* New York: Harper & Brothers.

Smitherman, G. (1977). *Talkin and testifyin: The language of Black America.* Detroit: Wayne State University Press.

Smitherman, G. (2006). *Word from the mother: Language and African Americans.* London & New York: Routledge.

Soja, E. (1990). *Postmodern geographies: The reassertion of space in critical social theory.* London: Verso.

Street, B. V. (1993). Introduction: The new literacy studies. In B. V. Street (Ed.),

Cross cultural approaches to literacy (pp. 1–21). New York: Cambridge University Press.

Street, B. V. (2005). Recent applications of new literacy studies in educational contexts. *Research in the Teaching of English, 33*(4), 417–423.

Tatum, B. D. (2003). *"Why are all the Black kids sitting together in the cafeteria?" A psychologist explains the development of racial identity* Rev. ed. New York: Basic Books.

Taylor, M. M. (2002). *Harlem: Between heaven and hell.* Minneapolis: University of Minnesota Press.

TimeOut New York. http://www.timeout.com/newyork/ [Accessed October 3, 2008 & October 29, 2008].

Tough, P. (2008). *Whatever it takes: Geoffrey Canada's quest to change Harlem and America.* Boston: Houghton Mifflin Harcourt.

Vasudevan, L. (2006). Making known differently: Engaging visual modalities as spaces to author new selves. *E-Learning 3*(2), 207–216.

Weis, L., & Fine, M. (Eds.). (2000). *Construction sites: Excavating race, class, and gender among urban youth.* New York: Teachers College Press.

Williams, T. (2008). Wall Street tremors leave Harlem shaken. *New York Times,* October 8, 2008. A21.

Wilson, W. J. (1987). *The truly disadvantaged: The inner city, the underclass, and public policy.* Chicago: The University of Chicago Press.

Wright, R. (reissued 1989). *Black boy.* New York: HarperPerennial.

Index

About the Respondents

Latoya Hardman currently teaches 11th grade English in Houston, Texas. She began her career as a teacher in New York City's Harlem communuity, where she taught 9th-, 11th-, and 12th-grade English. Latoya also teaches developmental reading and writing at Tomball Community College. She received her bachelor of arts in English from the University of Houston, Downtown, and has a master of arts in English eduction from the City College of New York. She is a 2009 recipient of the Early Career Educator of Color Leadership Award from the National Council of Teachers of English (NCTE).

Rebekkah A. Hogan received her master's degree from Teachers College, Columbia University, and her undergraduate degree from the University of Pennsylvania. Her field of study is international educational development, with a focus on gender identity in the Anglophone Caribbean. She lives and works in New York City.

Khaleeq Middleton is an African American male who resides in New York City and graduated from a high school in Harlem. He has an interest in history and has been contemplating a career in criminal justice.

Valerie Orridge is a longtime resident of the Harlem community of New York City. Persistently working with local organizations and activists for the civil and political rights of African Americans in Harlem, Valerie has been the president of the tenants' association of her apartment building for over 17 years.

Phillip Reece Jr. is an African American male from New York City's Harlem community. Interested in sports and photography, he is committed to protecting his community from gentrification.

Mimí M. Richardson is a seventh-grade language arts teacher in New Jersey. She earned her bachelor of arts degree in English literature from Binghamton University and her master's of arts degree in the teaching of English program at Teachers College, Columbia University.

About the Author

Valerie Kinloch is an associate professor in the School of Teaching and Learning at The Ohio State University. Her research interests include the spatial narratives, literacy practices, and democratic engagements of urban youth and adults in- and out-of-school spaces. Valerie's research has appeared in *College Composition and Communication, English Education, English Journal,* and *Language Arts Journal,* among others. She is the author of *June Jordan: Her Life and Letters* (2006) and coauthor of *Still Seeking an Attitude: Critical Reflections on the Work of June Jordan* (2004). Valerie has been awarded a Spencer Foundation Small Research Grant as well as a Grant-in-Aid from the National Council of Teachers of English (NCTE) to support her work on the literacy and activist practices of African American and Latino youth in New York City's Harlem. Her funded projects examine how gentrification and a politics of place can impact the lives, literacy practices, and survival strategies of urban youth of color.